IMMIGRATION NATION

IMMIGRATION NATION

RAIDS, DETENTIONS, AND DEPORTATIONS
IN POST-9/11 AMERICA

TANYA GOLASH-BOZA

Paradigm Publishers
Boulder • London

Copyright © 2012 Paradigm Publishers

Published in the United States by Paradigm Publishers, 2845 Wilderness Place, Suite 200, Boulder, CO 80301 USA.

Paradigm Publishers is the trade name of Birkenkamp & Company, LLC, Dean Birkenkamp, President and Publisher.

Library of Congress Cataloging-in-Publication Data

Golash-Boza, Tanya Maria.
  Immigration nation : raids, detentions, and deportations in post-9/11 America / Tanya Maria Golash-Boza.
    p. cm.
  Includes bibliographical references and index.
  ISBN 978-1-59451-837-9 (hardback : alk. paper) — ISBN 978-1-59451-838-6 (pbk. : alk. paper)
  1. United States—Emigration and immigration—Government policy. 2. Immigration enforcement—United States—History—21st century. 3. Immigrants—United States—Social conditions—21st century. 4. Immigrants—Civil rights—United States. I. Title.
  JV6483.G64 2011
  325.73—dc23

                                                            2011021055

Printed and bound in the United States of America on acid-free paper that meets the standards of the American National Standard for Permanence of Paper for Printed Library Materials.

Designed and Typeset by Straight Creek Bookmakers.

16 15 14 13 12   1 2 3 4 5

CONTENTS

To my mother, Deirdre Golash, herself an immigrant,
and my father, Michael Golash, grandson of immigrants.

PREFACE AND ACKNOWLEDGMENTS

I began to conceptualize *Immigration Nation* in the spring of 2006—the spring of immigrants in the United States. I was in my first year of a faculty position at the University of Kansas and was teaching courses on race and immigration. That spring, immigrants and immigrant-rights supporters marched *en masse* in cities and towns across the United States demanding immigration reform.

I found myself teaching my classes on immigration, yet knowing remarkably little about what the protests were about. I attended community meetings in Lawrence, Kansas, that criticized anti-immigrant legislative proposals and called for comprehensive immigration reform. I resolved that I needed to be more informed about immigration debates.

In May 2006, my department chair asked me to give a talk in honor of the retirement of one of our faculty members. I initially planned to deliver a talk from my research on Latinos' racial identifications on the Census. However, I saw this as an opportunity to force myself to learn more about the immigrant rights movement in the United States and agreed to deliver a paper on immigration reform.

A portion of that paper was published in the online magazine *Counterpunch,* which led to two coauthored publications on immigration and human rights with sociologist Douglas Parker. With those publications, I was on my way to becoming an immigrant rights scholar. More importantly, I was developing a vision of how immigration reform could be conceptualized with human rights at its core.

In spring 2008, while on a post-doctoral fellowship at the University of Illinois at Chicago, I had the opportunity to begin to write this book. I was in Chicago—in the heart of the immigrant rights movement—and I had plenty of material and inspiration. I began to volunteer at *Latinos Progresando,* a nonprofit organization that works for immigration reform, and I attended the meetings of local immigrant rights' groups.

I lived in Little Village, a community with a high percentage of undocumented migrants. I participated in the marches of the spring of 2008 and felt the solidarity and determination of the Latino community in Chicago. The more I read about the immigration raids occurring around the country and the heartless deportations happening every day, the more inspired I became to finish my book. By the end of the summer of 2008, I had a working draft of this manuscript.

At that point, I began the process of revision and benefited immensely from the feedback of many colleagues and friends. I especially would like to thank Holly Goerdel, Yajaira Padilla, Jorge Perez, Jessica Vasquez, Amalia Pallares, Ruth Gomberg-Muñoz, Nicholas de Genova, Brent Metz, Judith Blau, David Brunsma, Ian Golash, Joane Nagel, Dave Stovall, Bernard Headley, Victor Romero, Rekha Sharma-Crawford, Joanna Dreby, and Marta Caminero-Santangelo for their useful feedback on various portions of this manuscript. This manuscript has also benefited from the guidance of my editor, Jennifer Knerr, the two anonymous reviewers for Paradigm Publishers, and the two copy editors, Karen Gill and Kristy Johnson. I also must thank Kerry Ann Rockquemore, Angela Black, Eileen Diaz-McConnell, and other members of the National Center for Faculty Development and Diversity for allowing me to believe that writing this book was possible and for giving me a constant source of inspiration along the way.

Very special thanks also go to the tireless, dedicated staff at *Latinos Progresando*: Luis Gutierrez, Marcy Gonzalez, Juana Salazar, and Melissa Gonzalez, who have all helped tremendously with this project. The research for this book would not have been possible without generous funding from the Fulbright-Hays Faculty Research Abroad Award, the General Research Fund of the University of Kansas, and the College of Liberal Arts and Sciences at the University of Illinois at Chicago.

The human rights vision that is at the core of this manuscript is a vision I have learned from my long-standing mentor, Judith Blau. Judith is at the center of the human rights revolution in sociology. Her vision of how sociology can do more than simply diagnose social ills is the motivating force behind this text. From Judith and other members of the organization she founded, along with Alberto Moncada—Sociologists without Borders—I have learned that sociologists can work to shift the scholarly, political, and public discourse toward one that recognizes the fundamental dignity of all human beings. This is the project this book takes on.

How Punitive Immigration Policies Negatively Affect Citizens, Families, and Communities

While watching a YouTube video about a nine-month old infant, tears began to well up in my eyes. The baby had been taken to the hospital to be treated for dehydration, after being deprived of her mother's breast milk. The infant's mother had left for work that morning and never returned. She was arrested by Immigration and Customs Enforcement (ICE) in an immigration raid in New Bedford, Massachusetts, and was in ICE's custody. As a result, the baby refused to take a bottle, had a high fever, and was crying inconsolably. As I listened to the narrator explain, over the persistent wail of this child, that her mother was put in jail for working without proper documentation, I became increasingly upset. Perhaps I was so troubled because I, too, am a mother who has nursed her children, and I could imagine the distress this mother felt, or perhaps it was because the story was simply heartbreaking. I scrolled down the screen to read comments left by viewers. Many experienced an entirely different reaction to the video than I did. For them, the video evoked not sympathy, but disgust, and they sharply expressed their thoughts by writing comments such as these:

"Way to go ICE!! Arrest and deport the cockroaches!"
"Only tragedy here is that now the U.S. has to pay for some kids that freaking illegals left here."
"hahaha, am i supposed to feel bad for these people? ALL of this could have been avoided had they simply followed the laws of immigration. not our fault you wanna break the law when you got kids."[1]

I would like to think that these are just a few bigots willing to equate undocumented workers with insects. However, comments such as these are pervasive. The responses below nearly any YouTube video on immigration or any online article related to immigrants are filled with similar expressions of hate. One viewer disparages "Rosa" for getting prenatal care at the health clinic. Another complains his tax dollars are being used to pay for the education of children who are U.S. citizens but have parents who are undocumented migrants. How have we reached such a point? When did it become acceptable to chastise women for getting prenatal care and children for going to school? What compels my fellow citizens to fail to see the humanity of people, simply because they lack the proper documentation to remain in this country?

This book is a step toward restoring the dignity of undocumented migrants by focusing on the human rights of migrants and their families. I am primarily concerned with the human rights impact of the surge in interior enforcement of U.S. immigration laws. I take a close look at the costs of immigration law enforcement to individuals, families, and communities. The United States Department of Homeland Security (DHS) has drastically increased its efforts in raids, detentions, and deportations in the past few years. I attempt to make an in-depth assessment of the human costs these tactics have effected in migrant communities.

Immigration policies in the United States have had negative consequences for citizens, families, and communities. Even though family reunification has been at the core of U.S. immigration policy since 1965, our policies often tear families apart. Despite the perception that immigration policy primarily affects immigrants, frequently, it has devastating effects on citizens, such as the nursing infant mentioned earlier.

Human Rights, Citizens, and Immigration Law Enforcement

The passage of Senate Bill (SB) 1070 in Arizona renewed national debates and protests around immigration policy and reform. SB 1070—an immigration enforcement law—was controversial in part because it criminalized at the state level several federal immigration violations that carried no criminal penalty. The most vocal critics of SB 1070 pointed to the civil rights violations entailed by a law that mandated racial profiling. SB 1070 will continue to be contested in courts, and over the next two years it will become clearer the extent to which this law is unconstitutional. Those provisions that are in violation of standards set forth by the United States Constitution will be overturned in U.S. courts.

I will discuss these and other civil and political rights violations engendered by U.S. immigration policy. However, I also bring to light concrete examples of how other human rights, which are not included in the U.S. Constitution, have been violated. The United States has a strong tradition of civil and political rights, yet, unlike most other nations, it does not give much weight to the social, economic, or cultural rights that are also important to the human rights tradition (Blau and Moncada 2005). In the controversy over the Arizona laws, critics have claimed that SB 1070 would violate the civil rights of Latinos in the state, because they would be subject to racial profiling.

These claims were held up in court when Judge Susan Bolton of the Federal District Court ruled on July 28, 2010 that Arizona police officers would not be able to check the immigration status of people during the course of stops, detentions, and arrests, as SB 1070 had mandated. Her ruling also blocked provisions that allowed police officers to hold people arrested for a crime until their immigration status was determined. This ruling is based on the prohibition against arbitrary detention in the U.S. Constitution—a political right.

Other provisions blocked by Judge Bolton's injunction include the following:

1. The warrantless arrest of any noncitizen suspected of having committed a crime that could make them eligible for deportation
2. Those provisions that criminalized the failure to apply for or carry alien registration papers
3. Those provisions that criminalized undocumented migrants who solicited, applied for, or performed work

(In the United States, it is not a criminal offense for noncitizens to lack registration papers, nor is it a criminal offense for them to work. This law sought to criminalize these activities.)[2] These rulings marked a gain for the civil and political rights of Latinos and other immigrants in Arizona. However, human rights discourse—which includes cultural, social, and economic rights in addition to civil and political rights—did not form part of the debates over SB 1070. The discussions in this book will focus primarily on the human rights discourse and its important perspective in debates related to U.S. immigration law, policies, and law enforcement.

Human Rights Perspective

A human rights perspective presumes the fundamental dignity of all people, regardless of national origin. With this perspective in mind and for the purpose of this discussion, I work off the basis that all human lives are valuable. I will refer to the Universal Declaration of Human Rights (UDHR) and other human rights doctrines, using them as a moral compass to guide my analyses of the impact of immigration policies on citizens and noncitizens in the United States.

A human rights perspective presumes universal equality and dignity and recognizes that people are members of families and communities (Blau and Moncada 2005: 29). A consideration of the human rights impact of immigration policies in the United States requires recognizing that people have rights, not as citizens of a particular nation-state, but as human beings. A human rights analysis necessitates a consideration of how U.S. immigration policies affect all people—not solely or primarily U.S. citizens.

By applying a human rights perspective, we are compelled to see migrants not simply as workers, but as husbands, fathers, brothers, wives, mothers, sisters, and community members. As human beings, migrants have the right to be with their families and to be members of the communities in which they live. These family and community rights are enshrined in the UDHR. Article 16 mentions the right to found a family, and posits that the family is "the natural and fundamental group unit of society." Article 17 puts forth the notion that everyone has the right to "participate in the cultural life of the community." Article 25 reads, "Everyone has the right to a standard of living adequate for the health and well-being of himself and of his family, including food, clothing, housing and medical care, and necessary social services." Not only is the importance of these rights internationally recognized, but their realization is fundamental to creating a better society for all members. The UDHR is not a legally binding doctrine in the United States, because the U.S. Congress has not voted to ratify this convention. Nevertheless, it can serve as a moral compass for those of us who believe that all human beings deserve rights and dignity, regardless of national origin.

Immigration policy debates frequently revolve around the economic costs and benefits of immigration and ignore the human element. A human rights analysis compels us to calculate the human, and not simply the economic, costs of immigration policy. Putting human rights first often means asking a different set of questions. For example, some critics who argue that undocumented migration has a negative economic impact include the costs of education for U.S.-citizen children of undocumented migrants into their analyses.[3] A human rights analysis would see education as a fundamental human right. Others argue that undocumented migrants bring down wages. For example, George Borjas (2004) contends that low-skilled immigrants are only beneficial to their employers, while they bring down the wages of their native low-skilled counterparts. Steven Camarota (2004) of the Center for Immigration Studies argues that households with undocumented members pose a fiscal burden because undocumented migrants have low skill levels and thus low earnings potential. He notes that the fiscal burden is not due to low levels of employment or to heavy use of social services, but to the low wages undocumented workers earn. A human rights analysis would insist that all workers deserve a living wage. In addition, many of the costs that Camarota mentions are related to the care of children of undocumented migrants. These arguments are echoed by economist Barry Chiswick (1988), who points out that low-skilled foreign workers can be economically beneficial, so long as they do not bring their nonworking family members with them to the United States. A human rights analysis considers family unity to be an inalienable right.

The debate over the economic costs and benefits of undocumented migration is not settled. Frank Bean and his colleagues (1988) argue that undocumented workers do not bring down native workers' wages. Kjetil Storesletten (2000) contends that high-skilled immigration is not only economically beneficial, but also necessary to maintain the fiscal health of the United States. Overall, it appears that assessments of the economic advantages and disadvantages of immigration are based on what factors scholars choose to include in their analyses. Either way, a purely economic analysis ignores the human element. Migrants in the United States are not simply commodities. They are people with family and community ties in the United States.

Citizens, Families, and Communities

Most of us don't live in isolation; we're members of families and communities. Migrants, of course, are no different; they, too, live embedded in extensive networks. In this book, I consider the impact of immigration policy not only on migrants, but also on U.S. citizens, families, and communities—the collateral victims of punitive immigration policies. U.S. citizens who have close ties to migrants are severely affected by immigration policies in the United States. In many cases, they experience a diminishment or disregard of their citizenship rights, as well as their human rights, because of punitive immigration policies in the United States. For example, U.S.-citizen children have the right to territorial belonging. That right is devalued if their parents lose the right to live in the United States and decide to take the children with them.

Many immigration laws and policies have been designed to make life more difficult or impossible for noncitizens; this also, directly and indirectly, has a significant impact on citizens. Because families are made both by blood and by choice, any citizen could be affected by immigration policies. Two clear examples are adoption and marriage. The adopted children of U.S. citizens have been deported to their country of birth, as a result of the 1996 laws, especially the Illegal Immigration Reform and Immigrant Responsibility Act (IIRIRA), which made deportation mandatory for people charged with certain crimes. For some adopted children, youthful indiscretion has meant being severed from the only families they have known. Their parents must live with the grief and guilt of forgetting to naturalize their children. In other cases, plans to form a life together have been foiled when undocumented fiancés and spouses of U.S. citizens learn that they have no way to legalize their status, as punishment for having committed the civil infraction of crossing the border without permission.

In this book, I will also explore and explain how punitive immigration policies negatively impact citizens, families, and communities. I argue that this is because the divide between citizens and noncitizens is fluid. Noncitizens may be future citizens and are often also the family members of citizens. Laws that lead a noncitizen to unemployment, living in fear, incarceration, and their possible deportation inevitably have consequences for their communities and their family members who are citizens. These policies are detrimental not only for noncitizens, but also for citizens. I will explain how the punitive nature of U.S. immigration policies creates an unstable tension between human rights and citizenship rights.

Surge in Interior Enforcement

Immigration policy enforcement has infringed on the human rights of people in the United States in new and more pronounced ways because of a renewed commitment to interior enforcement: immigration law enforcement by various national security agencies, especially the DHS, within the borders of the United States. Interior enforcement includes home and worksite raids designed to find people who are deemed deportable, cooperation between police and immigration agents to locate "criminal aliens," and operations such as National Security Entry-Exit Registration System (NSEERS). NSEERS, instituted after 9/11, is a program that required male visitors from twenty-five Arab and Muslim countries and North Korea living in the United States to report to immigration officers and be fingerprinted, photographed, and questioned. Despite interviewing over eighty thousand people, no one was deported or denied entry on terrorism grounds, although many were deported for having overstayed their visas.[4] In the past few years, ICE has dedicated unprecedented resources to interior enforcement in these and other ways (Immigration and Customs Enforcement 2008c). The heavy enforcement of immigration laws and policies within the borders of the United States in small towns and large cities across the country marks a dramatic change from the past, when nearly all immigration law enforcement involved trying to prevent undocumented migrants from crossing the U.S./Mexico border.

When immigration policy is enforced primarily at the borders of the country, its most direct effects are on those people *outside* the country. Strong border enforcement makes it more difficult to enter the country. Many people who wish to enter the country have family members inside the United States and are desperate to rejoin them. Heightened border enforcement does not prevent them from entering the country (Cornelius 2006); it simply makes the passage more difficult. Those family members living in the United States are left to worry about the treacherous nature of the journey and hope that their relatives and loved ones are not among the four hundred or so people who perish each year in the deserts and mountains of Arizona.

By nature, the U.S.'s interior enforcement has a more immediate and direct effect on people *inside* the United States. Noncitizens inside the country often have their family members with them or are working to support their families abroad. Border enforcement makes it more difficult for families to unite, whereas interior enforcement often tears apart families that are already together. Tactics such as immigration raids instill fear in entire communities with a show of great force directed at community members.[5] In a raid, hundreds of immigration agents descend on a community in search of undocumented workers. Children bear witness to their parents being hauled off in shackles like criminals.

The spectacle of interior enforcement, especially since 9/11, has its precedents in previous shows of border enforcement. In the last decade of the twentieth century, the United States government engaged in a series of widely publicized operations designed to enhance border security. Despite an abundance of evidence that militarizing the border would not reduce border traffic, but redirect it and intensify the incentive for criminal organizations to engage in human smuggling, the border was increasingly fortified. Politicians were unwilling to vote against border militarization, because voting against securing the border would be viewed as politically unfavorable (Andreas 2000).

Many critics called on the U.S. government to dedicate more resources to interior enforcement. When asked in 1996 why the Immigration and Naturalization Service (INS) did not spend more money on preventing undocumented migrants from obtaining employment, INS Commissioner Doris Meissner responded that "the centerpiece of effective enforcement must be the border, and ... it must be backed up with employer enforcement" (Andreas 2000: 01). At the time, only about 2 percent of the INS budget was dedicated to enforcing employer sanctions. Peter Andreas (2000) argues that this emphasis was because of the symbolic importance of border enforcement and the lack of political will to enhance interior enforcement.

In the first few years of the twenty-first century, the focus, tactics, and emphasis of enforcement shifted. In the post-9/11 context, it is no longer intolerable for immigration agents to engage actively in interior enforcement. In the context of the War on Terror, there is no longer a lack of political will to enhance the policies and use of various operations of interior enforcement. Worksite enforcement operations, for example, increased twelvefold between 2002 and 2008—from 510 arrests to 6,287.[6] The escalation of interior enforcement has required increasing the number of beds available in immigrant detention facilities, having more interagency cooperation, and enhancing the capacity to deport people from the interior.

The escalation of interior enforcement means that both detentions and deportations increased considerably in the first decade of the twenty-first century. The DHS, which replaced the INS in 2003, has been able to secure funding for these operations by relying on a rhetoric of national security concerns. The detention of asylum-seekers and undocumented meatpacking workers has been made possible through claims that the DHS is "protecting the nation from dangerous people."[7] This heightened, yet unsuccessful, frenzy to find dangerous people has created a climate of fear in immigrant communities across the United States.

Even though, as stated, the DHS's primary goal is to "protect our nation from dangerous people," when the department issues statements regarding this objective, the focus is almost exclusively on immigration enforcement. For example, the first piece of evidence, put forth in a DHS document with a subsection titled "Goal 1: Protect Our Nation from Dangerous People," refers to the deployment of 6,000 National Guard to the border in 2008. From issues of border security, this DHS document goes on to talk about workplace enforcement of immigration laws and deportations and detentions of noncitizens.[8] By publishing documents such as these, the DHS's national security agenda seems clear: it is endeavoring to show concrete evidence of its success in protecting the nation from dangerous people. The documentation on the agency's prevention of undocumented migration and the increase in deportations and detentions of undocumented migrants is being used, more and more, by DHS as an excuse to enforce immigration laws in the name of national security. What is lacking, however, is evidence that worksite enforcement operations, road blocks, and home raids actually lead to the removal of dangerous people.

Immigrants and Citizens

In the United States, the DHS is charged with handling the transition of the foreign-born either into citizenship or into leaving this country. As indicated on the DHS official website (http://www.dhs.gov), the mission of the DHS is as follows:

> We will lead the unified national effort to secure America. We will prevent and deter terrorist attacks and protect against and respond to threats and hazards to the nation. We will ensure safe and secure borders, welcome lawful immigrants and visitors, and promote the free-flow of commerce.

The primary mission of the DHS is to protect citizens from terrorist attacks. This project involves protecting the borders and enforcing laws in the interior, while welcoming lawful immigrants, visitors, and international commerce. For the DHS, lawful immigrants are potential citizens, whereas unlawful immigrants are unwelcome. The DHS is charged both with enabling immigrants to become citizens and ensuring that those who are not eligible for citizenship are appropriately regulated.

The DHS is clear on its intent to regulate those who are not U.S. citizens and to protect noncitizens. It is virtually impossible, however, to create policies that exclusively regulate noncitizens and protect citizens. This is because there is not a clear boundary between noncitizens and citizens or between immigrants and citizens. Some U.S. citizens are immigrants, and some noncitizens may eventually become citizens. In addition, most noncitizens have citizen family members. As Fix and Zimmerman (2001: 400) point out, fully "85 percent of immigrant families (i.e. those with at least one non-citizen parent) are mixed status families. The meaning of this is clear: *most policies that advantage or disadvantage noncitizens are likely to have broad spillover effects on the citizen children who live in the great majority of immigrant families*" (emphasis in original).

People who are not U.S. citizens and are thus subject to regulation often have family members who are U.S. citizens. They also often live in communities with U.S. citizens. Some may have been in the country for a few days, but others have settled here and have been in the United States for decades. Their detention and deportation can cause tragic effects for those left behind. For this reason, the immigration policy debate cannot take a narrow view and focus simply on migrants; it also must consider the significant impact on citizens and recognize that immigrants and citizens are not mutually exclusive categories, but often stages in a person's migrant career.

Immigration Policy and Families

United States law allows any person born on U.S. territory to be a U.S. citizen, regardless of the citizenship or immigration status of her parents. Thus, when an undocumented migrant gives birth to a child within the United States, the child has the legal right to remain in the United States even though the undocumented parent does not. U.S. courts have ruled that the child's citizenship rights are not violated through the deportation of her parent, because the child is not legally obligated to leave the country (Colvin 2008). Technically, this is true. However, practically speaking, many parents and children have to choose between a *de facto* deportation and family separation when the undocumented parents of U.S.-citizen children are ordered to be deported. For this reason, I argue that U.S. immigration laws force families to choose between citizenship rights and human rights. Citizenship rights, in this case, include the right of citizens to remain in the United States. And human rights include the right of families to stay together as a unit. Human rights doctrines, however, are not currently legally binding in U.S. courts. Thus, until the laws are changed, the DHS will continue to have the ability to deport the undocumented parents of U.S.-citizen children, and many U.S. citizens will face *de facto* deportations.

Undocumented workers contribute greatly to our economy and provide a necessary labor force, yet they often live in constant fear of deportation. Moreover, most undocumented workers come to the United States because they, their families, and their communities have longstanding and extensive ties between the United States and their countries of origin. Nevertheless, migrants are often unable to acquire permission to live legally in the United States. The story of my neighbors in Chicago puts a human face on this dilemma.

Don Franco[9] came to the United States in 1985, with his wife, Doña Lucrecia, and their two youngest boys. They left their other two children behind in Morelos, Mexico, in the care of Doña Lucrecia's mother. They hoped to reunite with them once they were settled. They stayed at Doña Lucrecia's brother's house on the near west side of Chicago until Don Franco could save up enough money for them to move out and get their own place. Upon arrival, Don Franco's brother had already arranged employment for him. It didn't take long for Don Franco to save up the necessary funds for his family to move into their own apartment. Don Franco and Doña Lucrecia were able to establish themselves and their family in Chicago. Don Franco obtained a driver's license and social security number.

However, Don Franco and Doña Lucrecia never qualified for legalization; when the Immigration Reform and Control Act (IRCA) was passed in 1986 that gave amnesty to three million undocumented migrants, it specified that migrants must have arrived before 1982 to qualify. Because Doña Lucrecia and Don Franco had arrived in 1985 and there has not been another amnesty, they have lived tenuously in the United States for nearly three decades. They also cannot return to Mexico, for fear of not being able to reenter the United States. They have extensive family and community ties on both sides of the border. Unable to obtain legalization, they have not been able to reunite with the children they left behind in Mexico.

One evening I was talking to Don Franco, and he asked me if I enjoyed going to Peru, where I had been recently. I began to tell him about Peru, but he interjected to say that, although he did not have much money when he lived and worked in Mexico, it seemed he enjoyed life more then. Even though he worked, he still had time to hang out with his friends. In Chicago, he said, he works a lot and has little time to enjoy life. I asked him what he does on Sundays, his only full day off. He said that, because his driver's license has expired and he can't get a new one, he stays close to home. He fears getting on the interstate, so he no longer goes fishing in Indiana as he once did. He also does not visit his brother in Waukegan, just forty miles away. Neither has a valid driver's license, and both feel as though it is too risky to make the trip. They make do with phone conversations.

Don Franco and Doña Lucrecia have four grandchildren in Chicago. Their grandchildren come over most weekends and play in and around the house. Even though Don Franco has Sundays off, he never takes the kids outside of their neighborhood. He would like to take them to the beach when the weather is warm or to Waukegan to play with his brother's grandchildren, but it is not worth the risk that he would be stopped by the police, fined for not having a driver's license, and potentially deported to Mexico.

Don Franco says his life has gotten worse since 9/11. He asked me why the events of September 11 have had such a dramatic impact on his life, when he had nothing to do with what happened on that day. I, too, ask this question. Why is immigration being linked to security issues? Why do we, as a society, choose to make life less enjoyable for people like Don Franco? Wouldn't financially stricken Northwest Indiana like for Don Franco and his family to come to the beaches there on Sundays, thereby contributing to the economy through park fees, tolls, and likely a meal at one of the many *taquerías* in deindustrialized Northwest Indiana? The enhancement of interior enforcement of immigration laws has made people like Don Franco feel less secure in the United States yet has done little to reduce terrorism.

The terrorist attacks of September 11 made it clear that there are people who seek to harm civilians in the United States. There is no question that there is a need for a defense system to protect people in the United States from terrorists. However, these systems must be more elaborate than fences over which well-organized terrorist groups can fly and under which they can dig tunnels. Migrants from Mexico, Central and South America, or other countries in the Global South who walk across deserts, swim across rivers, or climb over fences in search of better employment prospects are not terrorists. Neither are undocumented workers who work in meat processing and garment factories. There is, of course, a need for national security in the United States, yet building fences, raiding factories, and terrorizing immigrant communities does not make the United States a safer place (Golash-Boza and Parker 2007).

Overview of Chapters

I open the discussion, in the first chapter, with an outline of the roots of immigration to the United States of America. This discussion involves a consideration of why we continue to have high levels of immigration despite restrictive laws. I argue that migrants come because migration decisions are not simply cost/benefit decisions made by individual migrants; they are influenced heavily by structural linkages between the United States and other countries.

In the second chapter, I discuss the enhancement of interior enforcement—specifically the surge in raids and detentions. Immigration raids are operations carried out by ICE, a division of the DHS that is responsible for enforcing immigration laws. These raids are designed to find people working without authorization and those found guilty of identity theft. The manner in which raids are executed often wreaks havoc on entire communities. I provide details surrounding four immigration raids carried out recently to demonstrate the effects such raids have had on migrant communities in the United States. I also look at the immigrant detention system. Migrants awaiting trial and deportation are housed in Detention and Removal Office facilities, private prisons, or other jails. The conditions in these facilities are often horrendous, and, in some cases, deadly. Drawing from a variety of human rights reports, I describe conditions in these detention centers and explore why these abuses continue to occur.

The third chapter looks at who is being deported and what the consequences of those deportations are. *Deportation*, or what the DHS calls *removal*, is when a migrant is formally removed from the United States, and, often, permanently barred from reentering. People can be deported for being in the United States without authorization. They also can be deported for having committed crimes, ranging from murder to shoplifting or drug possession. I describe who is being deported and why, and explain the consequences of these deportations on families in the United States.

In the fourth chapter, I demonstrate the strain immigration policy has on many couples, specifically, where one person is a citizen and the other is undocumented. Due to current provisions in the Immigration and Nationality Act (INA), some spouses of citizens are unable to legalize their status. This means that couples face hard decisions: U.S. citizens often have to choose between their family and their country. I present the stories of nine couples who must choose between living together as a family in the United States and deporting themselves to Mexico. The difficult choices these couples face make it clear that there is something fundamentally wrong with having to choose between your country and your family. Through these narratives, I explore the tension between citizenship and human rights created by U.S. immigration policies.

The fifth chapter is an introduction and discussion of what I call the immigration industrial complex. The *immigration industrial complex* refers to the public and private sector interests in the criminalization of undocumented migration, immigration law enforcement, and promotion of "anti-illegal" rhetoric. This concept is based on the idea that there exists a convergence of interests that drives the U.S. government to pass and then avidly enforce a set of immigration policies that have consistently failed to achieve their stated goals and have violated the human rights of migrants and their families in the process. The profit potential is at the root of this human rights crisis, yet political power also plays a significant role. This consideration of who benefits from undocumented migration allows us to develop an understanding of why legislators have not enacted viable immigration reforms.

I conclude with some recommendations for how we can improve our broken immigration system and create a system that respects the human rights of both citizens and noncitizens. Revisiting my argument that a human rights framework is essential for making changes to immigration policies, I contend that the immigration policy debate must take into account the human cost, in addition to security and economic needs. I make the case that the human rights of migrants and their families should be at the center of our analyses.

CHAPTER 1

ROOTS OF IMMIGRATION TO THE UNITED STATES

In 2010, there were more than ten million undocumented migrants in the United States (U.S. Department of Homeland Security 2011). The presence of large numbers of people who do not have the legal right to be in this country presents a variety of challenges. People in the United States are divided over how to solve the problem of undocumented migration. Some argue that all undocumented migrants are criminals and should be punished for their illegal activity. Others contend that undocumented migrants are simply people who have been unable to legalize their immigration status and should be given the opportunity to do so.

If the primary problem with undocumented migrants is that they lack legal status, one logical solution is to provide them with a path to legalization. If migration is only problematic insofar as it is illegal, legalization is an obvious solution. This proposal, however, is met with virulent criticism from many quarters. One of the primary bases for this criticism is that undocumented migrants are criminals and should not be rewarded for their illegal activity. The idea that undocumented migrants are criminals is gaining ground in both discourse and practice. Popular media pundits often refer to undocumented migrants as "illegals" and as "criminals," highlighting their purported criminality.[1]

Around the country, local police departments are entering into memorandums of understanding (MOUs) with Immigration and Customs Enforcement (ICE), allowing police officers to enforce immigration law. These programs, often called 287 (g) agreements, criminalize immigration violations by having police officers enforce immigration laws. In the spring of 2010, the criminalization of undocumented migrants reached new heights with the passage of controversial legislation in Arizona (Senate Bill [SB] 1070) that made undocumented migration a crime of trespassing and carried a punishment that involved a fine and jail time. The Arizona law was particularly controversial insofar as it criminalized what traditionally had been a civil offense—the lack of documents that permit a noncitizen to remain in the United States.

The trend toward the criminalization of undocumented migration evident in 287 (g) agreements and in SB 1070 is unwarranted because the distinction between legal permanent residents and undocumented migrants has little to do with criminal intent and much to do with the fact that U.S. immigration laws are not aligned with the reality of our position in a globalizing world. The stance that undocumented workers are morally reprehensible whereas legal residents are morally superior relies on the false assumption that some migrants have followed the "rules" whereas others have broken them. The reality is that many legal permanent residents and naturalized citizens have benefited from legalization programs—both directly and indirectly—even if they have broken the "rules" in the past. For example, a Dominican permanent resident may have come to the United States legally yet have been sponsored by his mother who was formerly out of status but able to legalize through the 1986 Immigration Reform and Control Act (IRCA). In contrast, a Dominican who came to the United States on a student visa in 1996 and then overstayed his visa would not be able to benefit from IRCA provisions and could continue to be undocumented and unable to sponsor family members.

Documented and undocumented migrants come to the United States for the same set of reasons—a range of connections to the country, family reunification, and the search for employment. Current provisions in immigration law allow some people to migrate legally for these reasons. Others either have to wait for years or have no option to migrate legally; still others come to the United States illegally but eventually are able to legalize their status.

By examining the laws, policies, and structural forces that bring migrants to the United States, we can see the extent to which immigration to the United States is closely related to our position in the global economy. Recognition of these longstanding structural linkages serves as an important reminder that immigration policies enacted in the United States will be ineffective insofar as they fail to account for conditions abroad. A report on how direct labor recruitment, military interventions, and foreign direct investment have drawn migrants to the United States renders evident the role of the United States in creating and sustaining migration flows. This chapter explains how the laws passed in the United States have given some migrants the opportunity to obtain legal status in the United States while denying others that opportunity.

Who Are the Immigrants?

The United States is often thought of as a destination for immigrants from all over the globe. It is true that the United States houses people from each of the 194 or so countries in the world, yet the majority of immigrants have come from only a few of these countries. Although the Statue of Liberty bears Emma Lazarus's poem that refers to immigrants as "poor huddled masses," the people who migrate to the United States are not always the most destitute in the world. In 2009, more than one million people became legal permanent residents of the United States. Only 6,718 of them came from the five poorest countries in the world. Nearly half (3,165) of the migrants from the five poorest countries hailed from Afghanistan, which is in the midst of a U.S. military occupation. Niger, the poorest country in the world, sent only 183 legal permanent residents to the United States (U.N. Human Development Report [HDR] and the Department of Homeland Security [DHS] Table 03 for 2009).[2]

Every year since 1990, between one-half and three-quarters of all people granted legal permanent residency in the United States in any given year have come from just ten countries. Mexico, China, India, the Philippines, and Vietnam have sent the most legal permanent residents over the past two decades; they have also sent large numbers of undocumented migrants. Forty-two percent of legal permanent residents came from those five countries in 2008, as did 64 percent of all undocumented immigrants. These data are displayed in Figures 1-1 and 1-2.

In 2009, an estimated 10,740,000 undocumented migrants were living in the United States (see Figure 1-1). Eighty-five percent of them came from just ten countries: Mexico (6,650,000), El Salvador (530,000), Guatemala (480,000), Honduras (320,000), the Philippines (270,000), India (200,000), Korea (200,000), Ecuador (170,000), Brazil (150,000), and China (120,000) (U.S. Department of Homeland Security 2010).

In 2008, there were an estimated 12.6 million legal permanent residents in the United States. Whereas undocumented migrants lack the legal right to be in the United States, legal permanent residents are those noncitizens who have been authorized by the Department of Homeland Security to remain permanently in the United States. According to estimates of the legal permanent resident population in the United States in 2008, 55 percent came from ten countries: Mexico (3,390,000) Philippines (570,000), India (520,000), China (510,000), Dominican Republic (420,000), Cuba (350,000), El Salvador (340,000), Canada (330,000), Vietnam (330,000), and the United Kingdom (290,000)

Figure 1-1 Undocumented Migrants' Countries of Origin: 2009

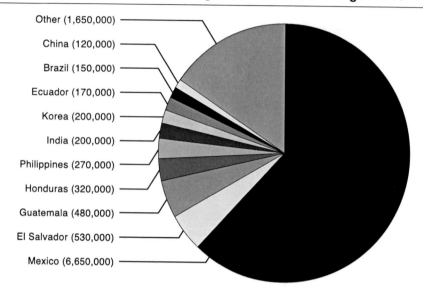

Other (1,650,000)
China (120,000)
Brazil (150,000)
Ecuador (170,000)
Korea (200,000)
India (200,000)
Philippines (270,000)
Honduras (320,000)
Guatemala (480,000)
El Salvador (530,000)
Mexico (6,650,000)

Data Source: U.S. Department of Homeland Security, 2010. http://www.dhs.gov/xlibrary/assets/statistics/publications/ois_ill_pe_2009.pdf.

Figure 1-2 Legal Permanent Residents' Countries of Origin: 2008

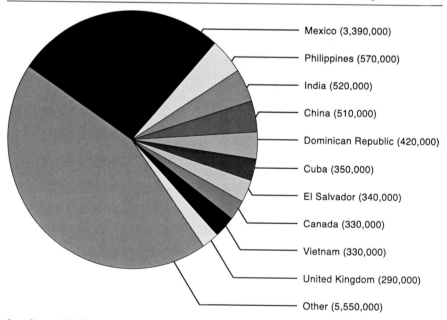

Mexico (3,390,000)
Philippines (570,000)
India (520,000)
China (510,000)
Dominican Republic (420,000)
Cuba (350,000)
El Salvador (340,000)
Canada (330,000)
Vietnam (330,000)
United Kingdom (290,000)
Other (5,550,000)

Data Source: U.S. Department of Homeland Security, 2010. http://www.dhs.gov/xlibrary/assets/statistics/publications/ois_lpr_pe_2008.pdf.

(U.S. Department of Homeland Security 2009b). Figure 1-2 shows these figures. It is interesting to note that the countries sending large numbers of undocumented as well as legally present migrants to the United States are countries with which we have close economic, political, and military ties.

Ties That Bind

Labor recruitment, military interventions, and foreign direct investment (FDI) create and sustain migration flows. Countries with long histories of labor migration, such as Mexico and the Philippines, continue to send us migrants because these long histories have created strong ties between our country and theirs. In addition, family reunification policies in the United States encourage further migration by giving preference to family members living in the country. This process is known as *cumulative causation*—migration begets more migration (Massey et al. 2002; Massey 1988). Military intervention can lead to an outflow of refugees because of the violence of military operations, amorous relationships between U.S. soldiers and locals, and the development of close ties between people in the United States and the country at hand, such as when Filipinos were recruited to join the U.S. Navy (Rumbaut 1994). FDI creates migration flows through its inevitable effects on the local economy and the integration of the country into the global economy. In an analysis of twenty-five developing countries, Sanderson and Kentor (2008: 529) found, "The stock of FDI has a long-term positive effect on emigration." These factors have led to both legal and illegal migration to the United States.

A Century of Labor Recruitment

Many contemporary migration flows into the United States go back to the mid-nineteenth and early twentieth centuries when U.S. employers recruited workers from Mexico, the Philippines, Korea, China, and India to work in agricultural sectors. The recruitment of workers from those countries planted the seed for the migration flows that continue to this day. Some employers are able to bring immigrant workers through the available legal channels to meet their labor needs. Many other employers find themselves obliged to recruit workers through illegal channels, because there is a severe shortage of work visas. Undocumented workers continue to come to the United States, at an average rate of more than a thousand per day. Some settle permanently; many form families here; many others send for their families from abroad, while still others return to their country of origin after a couple of years.

Today, Mexico is the largest single source country of immigrants in the United States. It by far outweighs all other countries in terms of the sheer number of migrants and the long, sustained history of migration. Mexicans account for more than a quarter of the twelve million legal permanent residents in the United States, and over half of the eleven million undocumented migrants (U.S. Department of Homeland Security 2009b; U.S. Department of Homeland Security 2010). The ties between the United States and Mexico run deep. The first Mexicans that came to be part of the United States never crossed a border. In 1848, the United States and Mexico signed the Treaty of Guadalupe Hidalgo, which resulted in Mexico's loss of almost half of its territory. Mexico surrendered its control over California, Nevada, Utah, Texas, and parts of Arizona, New Mexico, Colorado, and Wyoming in exchange for $15 million. In 1854, with the Gadsden Purchase, the United States bought what are now southern Arizona and southwestern New Mexico, making fifty thousand Mexicans residents of the United States (Massey et al. 2002).

After that substantial mid-century increase in the Mexican-origin population, in- and out-migration remained relatively stable until the early twentieth century. The instability engendered by revolution in Mexico, combined with increasing labor needs in the Southwest, translated into a tripling of the Mexican immigrant population between 1910 and 1930, from two hundred thousand to six hundred thousand. Immigration inspectors turned a blind eye to these flows in recognition of the fact that these migrants were meeting labor market demands in the southwest border region. Only in 1919 did Mexicans first have to apply for admission to the United States (Massey et al. 2002; Ngai 2004).

With the onset of the Great Depression in late 1929 and the very high rates of unemployment in the United States, many Mexican immigrants, as well as U.S. citizens of Mexican descent, were returned to Mexico. There were 1,751 expulsions of Mexicans in 1925. This number shot up to 15,000 by 1929. In the early 1930s, the Immigration and Naturalization Service (INS) mounted a repatriation campaign, and more than 400,000 people of Mexican origin were returned to Mexico in that decade. These exclusionary measures led to a temporary decrease in the Mexican population in the United States, as around 20 percent of the Mexican population returned to Mexico (Ngai 2004).

Just over a decade later, the demands of World War II produced labor shortages in the United States, and Mexicans were recruited to meet that labor need. The

U.S. Congress approved a seasonal worker program, called the *bracero* program, which brought in 4.6 million temporary Mexican *braceros* to work in agriculture from 1942 to 1964. The bracero program was terminated in 1964, partly in response to widespread publicity about the abuses engendered by the program. The dependency on Mexican farm workers, however, has not ended, and legal and illegal flows of Mexican and other farm workers continue to provide farms with vital labor in the United States (Massey et al. 2002).

The millions of braceros were not always enough to meet U.S. labor demands, and increases in braceros were accompanied by increases in undocumented migrants, colloquially referred to as *wetbacks*. The INS began Operation Wetback in June 1954 and deported 170,000 Mexicans in the first three months. This operation led to a temporary decrease in undocumented migration, yet it did not end the flows. The sustained recruitment of Mexican agricultural workers, both braceros and wetbacks, in the mid-twentieth century laid the basis for the establishment of migrant networks that persist to this day (Rumbaut 1994; Teitelbaum 1984; Ngai 2004).

Indian migration to the United States also goes back to the early twentieth century. Between 1907 and 1914, 5,943 Indians migrated to the United States. Many of these migrants were from the state of Punjab and came to work in the agricultural fields in California. The subsequent wars and Great Depression, accompanied by restrictive immigration laws in the United States, meant that there was very little immigration from India to the United States until after World War II, when we began to see small numbers of Indians coming to this country. Between 1945 and 1965, 6,371 Indians immigrated to the United States. This increase was due to the passage of the 1946 Luce-Celler bill, which lifted some of the restrictions on Asian Indians in the United States (Gonzales 1986). Those early migrants from Punjab, however, laid the groundwork for future Punjabis who would migrate to the United States once it became possible again.

The United States has a long-standing relationship with the Philippines, and a protracted migration history. This helps to explain why this relatively small (eighty-eight million as compared to China and India's billion-plus) and quite distant country sends large numbers of its nationals to the United States. The Philippines was a U.S. colony from 1898 until 1946. From 1898 to 1934, Filipinos were American nationals and could freely come to the States. Many were recruited by Hawaiian sugar plantations, and by 1931, around one hundred thirteen thousand had migrated to Hawaii alone. On the mainland, California manufacturers and vineyard owners recruited Filipinos as workers, attracting more than five thousand to the United States mainland by 1920. With the passage of the 1924 Immigration Act, which ended the flow of Japanese laborers, agribusiness turned to Mexican and Filipino labor, such that by 1930 there were fifty-six thousand Filipinos on the West Coast. The termination of the colonial relationship, combined with the onset of the Second World War and racial violence on the West Coast, slowed Filipino immigration until 1946. Between 1946 and 1965, 33,000 Filipinos immigrated to the United States, nearly half of whom were wives of U.S. servicemen (Liu, Ong, and Rosenstein 1991; White, Biddlecom, and Guo 1993; Ngai 2004).

Chinese immigrants in the United States predate many other immigrant groups; the large-scale migration of Chinese to the United States began when U.S. contractors recruited laborers to build railroads in the mid-nineteenth century. Around the same time, recruiters in Hawaii brought tens of thousands of Chinese to work in agriculture and other industries. Despite this early start, migration from China was slowed substantially for more than a century, beginning with the Chinese Exclusion Act of 1882. Between 1882 and 1943, when the Act was repealed, unskilled laborers from China who wished to migrate to the United States had no legal way to do so. However, once the doors reopened, the presence of Chinese immigrants and their descendants in the United States facilitated future waves of migration.

Korean migration to the United States also began in the early twentieth century. More than seven thousand Koreans migrated to Hawaii to work in sugar plantations between 1903 and 1905. U.S. plantation owners recruited Koreans in the hopes of mitigating the labor conflicts in which Japanese workers were engaged. However, their recruitment efforts were cut short in 1906, when emigration from Korea was prohibited by the Japanese imperial power (Patterson 1988). Nevertheless, about two thousand Koreans came between 1906 and 1923, mostly as picture brides for Korean laborers. Between 1924 and 1950, practically no Koreans migrated to the United States because of the 1924 restriction on Asian immigrants (Min 1990). These restrictions were lifted during the aftermath of the Korean War (1950–1953), and more than three thousand Koreans were admitted between 1950 and 1965, the vast majority of whom were wives of U.S. servicemen stationed in Korea.

These countries that were sources of labor migrants in the early twentieth century continue to send migrants to the United States today. Mexico, the Philippines, Korea, India, and China are among the top countries of origin of both undocumented migrants and legal permanent residents in the United States today.

Military Interventions and Immigration

U.S. military interventions often lead to immigration. Over the course of the twentieth century, the U.S. military has played a major role in the military and political arenas of many Latin American and Asian countries; and many of the countries that the United States has occupied and invaded are the same countries that have sent us immigrants. One of the most remarkable cases is Vietnam, as the Vietnam War (1963–1975) was the sole impetus for emigration from Vietnam to the United States.

Prior to the Vietnam War, there were very few Vietnamese in the United States, whereas today, there are more than one million. Between 1971 and 1980, 150,000 Vietnamese were admitted to the United States as refugees. By 1980, the U.S. Census counted two hundred forty-five thousand Vietnamese living in this country, nearly all of whom were recent arrivals (White, Biddlecom, and Guo 1993). Vietnamese refugees primarily came to the United States after the fall of the U.S.-backed Saigon government in 1975, when the U.S. government sponsored the evacuation of more than one hundred thousand Vietnamese refugees (Haines, Rutherford, and Thomas 1981). Beginning with the initial evacuation in 1975 until 1977, an average of eighteen hundred additional refugees arrived each month. The second wave came primarily out of opposition to the new government. The third wave began in 1978, when the Vietnamese government began to expel ethnic Chinese from Vietnam (Kelly 1986).

Dominican migration to the United States is closely related to the U.S. military intervention in the Dominican Republic in 1965. United States' relations with the Dominican Republic developed due to the interests of U.S. corporations in Dominican sugar plantations in the nineteenth century. The United States' grip on the sugar economy in the Dominican Republic was strengthened with the U.S. occupation from 1916 to 1924. Plantations remained primarily under the control of U.S. companies until the 1950s, when President Rafael Trujillo began to buy out their holdings to expand his family's control of the sugar economy (Gregory 2007). During the Trujillo regime, emigration was largely restricted by the Dominican government (Hernández 2004).

After the assassination of Trujillo, who had close ties to Washington, DC, Juan Bosch was elected to the presidency. Suspicion that he was Communist, combined with worries that he would ally with Fidel Castro and thus threaten U.S. control of the region, led the United States to intervene militarily in the Dominican Republic in 1965 (Brands 1987). U.S. troops arrived in the Dominican Republic on April 28, 1965, with the purpose of ensuring that Juan Bosch, who had since been ousted from power by a military coup, would not return to his position as president (Wiarda 1980).

The U.S.-organized elections in the Dominican Republic enabled Joaquin Balaguer to win the presidency. Balaguer's government was characterized by a reign of terror against any dissidents. Balaguer also opened the Dominican economy to more foreign investment, particularly from the United States. The economic changes led to growth in the industrial sector but also created unprecedented rates of unemployment in the Dominican Republic. The Pentagon and the CIA aided the squashing of dissidence, and the U.S. consulate granted visas to potential dissidents (Brands 1987; Wiarda 1980). This time of intense involvement of the United States in Dominican affairs—1961 to 1968—was also a time in which more Dominicans entered the United States than from any other country in the Western Hemisphere, except Mexico.

The U.S. military also has played a major role in the internal affairs of Cuba, a nation that continually sends many immigrants to the United States. Cuba was a colony of Spain until 1898, when the Cuban Army achieved victory over the Spanish forces. However, the U.S. government had intervened militarily in the conflict, and Cuba liberated itself from Spain only to become a colony of the United States. The U.S. occupation of Cuba was short lived, and on May 20, 1902, Cuba finally became a republic. North Americans, however, maintained a strong economic hold on Cuba, with North Americans owning about 75 percent of the Cuban cattle ranches and accounting for a large portion of the sugar production in the early years of the twentieth century. The economic influence of the United States continued, with some stops and starts, until the Cuban Revolution of 1959, when private holdings were expropriated by the Cuban government (Perez 2003). In the early twentieth century, around ten thousand Cubans lived in Tampa and another ten thousand in New York. By the end of the 1950s, about fifty thousand Cubans lived in the United States (Perez 2003).

The number of Cubans migrating to the United States increased dramatically with the victory of Fidel Castro in the Cuban Revolution in 1959. Cubans opposed to the revolution left in the tens of thousands, mostly to Miami. Cuban exiles, assisted by the CIA, organized an unsuccessful invasion of Cuba in 1961, known as the Bay of Pigs. This was followed throughout the 1960s by covert operations designed to sabotage Cuba and oust Castro (Perez 2003).

By the end of the 1980s, there were nearly one million Cubans in the United States (Perez 2003). Until August 1994, virtually all Cubans who fled Cuba were granted political asylum in the United States and permitted to attain permanent residency. This was a U.S. Cold War policy, designed to promote the benefits of capitalism as opposed to communism. President Bill Clinton changed this policy, such that Cubans found at sea attempting to come to the United States are now returned to Cuba, whereas those who land on U.S. soil are nearly always welcomed.

Cuban migration is the result of intimate social, political, and economic ties between the United States and Cuba. Cubans originally came to this country when the Cuban economy was strongly tied to that of the United States. The exiles, who came in the early 1960s, did so because of a long history of U.S. military interventions into Cuba, with the expectation that the U.S. government would assist in ousting Fidel Castro. Migrants today come mostly for economic rather than political motives, because of familial ties here in the United States, and a generally favorable immigration policy toward Cubans (Eckstein and Barberia 2002; Perez 2003; Pew Hispanic Center 2006b).

U.S. military intervention in Central America during the 1980s is the precursor to much of Central American migration to the United States. In the 1980s, migration to the United States from El Salvador and other Central American countries increased rapidly, both because of political violence in Central America and because of the economic setbacks that this violence entailed (Jones 1989). The civil war in El Salvador caused massive population displacements, and many displaced people came to the United States. Although the conditions in El Salvador have been the motivation for leaving, long-standing ties with the United States make this country a desirable destination for Salvadorans in search of refuge (Menjívar 2006). U.S. government and corporate interference in El Salvador not only helped to create the conditions that caused the displacement of Salvadorans, but also initiated the original ties that led refugees to the United States.

As part of Cold War strategy, the U.S. government supplied the Salvadoran government with more than $6 billion in military and economic aid between 1980 and 1992 (Quan 2003). This U.S. government-supplied military equipment was used to kill thousands of civilians and terrorize many more. Although it is well documented that Salvadorans were fleeing conflict in their country of origin, the U.S. government rarely granted them asylum. Between 1983 and 1990, only 2.6 percent of Salvadoran applicants for asylum in the United States were approved. Reagan officials were reluctant to create policies that would grant Salvadorans refugee status because to do so would be "to acknowledge that the governments it supported with millions of tax dollars were despotic regimes that violated human rights" (García 2006: 90). Instead of granting Salvadorans refugee status, they occasionally have been given temporary relief from deportation or other forms of temporary status. This created a situation, what Cecilia Menjívar (2006) calls *liminal legality,* which many migrants continue to experience. This uncertain legal status has led to prolonged family separations, limited access to higher education in the United States, and a disintegration of kinship networks.

Guatemalans began to migrate to the United States in large numbers during their long and bloody civil war, one in which the United States was heavily involved. In 1954, a CIA-sponsored military coup overthrew the democratically elected government of Jacobo Arbenz Guzman. This led to a civil war, which did not officially end until the peace accords were signed in 1996. During this time, a series of military officers ruled the country. Their rule frequently was challenged by guerilla armies, and this conflict caused intense violence, particularly in the countryside. Rural inhabitants suspected of being involved in guerilla activity were killed en masse. The U.S. government provided military aid to the government of Guatemala and trained Guatemalan military officers. The brutal practices of the Guatemalan military created an exodus of refugees (García 2006).

Many Guatemalan refugees settled in southern Mexico, with the hopes of eventually returning to their communities. However, violence in refugee camps and border settlements caused many to continue their trek northward to the United States, and for some, to Canada (García 2006). A 1976 earthquake propelled even more migrants to leave Guatemala, and about forty thousand Guatemalans entered the United States each year from that time through the 1990s. Today, although the civil war is officially over, poverty, high unemployment, and social disorder are left in its aftermath. The poor economic and social situation, combined with the strong ties to the United States, continues to push many Guatemalans to emigrate. Given the difficulties involved in acquiring permission to enter the United States, around half of the estimated one million Guatemalans in the United States lack the legal paperwork to remain in the country on a permanent basis (Menjívar 2007). Although Guatemalans ranked fifteenth in terms of the legal permanent resident population in 2007, they ranked third in the number of undocumented migrants in 2008, behind El Salvador and Mexico (U.S. Department of Homeland Security 2009a; U.S. Department of Homeland Security 2009b).

The United States government was heavily involved in Honduran politics and the Honduran economy throughout the twentieth century. In the 1950s and 1960s, the CIA funded labor unions in Honduras to ensure the failure of socialist movements. In 1954, the banana workers went on strike the same year that the

CIA aided in the ousting of President Jacobo Arbenz from his post in Guatemala. Fearful of the rise of socialism in Honduras, the United States Agency for International Development (USAID) and the CIA worked to take over Honduran labor movements, even granting U.S. visas to Honduran union leaders (Acker 1989).

The U.S. government and the CIA strengthened the Honduran military apparatus and set up a military training school in Honduras. Once the unrest in Central America began to settle down, with the help of U.S. military aid, U.S. corporations were quick to step in and set up shop in the free trade zones, orchestrated by the United States Agency for International Development (USAID) and funded by U.S. taxpayers. Today, Honduras is home to several free trade zones, where companies can set up manufacturing plants called *maquiladoras* (Jackson 2006; Acker 1989). The intense involvement of the United States in Honduran affairs has created and sustained migration flows; as of 2005, about twenty thousand Hondurans were migrating illegally to the United States each year (FONAMIH 2005). By January 2010, there were an estimated 330,000 undocumented Hondurans in the United States (U.S. Department of Homeland Security 2011).

The links between military intervention and migration to the United States are clear: U.S. military involvement in Asia and Latin America has sparked migration flows. However, these migrants have not been consistently welcomed into the United States, even when they have been fleeing conflicts that the U.S. military helped to create. During the Guatemalan civil war, for example, most Guatemalans were denied asylum or any other form of legal status in the United States. In contrast, in the aftermath of the 1965 Dominican Revolution, many Dominican dissidents were allowed to enter the United States legally. Both Guatemalans and Dominicans fled to the United States because of U.S.-sponsored military interventions. Because of the timing of the conflicts and the political orientation of the United States, Dominicans were favored in U.S. immigration policy.

Foreign Direct Investment

Military intervention and FDI often go hand in hand, and both are influential in creating migration flows. For example, the close economic ties between the United States and China are among the many possible explanations for Chinese migration. A centuries-long history of migration in combination with strong economic and social ties and trade relations has translated into tens of thousands of Chinese nationals coming to the United States each year, through whatever legal or illegal means available to them.

Although China is a vast country, the majority of Chinese immigrants in the United States come from just five of its thirty provinces. Prior to the 1940s, 90 percent of Chinese immigrants to the United States came from the Guangdong Province, which is somewhat isolated from the rest of China, yet close to large seaports, including Hong Kong. In fact, the majority of immigrants from China came from just one district within the province of Guangdong: Toishan (Skeldon 1996). With time, these flows changed, and by 1982, only 5 percent of emigrants came from Guangdong. This figure had gone down to 3 percent in 1995. By comparison, in 1982, less than 2 percent of Chinese immigrants came from the Fujian Province, yet by 1995, this figure had gone up to 28 percent (Liang and Morooka 2004).

In 2001, John Wang found that most undocumented Chinese came from the Fujian Province, and nearly all Fujianese come from just three counties—Changle, Lianjiang, and Minhou—all of which are just opposite Taiwan. Many undocumented Chinese immigrants travel on Taiwanese fishing boats at great personal risk. They often come to work in Chinatowns in major cities, both in the garment industry and the tourist sector. Their Chinese-language skills and familiarity with Chinese culture make them ideal employees. For unscrupulous employers, the illegal status of many Fujianese enhances their ability to abuse these employees, many of whom pay upward of $30,000 for their trip to the United States (Wang 2001).

The increase in emigration from Fujian appears to be related to two factors. The first is its close relationship with Taiwan. The second is the increase in foreign capital investment in this province, up from $379 million in 1990 to $4.1 billion in 1995 (Liang and Morooka 2004). The increase in capital investment by U.S. firms strengthens connections between these provinces and the United States and paves the way for emigration. Economic ties such as these increase the likelihood for emigration, because people are unlikely to migrate without strong financial linkages to their destination.

It's interesting to note the contrast between the types of emigrants coming from China. For instance, large numbers of Chinese immigrants also come from Beijing and Shanghai, which have many universities. Nearly all emigrants from Beijing are from the city, and 76.5 percent of them have some college education, as compared to emigrants from Fujian, 65 percent of whom are from rural areas, and less than 5 percent of whom have any college education. Immigrants from Fujian are much more likely to be undocumented.

Even more remarkable than the increase in emigrants from Fujian is the increase from the Yunnan Province. Emigrants from there accounted for less than

1 percent of Chinese immigrants in the United States in 1995. This jumped to nearly 30 percent of all Chinese emigrants in 2000 (Liang and Morooka 2004). Perhaps not incidental to this increase is the surge in foreign direct investment in the Yunnan Province. In addition, since the early 1990s, Yunnan has had a vibrant trading port and has become progressively more connected with the global economy, especially through its border with Vietnam (Biao 2003). In fact, all the major emigrant-sending areas in China are close to port cities, and many of these provinces have free trade zones. Of the four created in 1979, three were in the Guangdong Province, which is adjacent to Hong Kong, and the other zone was in Fujian and close to Taiwan (Biao 2003). In China, it is notable that foreign direct investment is related to emigration flows, and these flows are highly localized. Areas that see little FDI also see few emigrants.

Korean migration also has been motivated by continued participation of U.S. corporations in Korea's economy. Between 1962 and 1990, U.S. Foreign Direct Investment (FDI) accounted for about a quarter of all FDI in the Republic of Korea. In 2002, U.S. investment reached a peak, making up half of FDI flows in the Republic of Korea. The percentage of U.S. corporations in the Republic of Korea has ebbed and flowed, giving way, at times, to Japan and the European Union, but has been a constant presence since the 1960s (Min 2006). Correspondingly, we have seen continued flows of migrants from Korea to the United States.

Salvadoran migration to the United States goes back to the late nineteenth century, yet substantial numbers of Salvadorans did not begin to emigrate until the 1960s, about the same time that U.S.-based multinational companies began to invest heavily in manufacturing in El Salvador. These companies primarily set up factories in large urban centers in the departments of San Salvador, La Libertad, and Sonsonate. Industrialization attracted rural inhabitants to large cities, because it became increasingly difficult to make a living off of farming, especially in light of the fluctuations in coffee prices and the turbulence generated by increases in foreign investment. These changes in the Salvadoran economy led to increased emigration, both legal and illegal, to the United States during the 1960s and 1970s (Hamilton and Chinchilla 1991; Rickets 1987). Rickets (1987) uses multivariate analyses to demonstrate that growth in U.S. direct investment is positively correlated to increases in both legal and illegal immigration from countries in the Caribbean Basin.

Brazil has the tenth largest economy in the world in terms of GDP and the largest in Latin America; it is a major trading partner with the United States.

About 18 percent of its exports go to the United States, and about 16 percent of its imports come from the United States.[3] Brazil is the second greatest recipient of U.S. direct investment in the Western Hemisphere, trailing Canada by a wide margin. In 1995, Canada received 12 percent of all United States direct foreign investment, Brazil 3 percent, and Mexico 2 percent (U.S. Department of Agriculture 1998).

Overall, Brazil has a solid economy and strong ties to the United States. Emigrants to the United States from Brazil, however, come primarily from one state—Minas Gerais, the third wealthiest state in Brazil. Many of the migrants come from one municipality in Minas Gerais—Governador Valadares, one of the wealthiest municipalities in Minas Gerais.[4] In addition, 85 percent of people who emigrate from Governador Valadares go to the United States, compared to 42 percent of emigrants from Brazil as a whole (Fusco 2005).

Brazil was a net migrant receiving country until the early twentieth century, when it began to experience economic decline. By the mid-twentieth century, Brazil began to become a country of emigration. Emigration to the United States from Governador Valadares is a product of many factors, including exploitation of mica (a mineral used in the production of electronic devices) by U.S. companies in Minas Gerais, the involvement of U.S. corporations in the building of the railroad near Governador Valadares, and the experience of economic decline in Brazil in general. This flow of emigrants began in the 1960s and took off in the 1980s, when the Brazilian economy began to suffer. The people who migrated to the United States did not leave Brazil out of a need to survive; they saw migration as a way to accumulate enough capital to invest in a small business and attain a better standard of living in Brazil. Unlike Guatemalans, many Brazilians are able to go back to their countries of origin, and many do, once they have saved up enough investment funds. Not all have had financial success, however, and some have found it difficult to leave the United States after they and their families have become accustomed to living in the United States over many years (Siqueira 2007a, 2007b).

Migration from Brazil to the United States provides further evidence that migrant networks are crucial to promoting migration and shows the cumulative effects of ties between U.S. corporations and one Brazilian municipality, stretching back over fifty years. Relatively few Brazilians are legal permanent residents compared to other migrants for three primary reasons:

1. The relatively late start in migration flows from Brazil, which means many were not eligible for the 1986 amnesty
2. The fact that Brazilians, unlike the Cubans and the Vietnamese, were not granted refugee status

3. The relative ease with which Brazilians could obtain nonimmigrant (tourist or student) visas, up until the 1990s, when it became apparent that many Brazilians were overstaying their visas

In 1981, Brazilians were tenth among recipients of nonimmigrant (tourist or student) visas, and, by 1991, they climbed to fourth (Goza 1994). By 2005, Brazilians were among the top five among deportees, nearly all of whom were deported for illegal presence in the United States, and not for criminal activity (Dougherty et al. 2006).

Strong economic and political ties between the United States and Honduras have generated migration flows, even though Hondurans have great difficulty gaining legal entry to the United States. In 2000, U.S. businesses invested 42.5 percent of the total capital in Honduran maquiladoras, particularly in the textile industry. In that same year, more than one hundred thousand persons were employed in maquiladoras in Honduras, up from 9,000 in 1990 (Banco Central de Honduras 2001). U.S. laws work both to render Honduran migrants "illegal" and to prevent the migration of many other would-be migrants. Approximately eighty thousand Hondurans attempt to enter the United States each year, yet only about a quarter succeed. For every one hundred Hondurans who leave Honduras en route to the United States, seven enter legally, seventeen enter illegally, seventy-five return to Honduras, and one remains in either Mexico or Guatemala. Because of the difficulty of gaining legal status in the United States, Hondurans living in this country are three times more likely to be deported than to become naturalized as citizens (FONAMIH 2005; Sladkova 2007). In Repak's (1994) study of Central Americans in Washington, DC, she found that more of her informants were undocumented than not, and many had been recruited for work directly from their countries of origin. This relatively small country accounted for a disproportionate number of deportations in 2005—second in formal removals to Mexicans (Dougherty et al. 2006).

There has been a correlation between FDI and emigration from Mexico for over one hundred years. U.S. foreign direct investment in Mexico took off with the dictatorship of Porfirio Diaz (1876–1911), and Mexico experienced an economic boom. The uneven nature of the developments, however, led to the Mexican Revolution, and thus a temporary stall to FDI. However, despite the relatively nationalistic approach toward foreigners of the 1917 Constitution, FDI continued, in stops and starts, throughout the twentieth century in Mexico (Emiliano del Toro 1997). FDI in Mexico reached a peak with the signing of the North American Free Trade Agreement (NAFTA) in 1994.

Although NAFTA purportedly was designed to reduce immigration, it has caused a large upsurge in the numbers of Mexican immigrants in the United States for various reasons. First, NAFTA has had a devastating effect on the profitability of grain agriculture in Mexico. The entry of heavily subsidized and capital-intensive U.S. corn and other grains into the Mexican market has made it unprofitable to grow these grains in Mexico. Around two million Mexican peasants have been forced out of agriculture to find work in the cities and the United States. Second, NAFTA created favorable conditions in Mexico for large transnational retail corporations such as Walmart, which pushed smaller businesses to bankruptcy and forced their employees and owners to migrate. Finally, NAFTA has resulted in the reduction of wages along the Mexican border. When workers are earning lower than the subsistence level, they are also more likely to send a family member abroad to work or to migrate themselves to survive (Bacon 2004; López 2007).

Prior to the passage of NAFTA, Mexican immigrants came almost exclusively from Mexican states in what are known as the *traditional region* of migration and the northern states close to the border. The states in the traditional region include Aguascalientes, Colima, Durango, Guanajuato, Michoacán, Naryarit, San Luis Potosí, and Zacatecas. The northern border states include Baja California, Baja California Sur, Coahuila, Chihuahua, Nuevo León, Sinaloa, Sonora, and Tamaulipas. In 1993, 80 percent of Mexican migrants to the United States came from these states, meaning only 20 percent came from other Mexican states; by 1997, 25 percent came from other states; and by 2002, 31 percent came from other states of Mexico (Zúñiga Herrera 2006a).[5] In three of these states—Veracruz-Llave, Hidalgo, and Tlaxcala—the number of emigrants tripled between 1990 and 2003.[6]

Just as emigration has spread across Mexico, immigration has spread across the United States. Mexican immigrants were previously concentrated in a few states. Today Mexican immigrants can be found in every state of the United States. In 1970, 85 percent of Mexican immigrants lived in the traditional receiving region, which includes Arizona, California, New Mexico, and Texas. By the year 2000, only 69 percent of Mexican immigrants lived in those states, and Mexicans were the most predominant immigrant group in over half of the states in the United States (Zúñiga Herrera 2006b).

On July 28, 2005, President George W. Bush signed into law a new free trade agreement called the Dominican Republic–Central America–United States Free Trade Agreement (CAFTA-DR). CAFTA-DR is a free trade agreement between the United States, Costa Rica, El Salvador, Guatemala, Honduras,

Nicaragua, and the Dominican Republic. It is reasonable to expect that the further merging of the economies of the United States with migrant-sending countries will lead to more legal and illegal migration from these countries to the United States.

Legal permanent residents and undocumented migrants come to the United States because of similar structural forces. Labor recruitment, military interventions, and FDI create great incentives for migration; and these three factors have been responsible for both the legal and illegal flows. However, it is the immigration laws of the United States that determine the extent to which migration is legal or illegal. The following overview of the history of immigration law will make this point clearer.

Laws That Bind

What renders some migrants "illegal" is the lack of legislation that enables undocumented migrants to obtain proper documentation. Thus, when critics claim that the problem is the "illegals," we would do well to point out that the difference between the two classes of migrants is not that some are more willing to go to the "back of the line." It's that the primary distinction, as we've discussed, can be found in the historical relationship between their countries and ours, and the more or less punitive nature of U.S. immigration laws. Therefore, it is crucial to consider the laws and policies that have created the unfortunate distinctions between legal and undocumented migrants.

The idea that a person could be an "illegal alien" is based on the premise that some people have no right to be within a nation's borders and deserve to be deported. The concept of an illegal alien thus became meaningful to U.S. law and policy in the early twentieth century, when the U.S. Congress passed laws that appropriated funds for deportations and created such proceedings. Prior to that, the idea of an illegal alien had little substance. From the time the United States was created in 1776 until 1882 when Congress enacted the first federal immigration restrictions, there were no immigration policies to speak of. The passage of the 1882 Chinese Exclusion Act set the stage for U.S. immigration law in two significant ways:

1. It was racially exclusive.
2. It set the precedent that Congress would be able to decide who could enter and remain in the United States (Romero 2009).

Although the first restrictive laws were passed in 1882, there were not large numbers of deportations until the late 1920s. Between 1892 and 1907, the Immigration and Naturalization Service processed only a few hundred deportations each year, even though there were high numbers of immigrants. From 1908 to 1920, between two and three thousand deportations occurred per year, even though about one million immigrants entered the country between 1907 and 1917. As immigration restrictions sharpened, deportations increased. There were 9,495 deportations in 1925, and this number shot up to 38,796 in 1929. In 1929, Congress passed a law that made illegal entry a violation of U.S. laws. Prior to that, deportation was an administrative procedure. The laws passed in the 1920s fundamentally changed the nation's position toward immigrants and their potential contribution to society (Ngai 2004).

National Origins Quota System

One claim we often hear from nativists in the United States is that their ancestors went through the proper legal proceedings when they migrated to the United States. However, prior to 1924, when the bulk of Europeans came to the United States, there were no legal proceedings to speak of, and passports and visas were not necessary. It was not until 1924 that Europeans were required to apply for admission, and, by that time, immigration from Europe had already begun to decline (Ngai 2004).

The Johnson-Reed Act of 1924 established, for the first time, national-origin quotas for Europe, aimed at keeping undesirable immigration from Southern and Eastern Europe at bay. These quotas were calculated based on the composition of the United States in the early twentieth century, with the notable exception of the descendants of African slaves, American Indians, Asians, and all the countries in the Western Hemisphere. The national origin quotas were based on previous waves of European immigration, giving immigration laws an explicit racial bias that continued until 1952.

Asian immigrants were excluded from the United States between 1924 and 1952. The Johnson-Reed Act prohibited immigration from China, Japan, India, and other parts of Asia, on the grounds that Asians were not eligible to become U.S. citizens. After World War II, Congress passed the Chinese Exclusion Repeal Act of 1943, which lifted some exclusions and permitted Chinese nationals already in the country to become naturalized citizens. In 1946, Congress extended the right of citizenship to other Asians (Reimers 1981; Ngai 2004). The Immigration and Nationality Act of 1952 (the McCarran-Walter Act) lifted other restrictions on Asian immigration, yet it gave the government more power to deport suspected Communists. Finally, the Immigration and Nationality Act of 1965 discontinued the quotas based on national origin established by the 1924 Johnson-Reed Act.

1952 Immigration and Nationality Act

The Immigration and Nationality Act (INA) forms the basis for our immigration policy today. The INA established a structure that determined which immigrants could enter the United States, how many could enter, how they could obtain naturalization, and on what grounds they could be deported. The INA continues to be the statutory basis for immigration law today, although subsequent laws and reforms have modified it (Fragomen and Bell 2007).

1965 Immigration and Nationality Act

One of the most significant changes to U.S. immigration law in the twentieth century was the 1965 Immigration and Nationality Act, also called the 1965 Hart-Celler Act. This Act fundamentally changed the face of migration to the United States—from primarily European to mostly Asian and Latin American. The 1965 Act established a system of preferences based on family ties and skills and removed many former racial restrictions on immigration.

After the passage of the 1965 Act, Mexicans became more likely to settle in the United States, as opposed to coming as temporary workers. Until the 1970s, over 80 percent of Mexican immigrants were temporary workers who came to the United States to work in the agricultural sector for a few months and then returned to Mexico with their savings. By 1997, only 40 percent of Mexican migration was for temporary work in the agricultural sector (Avila, Fuentes, and Tuirán 2000). The 1965 Act encouraged the permanent settlement of Mexicans by granting preferences to family members of people already living in the United States.

The 1965 Act also created the "problem" of undocumented migration by placing quotas on immigrants from the Western Hemisphere. Prior to 1965, there were no numerical limits on the number of immigrants to be admitted from any country in the Western Hemisphere. The 1965 Act established a ceiling of one hundred twenty thousand immigrant visas. In 1976, a quota of twenty thousand immigrants per year was extended to all countries in the Western Hemisphere (Joppke 1998). The imposition of a quota of twenty thousand on immigrants from Mexico was unrealistic in the 1970s because of the need for Mexican labor and the desire of many Mexicans to work in the United States. As such, this quota led to substantial flows of undocumented migrants.

The 1965 Immigration Act also was a catalyst for increasing immigration from India and for attracting immigrants from states other than Punjab. This legislation gave greater importance to family ties and to higher skill levels among immigrants than did previous laws (Keely 1971). Together, these provisions have increased the number of Indian immigrants in the United States. Between 1966 and 1981, 215,640 Asian Indians came to the United States. This rate of 14,376 per year is twenty times higher than the rate at the previous peak in the period just before World War I. The majority of these new immigrants were professionals, with less than 1 percent working in farm labor occupations (Gonzales 1986).

Indian migrants continue to be primarily high skilled. In recent years, they have been the primary recipients of the H1-B visas, which are skills-based visas that require an employment contract and the condition that no national workers can be found to fill the jobs. In 2003, 37 percent of the recipients of these visas—75,964 people—were from India (Chellaraj, Maskus, and Mattoo 2006; Khadria 2006). Prior to security measures enforced after 9/11, even more Indians were admitted under this visa program—104,543 in 2001.

Similar to other countries, the 1965 Immigration Act changed immigration patterns from the Philippines to the United States. Between 1965 and 1985, about 667,000 Filipinos obtained visas to come to the United States. These Filipino migrants consisted of two distinct groups of people. The first group came on family reunification visas from the networks of the pre-1965 migrants. The second included highly trained migrants who obtained employment visas. During the first ten years after the passage of this Act, about two-thirds of Filipino immigrants came on family reunification visas. The remaining third came on employment-based visas, mostly as professionals and other highly trained individuals (Liu, Ong, and Rosenstein 1991).

With the passage of the 1965 Immigration and Nationality Act, Koreans quickly became one of the largest immigrant groups in the United States. In 1965, 2,165 Koreans entered the United States. In 1970, 9,314 came. In 1977, 30,917 entered (Reimers 1981; Min 1990). Between 1975 and 1990, Korea sent more immigrants to the United States than any other country, with the exception of Mexico and the Philippines. Korean immigrants were relatively highly educated, and 30 percent in the 1970s came on skills-based visas. The remaining 70 percent came on family reunification visas. Korean immigrants also tend to come from urban centers in Korea; more than half of the Koreans in the United

States in the 1980s came from Seoul, and more than three-quarters were from the three largest cities in Korea (Min 1990).

The reunification provisions of the 1965 Act also led to the growth of the Vietnamese population in the United States well after the Vietnam War ended. The flow of refugees from Vietnam slowed substantially after 1981, when the U.S. government placed restrictions on their entry (Kelly 1986). Those who were in the United States already, however, had the right to bring their family members to the United States under the family reunification provisions of the Immigration and Nationality Act. Legal immigration through family reunification policies, combined with illegal immigration, led to the continued growth of the Vietnamese population. According to the 1990 Census, there were 614,547 people of Vietnamese descent living in the United States. By the 2000 Census, there were more than one million, nearly a quarter of whom had been born in the United States. Yet, there were an estimated 160,000 undocumented Vietnamese in the United States in January 2006 (U.S. Department of Homeland Security 2007).

The numerical restrictions for immigrants from countries in the Western Hemisphere put in place with the 1965 Immigration Act consistently have been lower than the number of immigrants needed to sustain economic growth in the United States. This imbalance has led to increased undocumented migration (Massey, Durand, and Malone 2002). Undocumented immigration reached unprecedented levels and became a matter of public debate for the first time in the 1970s. During the 1980s, public opposition to undocumented immigration grew, and politicians began to get tough on immigration. Eventually, another major legislative change took place in 1986.

IRCA

IRCA came about in the context of concern over rising numbers of undocumented immigrants in the United States. The tightening economy, combined with the arrival of increasing numbers of Latin Americans, generated waves of nativism and anti-immigrant sentiment. The concern over large numbers of undocumented migrants often had a racial tenor insofar as the debates made it clear that the "problem" with immigration was the high and increasing numbers of Mexicans in the United States (Inda 2006). These concerns translated into Congressional action, and IRCA was enacted in 1986.

As the name implies, IRCA included immigration reform and control provisions. The twin prongs of IRCA were as follows:

1. To offer a legalization option for people who lived in the United States but did not have proper authorization to work in the country
2. To impose sanctions on employers who hired people not authorized to work in the United States

The imposition of sanctions was meant to deter employers from hiring undocumented workers. The backlash proved, instead, to create an industry that produced fraudulent documentation, making it easy for anyone to obtain the (false) documents they needed to work (Fragomen and Bell 2007). The legalization of temporary workers encouraged more migrants to settle permanently in the United States and to bring their families with them (Massey et al. 2002). Once migrants obtained legal residence or citizenship, they were able to bring over family members, under family reunification provisions.

1990 Immigration Act

The Immigration Act of 1990 changed some parts of the immigration selection system, revised the grounds for deportation, and created some protections for asylees. The 1990 Act expanded the definition of who should be deported for engaging in criminal activity and made many immigrants ultimately deportable for having committed "aggravated felonies" (Fragomen and Bell 2007). It also eliminated some grounds for deportation, such as participation in the Communist Party (Gordon, Mailman, and Yale-Loehr 2008).

1996 Laws

In 1996, Congress passed two laws that fundamentally changed the rights of all foreign-born people in the United States: the Anti-Terrorism and Effective Death Penalty Act (AEDPA) and the Illegal Immigration Reform and Immigrant Responsibility Act of 1996 (IIRIRA). These laws were striking in that they eliminated judicial review of some deportation orders, required mandatory detention for many noncitizens, and introduced the potential for the use of secret evidence in certain cases. Two of the most pernicious consequences of these laws are related to the treatment of refugees and the deportation of legal permanent residents (Welch 2002). Refugees and asylees are noncitizens who are unable or unwilling to return to their country of origin because of persecution or fear of persecution. Legal permanent residents are noncitizens who have been granted legalization and have the right to remain in the United States, so long as they do not violate provisions in the INA. Legal permanent residents are commonly referred to as *green card holders.*

The 1996 laws greatly increased the likelihood that refugees and asylees would be placed in detention. Since the passage of these laws, asylees who arrive at the U.S. border have to convince the border inspector that they have a credible fear of persecution. They have no right to a hearing if the border inspector does not believe that they have such a credible fear. If the border inspector does think they may have a case, the applicants for asylum are placed in detention while they wait for decisions on their cases. If the border inspector determines that they do not have a credible fear of persecution, they face immediate deportation, with few options for appeal (Fragomen 1997).

The 1990 Act expanded the grounds for deportation, but the 1996 laws were more draconian. Under IIRIRA, legal permanent residents who are convicted of an array of crimes are subject to detention and deportation. Legal permanent residents who have been in the United States for less than seven years face detention and deportation for relatively minor crimes; for example, jumping a turnstile in the New York subway could render a person deportable (Morawetz 2000).

Legal permanent residents who have been in the United States for more than seven years face mandatory deportation if they are convicted of "aggravated felonies." These include any felony or misdemeanor where the person is sentenced to at least one year in prison, regardless of whether the sentence is served or suspended. These crimes can also be relatively minor, such as the theft of baby clothes from a department store. These cases do not require judicial review, meaning that people do not have the right for a judge to take into account the specifics of the case or the ties that person has to the United States. Further, the law applies retroactively. This means that any legal permanent resident charged with a crime at any time during his stay in the United States could be subject to deportation. For example, a person could have come to the United States legally at age two, been convicted of resisting arrest at age seventeen, and—twenty years later, *after* the passage of IIRIRA—could be subject to deportation at age thirty-seven. Even adopted children of U.S. citizens have faced deportation under these laws, in those cases where parents failed to naturalize their children prior to age eighteen (Morawetz 2000; Master 2003). In light of the heavy policing of black and Latino neighborhoods and of black and Latino youth in particular, immigrants from Latin America and the Caribbean are more likely to face deportation because of these laws.

These laws eliminated judicial review of aggravated felony cases. Judges have no discretion once a determination is made that a crime is an aggravated felony.

In criminal proceedings, judicial review serves as a safeguard against abuse of power by law enforcement agents, because it requires officers to justify their actions to a neutral decision maker: a judge. Doing away with judicial review entails eliminating the separation of powers between the courts and law enforcement. The separation of powers is a fundamental part of the U.S. Constitution and is intended to maintain a balance of powers and thus a fairer system of justice. Practically speaking, the absence of judicial review in immigration cases means that legal permanent residents who have lived in the United States for decades, have contributed greatly to society, and have extensive family ties in the country are subject to deportation for relatively minor crimes they may have committed years ago.

Judges do not have the opportunity to take people's family and community ties into account. Nor can judges take into account weak or nonexistent linkages to their countries of birth. The only recourse that people facing deportation, on aggravated felony charges, have is to hire their own lawyer (often paying thousands of dollars) to argue that the charge they face is not in fact an aggravated felony. If the judge determines that the crime is indeed an aggravated felony, the defendant cannot present evidence that, for example, he is the sole caregiver of a disabled U.S.-citizen child. Without judicial review, the judge cannot take family ties or the needs of U.S.-citizen children into account in aggravated felony cases.

Homeland Security Act of 2002

In early 2003, the operations of immigrant detention and removal were transferred to ICE, as part of the overall restructuring of the INS and the creation of the DHS under the Homeland Security Act of 2002 (Dow 2004: 11). With immigration enforcement operations inside the Department of Homeland Security, the budget allocated to arresting, detaining, and deporting noncitizens has increased substantially. In the absence of Congressional action on immigration policies, existing immigration laws have been enforced more vigorously.

USA PATRIOT and REAL ID Acts

Two more laws were passed in the wake of 9/11 that increased the number of people who must be detained by ICE: the USA PATRIOT and the REAL ID Acts. The Uniting and Strengthening America by Providing Appropriate Tools Required to Intercept and Obstruct Terrorism Act of 2001 (USA PATRIOT Act) increased the budget for immigration enforcement, both on the border and internally, which has led to more detentions and deportations. The REAL ID

Act, of 2005, includes provisions that require proof of legal presence for people to obtain driver's licenses. Together, these Acts enact further restrictions on the judicial review of immigration cases and make the asylum-seeking process more difficult (Hines 2006).

Both of these Acts continue the trend of vesting more power in the executive branch and thus further disrupting the balance of powers that is the foundation of our democracy. The USA PATRIOT Act was passed in just six weeks—from its initial draft to the final vote. Moreover, many of the deliberations were conducted behind closed doors, and most legislators were not given sufficient time to read the 131 pages of the bill before being asked to vote.[7] Although these laws were passed quickly and without much deliberation in the interest of fighting terrorism,[8] the Department of Homeland Security has used the immense resources it has been endowed with to capture scores of undocumented migrants.

ICE has made internal strategic decisions that have led to a continued escalation of the number of detainees and deportees. In fiscal year 2007, an average of 29,786 people were detained by ICE, and more than 322,000 migrants passed through ICE detention facilities, 276,912 of whom were deported (ICE Fiscal Year 2007 Annual Report). In Fiscal Year 2007, ICE implemented a comprehensive interior enforcement strategy focused on more efficient processing of apprehended illegal aliens and reducing the criminal and fugitive alien populations. These "successes" allow ICE to request more funds to enhance its operations. This enhancement of interior and border enforcement has had a disproportionate and adverse impact on black and Latino immigrants.

Criminalizing the Undocumented: Arizona's SB 1070

The laws discussed earlier are federal laws—as immigration law is in the domain of the legislative branch of the federal government. However, in the absence of any major legislative changes since 1996, states have begun to take immigration laws into their own hands. Arizona's SB 1070 is one example. Arizona SB 1070 went into effect on July 29, 2010; its passage sparked national debate, protests, and boycotts. A month later, twenty cities or counties had issued official boycotts of the state of Arizona.[9] When Arizona Governor Jan Brewer signed SB 1070 on April 23, 2010, the law required local law enforcement agents to determine the immigration status of any person with whom they interacted during the course of their duties. This meant, for example, that if a police officer responded to a call for domestic violence, he would be required to check the immigration status of both the perpetrator and the victim, if he had reason to believe that either may be in in the country unlawfully.

SB 1070 was subsequently modified with the enactment of House Bill (HB) 2162 on April 30, 2010, which changed the language such that police officers would only be required to check the immigration status of people during a lawful stop, detention, or arrest. With these modified provisions, SB 1070 only required intervention in those cases in which a person was suspected of violating state laws. These modifications relieved some concerns that those victims of such crimes would be unlikely to contact law enforcement officials, yet the possibility of racial profiling remained a substantial problem.

Section 2 of SB 1070, as amended by HB 2162, requires law enforcement officers to determine the immigration status of a person "where reasonable suspicion exists that the person is an alien who is unlawfully present in the United States." The question remains: how will a police officer establish reasonable suspicion that a person is unlawfully present? Lawful or unlawful presence in the United States is a legal distinction that is not discernable to a law enforcement official. A noncitizen may not even know herself whether or not she is lawfully present, because she may be unaware of having violated the provisions of her visa. Someone could even be a U.S. citizen and not be knowledgeable of citizenship status. Insofar as it is impossible for a law enforcement official to determine a person's legal status based on her appearance, Arizona police officers must rely on either documentation or their preconceived notions as to what an undocumented migrant looks like. In the United States, U.S. citizens are not required to carry proof of their citizenship. This makes relying on documents problematic.

How, then, will police officers determine whether a person is lawfully present? According to an *amicus brief* filed by the American Immigration Lawyers Association (AILA), "There is simply no unbiased means of implementing the term 'unlawful presence,' because as a *legal* status there are no observable characteristics of 'unlawful presence' or readily available means by which a police officer could discern 'unlawful presence' in any stop, detention, or investigative encounter." (Emphasis used in original text.)[10]

Another controversial provision of SB 1070 can be found in Section 6, which states that Arizona police officers can make warrantless arrests if they have probable cause to believe that an individual has "committed any public offense that makes the person removable from the United States." This provision is problematic because it is often impossible for a police officer to determine whether a noncitizen could be deported for committing a particular offense. There is not a clear list of crimes that render people deportable. Whether noncitizens will be ordered deported for criminal activity depends on the nature of the crime, their length of stay in the United States, their ties to this country, the possibility of persecution in their home country, and a host of other factors. It is practically impossible for police officers to determine, in the course of duty, whether noncitizens could in fact be removable.

The day before SB 1070 was scheduled to take effect, Judge Susan Bolton of the Federal District Court issued a preliminary injunction against sections of the law. This ruling stopped the requirement that police check the immigration status of people during the course of stops, detentions, and arrests and blocked provisions that allowed police officers to hold anyone arrested for any crime until the individual's immigration status was determined. It also blocked the provision that authorized the warrantless arrest of anyone suspected of having committed a removable offense and those that made it a crime to fail to apply for or carry alien registration papers or for an undocumented migrant to solicit, apply for, or perform work.[11] For the time being, SB 1070 has lost its teeth. However, the rhetoric on which it was based lives on—especially the idea that all undocumented migrants are criminals.

Creating *Illegals*

The analyses discussed here demonstrate that U.S. military and economic policies have played a critical role in generating and directing migrant labor flows—both legal and illegal. Seen in this light, the criminalization of undocumented immigrants is both shortsighted and unwarranted, whereas changes in immigration policy are essential. The distinction between legal permanent residents and undocumented migrants has little to do with the level of criminality of the individuals in question and much to do with the extent to which U.S. foreign relations and labor needs are in line with U.S. immigration policy. Nearly all people who came to the United States prior to 1980 are legal permanent residents or citizens by now. Those people are more likely to be Cuban or Dominican than Brazilian, Honduran, or Guatemalan. This is because of the timing of the historical relationships between the United States and these countries.

A consideration of immigrants' country of origin and time of arrival in the United States provides a much better explanation of why some immigrants are "illegal" and others are not, rather than the uninformed idea of individual migrants' propensity to criminality. A comparison of Brazilians to Dominicans, for example, demonstrates this point. Few Brazilians came to the United States prior to the 1980s because the Brazilian economy was doing fairly well. When the economy began to decline, the relationships between people in Minas Gerais,

Brazil, and Massachusetts translated into chain migration. Brazilians were able to obtain tourist visas to come to the United States, and many overstayed their visas, transforming them into undocumented migrants. The inability of many Brazilians to obtain legal permanent residence is a consequence of the laws in place, which make this nearly impossible for most people.

In contrast, many Dominicans came to the United States between 1961 and 1968, when the U.S. military was heavily involved in their country. The facility with which many Dominicans obtained visas and legalization is a product of the laws in place, at that time, which facilitated this process. Dominicans who came to the United States on tourist visas were able to adjust their status and obtain legal residence, either based on their family ties in the United States or through the provisions for amnesty in the Immigration Reform and Control Act of 1986. Others came to the United States through family migration policies established by the 1965 Act. The changes in immigration policy in 1986, 1996, and subsequent years have made the process of legalization much more difficult. The problem of illegal immigration, then, does not lie in the criminality of the individual migrant,[12] but in the fact that current laws and policies are out of sync with both U.S. foreign relations and labor needs in the United States.

Importantly, these laws have been out of sync for a long time. As Europe underwent modernization and industrialization at the end of the nineteenth century, it sent millions of emigrants abroad. Douglas Massey (1988) argues that mass emigration from Europe was fundamental to the modernization process. Emigration from Europe ended before modernization was complete, in the 1920s, due to the introduction of restrictive immigration policies. Prior to the introduction of these policies, migration was a win-win situation for many in the United States and in Europe. Employers in the United States had access to a large labor force, and European countries were able to ease some of the pressures of rapid economic development through emigration. Since the introduction of restrictive immigration laws, immigration to the United States has, of course, continued, but with consequence that these restrictive laws have created vulnerability for many migrants and have done more to marginalize migrants than to influence migration flows. It's important to document the consequences of this criminalization. A consideration of how immigration law enforcement terrorizes immigrant communities and tears apart families, in the following chapters, gives examples of the effects of such consequences.

CHAPTER 2

THE DEPARTMENT OF HOMELAND SECURITY AND THE IMMIGRATION ENFORCEMENT REGIME OF THE TWENTY-FIRST CENTURY

For most of the twentieth century, immigration enforcement in the United States focused primarily on the U.S./Mexico border. In the last decade of the twentieth century, the process of border militarization accelerated. Presidents ordered walls to be built and fortified. Thousands of Border Patrol agents were stationed along the southern border. The Border Patrol placed a variety of technological innovations designed to detect unauthorized migrants at strategic locations near the border (Andreas 2000). Ground troops were deployed to assist police in the southern border region (Dunn 2001). Despite criticism from immigrant advocates and researchers, border militarization continues apace.

In addition to border militarization, we are now witnessing an unprecedented surge in interior enforcement. Whereas *border militarization* refers to the use of military-style techniques along the border to prevent the entry of undocumented migrants, *interior enforcement* describes policing strategies designed to find undocumented migrants within the borders of the United States. The only time we have seen such large-scale enforcement of immigration laws within the borders of the United States was during the Great Depression when the United States engaged in a mass repatriation of Mexicans.

In 1930, there were about 1.5 million Mexicans and Mexican-Americans in the United States (as compared to nearly 30 million today). Balderrama and Rodríguez (2006) estimate that the majority of the 1.5 million people of Mexican origin residing in the United States were deported in the 1930s; as many as one million Mexicans and their children were repatriated to Mexico in this decade. This repatriation has been heavily criticized. In 2003, for example, the

California Senate Select Committee on Citizen Participation held hearings on the repatriation, and the California legislature passed a bill that authorized the creation of a commission to explore and document the repatriation. The bill never became law, however, due to a veto by Governor Arnold Schwarzenegger (Johnson 2004). In recent years, advocates have demanded an apology at the national level for the inhumanity of these mass deportations.[1]

In the first decade of the twenty-first century, DHS deported more than two and a half million people, and nearly three-quarters of them were Mexican.[2] The current era of mass deportation remarkably has led to more deportations than the mass repatriation of the 1930s. The mass repatriation of Mexicans in the 1930s is different from the current era, however, in two ways. First, it accounted for a much larger portion of the Mexican population. Second, many more legally present Mexicans and even U.S. citizens of Mexican descent were deported as a matter of course. Today, most Mexican deportees are undocumented, and citizens are only rarely deported, usually due to bureaucratic errors. This mass repatriation of people of Mexican origin in the 1930s is similar to the current era of deportation insofar as it was accomplished through raids that terrorized communities. Unfortunately, this aspect of the story has not changed, to any great extent, in the twenty-first century.

An examination of what happens during immigration raids and inside immigrant detention facilities reveals startling results regarding the human consequences of the increases in U.S. interior enforcement. The escalation of raids and detentions has worsened the lot of noncitizens in the United States. Immigration raids terrify communities. For instance, the day after a large-scale immigration raid in Postville, Iowa, half of the children did not report to school. It took weeks for normal school attendance to resume. Many noncitizens have undergone brutal mistreatment in immigrant detention facilities, and many more have faced verbal abuse, neglect, and illness.

Although the assumed goal of immigration raids is to target noncitizens, they also affect citizens. Jeffrey Abram Hernandez, for example, was born in the United States in 2005, and he now lives in Xicalcal, Guatemala with his parents, Viviana and Filiberto. They live with Filiberto's mother, sisters, and brothers because they cannot afford a place of their own. Since their return to Guatemala in late 2007, Filiberto has not been able to find work, and the family struggles to survive. Although Jeffrey is a U.S. citizen, his parents entered the country illegally and were deported after a raid at the Michael Bianco Inc. factory in New Bedford, Massachusetts.[3] Jeffrey is one of many children whose, as a migrant mother adeptly put it, "wings have been cut"[4] due to immigration policy. Their lives have been severely and often irreparably affected by raids carried out by the U.S. Immigrations and Customs Enforcement (ICE). In Guatemala, Jeffrey will not find the same educational opportunities that he would have in the United States. Although he will have the right to return to the United States when he is able to do so, on his own, he most likely will have to enter the low-wage sector of the economy, because his chances for getting beyond the sixth grade are slim.

Raiding Our Communities

Immigration raids are one of the most visible aspects of the increases in immigration enforcement. These raids lead to the *de facto* deportation of U.S. citizens and wreak havoc on immigrant communities by creating a fearful and distrusting climate. A de facto deportation of a U.S. citizen occurs when a noncitizen parent or spouse of a U.S. citizen is deported, and the U.S. citizen's best or only alternative for survival is to accompany this person back to his homeland.

Worksite and home raids have occurred with growing frequency over the past few years, despite limited evidence of their efficacy at removing dangerous people or reducing the numbers of undocumented employees in the United States. In fiscal year (FY) 2002, worksite raids led to just over 485 arrests; in 2007, they led to 5,184. To achieve such marked escalation, ICE has had to implement a sixfold increase in the number of officers it employs to carry out worksite operations.[5] These new tactics were put into place in 2006 and continued throughout 2007 and 2008, with devastating effects on immigrant communities.

Such massive immigration law enforcement efforts have been possible because of an enormous infusion of money, in recent years, into both the established and newly created agencies. In the aftermath of the terrorist attacks of September 11, 2001, the U.S. government's launch of the "war on terror," with its mission to prevent such attacks in the future, created the Department of Homeland Security (DHS) in 2003. This new government agency was specifically designed to subsume all aspects of homeland security. DHS took over all the operations of the Immigration and Naturalization Service (INS) as well as those of other agencies, including the Federal Marshall Service, the Secret Service, and the U.S. Coast Guard, that were not part of the INS. The creation of such an overarching and broad-based agency as DHS was the most significant transformation of the U.S. government's security structure in over a half-century. For immigration policy, the transfer of immigration law enforcement from the Department of Justice (DOJ) to the DHS was a critical moment; the policy took on new meaning when it became central to the United States' efforts in fighting terrorism.

The DHS has a much bigger budget, being a much larger agency than its predecessor, the INS. Moreover, this budget has steadily increased since its creation in 2003—from $31.2 billion to $50.5 billion in 2009.[6] Of the $50.5 billion DHS budget for FY 2009, about $10.9 billion went to Customs and Border Patrol (CBP), $5.7 billion to ICE, and $2.7 billion to Citizenship and Immigration Services (USCIS). ICE's budget of $5.7 billion means that unprecedented amounts of money are put into interior enforcement. ICE's budget alone is now larger than the entire budget of the INS. In 2002, the last full year of the existence of the INS, its budget was at an all-time high of $6.2 billion, up from $1.5 billion in 1993. Based on the dollar value of that year, this represented a growth of 223 percent.[7] In the early 1990s, less than 10 percent of the INS budget was dedicated to interior enforcement.[8] Now that the DHS has replaced the INS, 10 percent of the much larger DHS budget goes to interior enforcement. This budget is used for home and worksite raids as well as a variety of other enforcement operations.

Home Raids

ICE agents use home raids to go into private homes in search of suspected undocumented migrants or "criminal aliens." The agents typically conduct the raid in the following format. Early in the morning, when most occupants are sleeping, the agents surround a house and pound on the door and windows. If the occupant opens the door, the agents enter the home, frequently without properly identifying themselves or gaining the consent of the occupant. Once the agents enter the house, they order all the occupants—including children and the elderly—to a central location. Although the agents are often looking for a particular person who is suspected to be a fugitive or criminal alien, they frequently interrogate all occupants of the house and arrest anyone who they suspect is unlawfully present in the United States. Such an act is roughly equivalent to police agents entering a house where a suspected robber lives, finding the robber does not live there, yet arresting other people in the house, simply because they are suspected of having the same criminal tendencies. ICE refers to these literally "unwarranted" arrests of suspected undocumented migrants as *collateral arrests*. Because you cannot tell whether someone is undocumented simply by looking at them, many U.S. citizens and legally present people of Latin American origin have been arrested in these raids (Azmy, Farbenblum, Michelman, et al. 2008).

ICE home raids, over the past decade, have involved a series of violations both of people's constitutional rights and of ICE's own policies. According to a recent report, aptly titled "Constitution on ICE," ICE agents routinely fail to observe constitutional rights during home raids. The Fourth Amendment to the Constitution implicitly protects citizens and noncitizens from unreasonable searches and seizures. When ICE agents with an administrative warrant enter a person's home without consent, they are violating that person's constitutional rights, as well as ICE's own guidelines. Chiu et al. (2009) point out that ICE's Field Manual is clear in its stipulation that administrative warrants do not grant officers the authority to enter private homes without consent and that ICE agents are also not allowed to arrest people without probable cause. However, according to a vast amount of evidence—including eyewitness accounts of home raids, lawsuits, media reports, and ICE's own documentation—these rights are violated on a consistent basis.

Attorneys, from the Seton Hall School of Law, filed a civil rights action in which the plaintiffs claimed they were victims of unconstitutional practices in the course of several home raids. Some of the plaintiffs were U.S. citizens or lawful residents. They reported that ICE agents gained unlawful entry to their homes through deceit or force and detained the occupants of the home without a judicial warrant. One of the plaintiffs in this case, Maria Argueta, had valid Temporary Protection Status (TPS), which allowed her to remain lawfully in the United States. Maria reported that around 4:30 a.m. on January 29, 2008, ICE agents banged loudly on the doors and windows of her home. When she opened the door, they told her they were police agents (which is inaccurate) and that they were looking for a certain man who Maria did not know. Although she told them she did not know the man, and the officers did not have a search warrant, they proceeded to search her entire apartment. After not finding the man in question anywhere in her apartment, they asked Maria about her immigration status. She told them about her TPS and that she was waiting to receive her card in the mail. Despite producing a letter that indicated her card would arrive soon, the ICE agents seized her passport and arrested her. She was placed in detention where she remained for 36 hours before being released. In FY 2007, similar operations resulted in 2,079 arrests in New Jersey alone. Fewer than 15 percent of these arrestees had any criminal history, even though these raids are designed to find criminal fugitives (Azmy, Farbenblum, Michelman, et al. 2008).

Maria Argueta's home raid was part of the National Fugitive Operations Program (NFOP), an initiative led by ICE that has come under harsh criticism for its inefficacy. NFOP is intended to enhance national security by finding and deporting dangerous "fugitive aliens." A *fugitive alien,* as defined by the NFOP, is a noncitizen who has been ordered to be deported yet has not left the country. NFOP's budget has increased dramatically since its inception in 2003—from $9 million to $218 million in FY 2008. A recent report by the Migration Policy Institute criticizes the program, primarily because of its failure to arrest dangerous fugitives—"NFOP has failed to focus its resources on the priorities Congress intended when it authorized the program. In effect, NFOP has succeeded in apprehending the easiest targets, not the most dangerous fugitives" (Mendelson, Strom, and Wishnie 2009: 2). Although NFOP is designed to deport dangerous criminals, nearly three-quarters of the people they apprehended through February 2008 had no criminal records. In 2007, with a $183 million budget, NFOP arrested only 672 fugitive aliens that ICE considered to be dangerous. The other 30,000 arrested were people with deportation orders (15,646), undocumented migrants (12,084), or noncitizens who had been convicted of nonviolent crimes, such as shoplifting (2,005). Mendelson et al. of the Migration Policy Institute point out that "the number of fugitive aliens with criminal convictions arrested … remained relatively constant between FY 2004 and FY 2008. Congressional allocations to NFOP, by contrast, grew 17-fold over the same period" (2009: 15).

NFOP has been given the money and the authority by Congress to search homes for dangerous criminal and fugitive aliens who threaten national security. However, in FY 2007, 40 percent of people arrested by these agents were ordinary undocumented migrants who were neither fugitive aliens nor convicted criminals. These noncitizen arrests occurred even though there was no warrant for their arrest, nor were they given a hearing before an immigration judge.

Such arrests happened because the executive branch has given ICE agents the authority to enforce immigration law, and they do not need a warrant to arrest noncitizens. Although it seems improbable that lawmakers in the United States Congress would approve legislation that permitted federal agents to roam the streets in search of immigration status violators because of the civil rights implications of such practices, this is, in effect, what NFOP has done (Mendelson, Strom, and Wishnie 2009).

Despite criticism from legal advocates and immigrant rights organizations, these practices continue. I learned firsthand the effects of these home raid practices when, in February 2010, I spoke with "Maximo," a Dominican citizen who lived in Puerto Rico. Maximo shared an apartment in San Juan with two other men—a Venezuelan and a Puerto Rican. Early one morning in January 2010, they heard loud banging on the door. Maximo tried to sleep through it, but the banging got louder. Finally, he got up to answer the door. Just before he reached the door, the people knocking decided to break down the door. Maximo found himself surrounded by several officers, some of whom had jackets with *ICE* stamped on them. The agents did not indicate that they had a warrant for the arrest of a specific person. Instead, they demanded to see all occupants of the house, pointed guns at them, and ordered them to sit on the floor. Finally, they gave Maximo his clothes and allowed him to get dressed. When they asked him for identification, he gave them his Dominican passport. They asked if he was in the country illegally, and he said he was.

Once the search was over, Maximo was arrested and taken to an immigration detention center. He signed a voluntary departure form and was deported to Santo Domingo two days later. From Maximo's recounting of the story, it would seem his constitutional rights against search and seizure were violated. By law, immigration agents have administrative warrants that do not permit them to enter houses without the consent of the occupants. They definitely were not looking for Maximo, as he had never had previous encounters with immigration agents, and thus could not have had a deportation order. He just happened to be there and was arrested when he revealed that he was undocumented. Maximo's arrest is one of the many collateral arrests made by ICE agents during home raids. These sorts of arrests account for a substantial portion of arrests during home raids. Apart from reports by human rights advocates, these home raids have not received much national attention. In contrast, worksite raids or *worksite enforcement operations,* as ICE calls them, were something of a media spectacle between 2006 and 2008.

Worksite Raids

The stated goals of worksite enforcement operations are to ensure fair labor standards and eliminate the "job magnet": the existence of jobs that attract undocumented labor migrants to the United States. ICE has a goal or internally set quota of 18,000 arrests per year through these raids. Each year, Congress appropriates billions of dollars for worksite raids. In this type of raid, hundreds of ICE agents descend on a workplace and inspect the documents of the workers present to determine who should be taken into custody. This process often takes several hours, and normal operations of the workplace are stopped. These raids are intrusions to workflow. Those that are on a larger scale have immediate effects on the entire community. When word gets out that a raid is taking place, community members assemble outside of the plant or other site to find out if their loved ones are being apprehended or if they will be released. A general sense of panic and fear pervades the community, because many in the community are either undocumented or have family members or friends who are.

Once ICE officials have determined which of the workers they will take into custody, the workers are put onto buses and taken to an ICE processing facility. Some of these workers agree to be deported immediately without a hearing (voluntary departure), some are put into detention facilities, others are referred to federal or state authorities for criminal charges, and some are released on their own recognizance pending an immigration hearing. Those workers who are not immediately deported are eventually allowed to stay in the United States legally or are formally deported later, depending on the outcome of their immigration trial.

To shed light on this particular era of immigration law enforcement, it is useful to take a close look at four highly publicized raids—Greeley, Colorado; New Bedford, Massachusetts; Little Village, Chicago; and Postville, Iowa. The raid in Greeley, Colorado, in December 2006 marked the beginning of this era of ICE raids, and the raid in Postville, Iowa, marks the end. These are four of the largest raids in the history of immigration law enforcement. Although these raids represent less than 1 percent of all people deported during this time period, they received substantial media attention and came under harsh criticism for human rights violations; fortunately, these types of raids seem to have come to an end.

Greeley, Colorado—December 12, 2006

On a cold morning in December, workers at Swift Meatpacking Co. got up early and went to work as they did every morning, where they earned between $10 and $15 per hour for full-time work and had health and other benefits. At 7:25 a.m., shortly after everyone had begun to carry out their daily tasks, ICE agents surrounded the plant and sealed all the exits. When the heavily armed agents stormed into the plant, many of the workers were frightened; some even threw themselves into the cattle pens. All of the workers were led into the cafeteria and separated into two groups—those who claimed to have the proper documents to work and those who did not. Workers, both men and women, were frightened, and many were reduced to tears (Bacon 2007; Capps et al. 2007).

Word about the raid spread quickly to the community, and family and community members massed around the gates of the plant. Some people brought their family members' documents to the plant for them, while others shouted at the ICE agents not to take away their loved ones. Onlookers screamed that children were crying in school for their parents, that they were not terrorists, simply workers. Outside the factory gates, a priest led a vigil, as was particularly appropriate, because this was the day of the Virgin of Guadalupe.[9] Some high school students learned about the raids via their mobile phones and left school to come to the factory to find out what was happening to their parents (Capps et al. 2007).

ICE processing of the nearly 3,000 employees took about four hours. By 11:30 a.m., ICE agents had arrested 262 Swift employees. By noon, the ICE agents left the plant, with 262 people boarded onto buses to be taken into custody (Bacon 2007). As the buses rolled away, one young woman watching the bus leave wiped away her tears and asked who was going to care for her and her three-month old daughter. The woman said she did not want to go on welfare to support her family.[10]

The arrestees were given the option of signing voluntary departure orders. Of the 128 Mexican arrestees, 86 signed voluntary departure orders and were sent to Mexico within two days. The deportation of Mexicans is the easiest because of the country's proximity to the United States. Of those who did not sign voluntary departure orders, some were released on their own recognizance; some were released with bail; and others remained in ICE detention. Those who were released the quickest were people who were the sole caregivers for minors and those who had authorization to work but could not prove it at the time of the raid (Capps et al. 2007).

Lucia, from Guatemala, was among those detained. She was taken to Texas and then to New Mexico, where she was in jail for more than a month. During that time, she worried a great deal about her minor son, who was left alone. After being released on bond, Lucia was concerned that she would be deported to Guatemala, where she did not expect to be able to find work to support herself and her son.[11]

ICE had warrants to search the plant for people charged with identity theft. A lengthy investigation had shown that twenty-five people were using other people's social security numbers. ICE obtained the warrants to look for those people. In the course of the raid, ICE agents arrested eighteen people who they suspected of identity theft and fraud. Later, eleven of those people were charged, and seven had their charges dismissed (Bacon 2007). Although the raid took the workers by surprise, the owners of Swift had been informed by ICE that such an operation was imminent. Swift tried to prevent the raid, citing its potential losses (Dyer 2006).The raid on the Swift plant greatly affected the workers' children and families as well. Many workers who were deported or detained were the sole breadwinners for families. For many families, this meant not only sparse pickings on Christmas day, but also not having money to meet their basic needs for months to come. Helen Somersall, of Catholic Charities in Greeley, reported having helped 109 households with basic needs. In these households were more than 250 children, many of whom were U.S. citizens (Capps et al. 2007).[12] With the primary breadwinner gone, many of these families were not sure where their next meal would come from. The children began to eat less, especially because they could not have the foods to which they were accustomed. In addition, many of these families faced severe emotional distress, especially in those families where the sole caregiver of children was not able to return immediately. Family members and friends stepped in to care for children when parents did not return from work after the raid; some children remained in these situations for several months. The raids created an atmosphere of fear in Greeley, even among kids whose parents were not arrested (Capps et al. 2007).

In sum, ICE officials obtained warrants to arrest 25 people and thus were able to conduct this raid on Swift Meatpacking Co. In the course of this operation, they verified the documentation of more than 3,000 workers and arrested 262 people. As a result, they were able to deport 132 people, and 11 faced criminal charges. In addition, this raid had substantial economic and emotional impacts on Greeley.

According to a recent report, there have been upwards of eight million cases of identity theft in the United States since 2005.[13] Another report indicates that there were seven million undocumented workers in the United States in 2006 (Passel 2006). Thus, this operation surely was not intended to put a dent in either identity theft or in the use of undocumented labor. It was meant to serve as a deterrent to both of these activities. The cost, however, has been borne by many more than those who are the targets of ICE strategies. The affected include the family members of the workers, the twenty-eight hundred workers who were in the plant at the time of the raid, community workers and leaders, and immigrants and families across the country who live more fearfully every day as a result of these scare tactics.

New Bedford, Massachusetts—Tuesday, March 6, 2007

Just before dawn on Tuesday, March 6, 2007, 300 heavily armed ICE agents stormed into Michael Bianco, Inc., a leather factory, demanding to see the work documents of all 500 employees. All the machines were turned off. Panicking, people began to run and hide. ICE agents ran after people, shouting at them to sit down. The agents then proceeded to handcuff the workers (Bacon 2007). Reports indicate that some employees became ill and vomited. Others testified that they were mistreated and abused both at the factory and later during detention.[14]

After screening each of the employees, the agents determined that 361 of them were to be placed in ICE custody. These 361 workers were handcuffed and taken to Fort Devens, in Ayer, Massachusetts for processing around 3pm. The following day, sixty of these workers were released for humanitarian reasons; ninety were sent to a detention center in Harlingen, Texas, thousands of miles away. On March 8, another 116 workers were flown to a detention center in El Paso, Texas. Over the next few days, 31 more workers were released from Texas for humanitarian reasons, primarily because they are the sole caregivers of children.[15]

As a result of this raid, many children spent at least one night without their parents. Since many of the children were in the same childcare setting, family and community members took charge of those children whose parents did not come to pick them up.[16] At least one mother was not able to convince ICE that she had a toddler, and thus was not released until late at night. About twenty other parents were flown to Texas and waited several days before they could be reunited with their children (Capps et al. 2007). Among these was Marta Escoto, the mother of two young children. Both Daniel, 2, and Jessie, 4, were born in the United States and were in day care when their mother was arrested. Jessie suffers from a debilitating illness and cannot walk. Marta's sister, Andrea, heard of the raid, and was able to care for Marta's children in her absence. On Wednesday, March 14, over a week after the raid, Marta was released pending her trial and was flown back to Massachusetts to care for her children.[17]

Another woman who is a sole caregiver reported that ICE agents in the factory and in the detention center in Massachusetts would not listen to her when she insisted that she had a daughter and that she was the sole caregiver. Upon being sent to Texas with the other detainees, she was able to explain that she has a six-year old daughter who was ill and had to be taken to the doctor the next week. On her second day in Texas, she was permitted to contact her babysitter, who did not know what had become of the mother. Her daughter was worried about her mother's whereabouts and told her mother she was going to kill herself if she didn't come home. On Monday, the woman was released. This woman reported that she had experienced minor mistreatment but was particularly disturbed by the treatment of the breastfeeding mothers. She reported that women who said that they were breastfeeding had to prove it by showing the milk secretions. She said that the guards made fun of the women when the milk was excreted, by laughing and asking other guards to bring out the Oreo cookies.[18] At least one of the breastfeeding mothers' babies was hospitalized as a result of dehydration. Her eight-month old child could not be convinced to take a bottle in her absence and was taken the hospital to be treated for dehydration.[19]

Mistreatment in immigrant detention facilities is known to be widespread, as detailed in the next section. Detainees from the New Bedford raids reported abusive treatment. Some detainees testified that they were given dirty clothes and were not given proper medical attention.[20] Others claimed that they were treated badly by the prison guards in El Paso. One woman reports that the guards threw bags of food at them when it was time to eat.[21] The stress of the detention has had long-term effects, especially for those people who had to wear ankle bracelets when released, which further enhances their status as criminals. It also causes financial stress, as many detainees had to borrow several thousands of dollars to pay bail.[22]

Two months after the raid in New Bedford, 42 of the workers had been deported, 181 had been released pending their immigration hearings, and 137 remained in detention.[23] One year after the raid, only one worker remained in detention, and 165 of the detainees had been deported.[24] The remaining workers had been released pending their trials. Hector Mendez, for example, spent three months in prison before he was released upon borrowing $10,000 to post bail. When released, Mendez saw his wife and three children for the first time in three months.[25] Immigration attorneys expect that many of those awaiting trial will be granted stays of deportation, because they have unearthed stories of rapes and killings that occurred in the civil wars in Guatemala and El Salvador. Women who experienced sexual violence during these conflicts may be eligible for refugee status under the Violence Against Women Act (VAWA). Ten arrestees have been allowed to stay in the United States thus far under these and other provisions in immigration law.[26]

Little Village, Chicago—April 24, 2007

Shortly before 2 p.m., hundreds of heavily armed federal agents, dressed in bulletproof vests, descended on the Little Village Discount Mall in a predominantly Mexican neighborhood in Chicago. On most weekday afternoons, this mall is frequented by mothers of small children, the elderly, and others who live in the vicinity and are in need of any of the wide variety of things sold here—from quinceañera gowns to cowboy boots, and from roast chicken to *pan dulce*. On April 24, 2007, agents from ICE, the FBI, and the Secret Service closed off all the exits to the mall and proceeded to search for suspects in a fraudulent ID ring that allegedly was being run out of the mall. All the shoppers and workers had to show their IDs to prove they were not the suspects. Once that was established, they were allowed to leave the mall. Those who did not have IDs were detained and questioned.

Women in the health clinic with small children reported that armed federal agents stormed in, yelling at people and terrifying everyone—especially the children. Others testified that agents stormed into bathrooms and instilled fear in the shoppers and workers. A beauty salon owner reported that innocent people were placed in handcuffs. Word got out quickly about the raid, and community members and activists soon showed up. Over two hundred people staged a protest in front of the mall that lasted until around 11:00 p.m.[27]

Community members came out to the mall to protest what many perceived to be an attack on the Mexican community in Chicago. ICE officials threw men, women, and children on the ground and pushed others onto fences. The use of force and the large weaponry instilled fear in people in the mall, in those who were looking on, and even in those who heard about the event later. At a one-year anniversary of the raid, one speaker said that she would never forget the day that the *migra* intimidated her community.[28]

At the time of the raid, not even the local police were aware of why the raid was taking place. At a press conference the next day, however, Patrick Fitzgerald, from the Chicago U.S. attorney's office, announced that the raid was designed to arrest an identity-theft ring that operated in this mall. For many years, a crime ring sold fake driver's licenses and "green cards" to people who needed them. Undocumented people require proof of legal status for most jobs and thus rely on places such as these to secure fake "green cards" to work.

In conjunction with the raid at the mall, ICE agents raided two other houses that were connected with the making of the false identifications. On April 24, they were able to arrest twelve people; the other ten people named in the investigation remained at large. Elissa Brown, from ICE, insisted that similar measures would have been taken, were this illegal activity to have been taking place on State Street, in downtown Chicago, but many Latino leaders and activists in Chicago found this implausible and decried ICE's actions as a direct attack on the Latino community in Chicago.

The purpose of this raid was not to find undocumented workers, but to arrest the perpetrators in an international crime ring. ICE had the names of the suspects and had been studying the organization for years. Their main targets were the leaders of the ring. Nevertheless, ICE chose the strategy of closing off the entire mall, using heavy weaponry, and instilling fear in the hearts of the shoppers at the mall, many of whom were young children. ICE reports describe the raid as an operation directed at one photo shop in the mall—Nuevo Foto Muñoz—that was suspected of producing false identification documents.[29]

The raid in Little Village was not designed to reduce the pull of the "job magnet," but to find people who produce false identification documents. This operation was successful at finding many of the ringleaders of this particular crime ring, both in the United States and in Mexico. Nevertheless, as argued in a recent *Newsweek* article, the availability of false documentation in Chicago or other cities around the nation has not declined.[30] Furthermore, judging from the widespread community protests in the wake of the raid, the raid was interpreted by many locals as an attack on their community.

Postville, Iowa: Monday, May 12, 2008

In December 2006, federal agents began to plan a worksite enforcement operation in Postville, Iowa, a town with 2,273 inhabitants, 968 of whom worked at the Agriprocessors slaughterhouse. On Monday, May 12, 2008, the federal plan became a reality and 900 agents descended on Postville, armed with warrants for nearly 700 workers. This worksite raid led to a humanitarian and economic disaster for the town and for much of the region. The raid led to the closing of Agriprocessors, Inc., a kosher meat processing plant, which had a ripple effect throughout the region for its suppliers and within Postville for local stores that sold products to its former employees (Camayd-Freixas 2008; Grey, Devlin, and Goldsmith 2009).

The ICE raid in Postville, Iowa, was an enormous undertaking that involved the cooperation of several federal and local agencies. It was the largest raid that ICE had carried out, in the largest meatpacking plant in Northeastern Iowa. In all, 389 immigrant workers were arrested at the Agriprocessors plant on a Monday in the middle of May. The following day, Tuesday, half of the school system's 600 students were absent because their parents were in hiding or had been arrested (Hsu 2008).

Around 10 a.m. on Monday morning, dozens of helicopters, buses, and vans began to encircle the western edge of town. Within ten minutes, hundreds of agents surrounded the plant (Hsu 2008). One Postville worker reported that agents entered the plant with their guns drawn, shouting, "Don't run, because we are going to chase you like rats!" The armed agents called the workers donkeys and other names.[31] Within a couple of hours, 313 male suspects were taken to the National Cattle Congress grounds in Waterloo, Iowa, for processing. The 76 female suspects were taken to local jails. 290 of the arrestees were Guatemalan. The remaining included 93 Mexicans, 2 Israelis, and 4 Ukranians (Hsu 2008).

What differentiates this raid from previous ICE raids is the decision of ICE officials to work with the DOJ to pursue criminal charges against nearly all the detainees. In previous raids, ICE charged most of the workers with administrative violations, and the workers were placed in deportation proceedings. In Postville, nearly all the workers were charged with aggravated identity theft and placed in criminal proceedings. These charges were not because the workers had done things any differently in Postville than in the other sites of the worksite raids, but because ICE decided to pursue a new strategy. This new strategy, however, came under great scrutiny. The scrutiny and negative attention caused ICE to decide not to continue this tactic of criminally charging undocumented workers, at least for the time being.

The decision to pursue criminal charges was made well in advance of the raid at Postville. Through a lengthy investigation, ICE officials learned that the majority of workers at the Agriprocessors plant did not have the right to work legally in the United States and had used fraudulent documents to gain employment at the plant. Thus, ICE was able to obtain a criminal search warrant for evidence related to identity theft and fraudulent use of social security numbers, and a civil search warrant to arrest people illegally present in the United States (U.S. House of Representatives 2008c).

On the day of the raid, 83 of the employees were arrested for immigration violations, and 306 were detained on criminal charges (U.S. House of Representatives 2008c). After placing the employees under arrest, ICE transported them to a fairground in Waterloo, about two hours away from Postville. As mandated by law, ICE had only 72 hours to press charges against all 306 people. To avoid having to release detainees, ICE created a new system called *fast-tracking*. In this system, ICE offered the same plea agreement to all the detainees and told them they had to accept or reject it fully. The plea agreement offered to drop the charge of aggravated identity theft and for the detainees to serve only five months of the six-month sentence of Social Security fraud. In exchange, the detainee would agree to be deported from the United States. Because of the short time period and the complicated nature of immigration law, many of the detainees and their criminal defense lawyers were unaware that "accepting a plea for a felony involving fraud has immense immigration consequences, most notably that the detainee can never become a U.S. citizen" (Peterson 2009: 334).

In all, there were 18 defense attorneys for the 306 defendants. Most of the 306 workers faced charges of aggravated identity theft because the social security numbers they had been using belonged to someone else. Aggravated identity theft carries a two-year prison sentence. The workers were offered a plea bargain where they could plead guilty to a lesser charge, not have a jury trial, and spend five months in jail. Subsequent to serving their sentences, they would be deported. They were given seven days to make a decision (U.S. House of Representatives 2008c).

After consulting with their attorneys, 233 defendants pled guilty to the use of false identification to obtain employment, 30 pled guilty to false use of a social security number, and 8 pled guilty for illegal reentry to the United States. These 271 defendants were sentenced to five months in prison and three years of supervised release. Two other defendants were sentenced to twelve months in prison for using false identification to obtain employment. Twenty-seven defendants were sentenced to five years of probation for using social security numbers that did not actually belong to any one, or for illegal reentry (U.S. House of Representatives 2008c).

The way this raid was handled led to a public outcry, and eventually a Congressional hearing. Lawyers, human rights activists, immigrant rights activists, and others decried the way that the criminal cases were handled. These claims of injustice result from the government officials' treatment of the slaughterhouse workers. Government bureaucrats in Washington, DC, decided, before the raid began, that the workers would be charged with aggravated identity theft. This federal offense (U.S. 18: I: 47 § 1028) involves knowingly using a false identification with the intent to commit an unlawful act. The undocumented workers were given the option to plea to a lesser charge—using a false social security number—which carries a sentence of 0 to 6 months. Prosecutors offered the workers five months in jail in exchange for the plea—hardly a bargain (Peterson 2009).

Erik Camayd-Freixas, a federally certified interpreter who was present for much of the criminal proceedings, contends that these court proceedings constituted a tremendous travesty of justice. His reasons are compelling.[32] Camayd-Freixas argues that, because most of the workers did not know what a social security number actually was, and because obtaining work is not unlawful activity, it is extraordinarily unlikely that a grand jury would find probable cause of identity theft. "But with the promise of faster deportation, their ignorance of the legal system, and the limited opportunity to consult with counsel before arraignment, all the workers, without exception, were led to waive their 5th Amendment right to grand jury indictment on felony charges" (Camayd-Freixas 2008: 15).

In the aftermath of the raid, allegations surfaced that an Agriprocessors supervisor had charged plant employees $220 for work authorization, which turned out to include a fake "green card." Legal scholar Peterson argues that, "ICE's fast-tracking model cut off the need to determine whether the detainees knowingly used the identification of another person in the Postville cases, because almost all of the detainees accepted the plea agreement" (2009: 341).

On May 4, 2009, nearly a year after the raid, the U.S. Supreme Court decided that defendants must know that a social security number belongs to another person to be charged with identity theft.[33] The Court argued that the distinction between using an invalid social security number and one that belonged to an actual person was meaningless, and that the charge of identity theft does not apply to workers using false social security numbers. However, this decision came too late for the majority of the Postville arrestees, who had long since served their sentences and been deported (Chaudry et al. 2010).

This raid provides a prime example of how the current enforcement regime threatens the balance of powers—a pillar of our democracy. Executive branch officials—primarily from DHS and the DOJ—were the main decision-makers in this case. They decided beforehand to use an "inflated charge" to have more "bargaining leverage" (Camayd-Freixas 2008: 14). The fast-tracking system not only left the defendants with little choice but to plead guilty, it also took away the decision-making authority from the judge. The inflated charge "reduced the judges to mere bureaucrats ... [with] absolutely no discretion or decision-making power.... When the executive branch forces the hand of the judiciary, the result is abuse of power and arbitrariness, unworthy of a democracy founded upon the constitutional principles of checks and balances" (Camayd-Freixas 2008: 14).

The defendants in this trial were not fully accorded the rights we normally ensure criminal defendants—adequate access to legal counsel, the presumption of innocence, and judicial review. The workers' inadequate access to legal counsel was exacerbated by their complete lack of access to immigration counsel. David Wolfe Leopold of the American Immigration Lawyers Association, who testified at the same hearing as Camayd-Freixas, argued that the criminal defense attorneys were not aware of the immigration consequences of the guilty pleas they advised their clients to accept (U.S. House of Representatives 2008a).

Some of the workers may have been eligible for legalization. For example, if the workers had a U.S.-citizen spouse or child, they may have been eligible for legalization under immigration laws that take family ties into account. If the workers had been in the United States for more than ten years, they may have been eligible for a cancellation of their deportation order on the basis of the needs of a U.S.-citizen family member. Finally, the workers may have been eligible for asylum, based on humanitarian concerns in their countries of origin. The workers were not able to pursue any of these options because pleading guilty to a crime of fraud rendered all the workers ineligible for any of these paths to legalization. The lack of immigration counsel combined with the speed with which they had to make decisions left the defendants without the opportunity to benefit from any of the provisions in immigration law (U.S. House of Representatives 2008a).

The Social Costs of Worksite Raids

The raid in Greeley, Colorado, marked a new era for DHS in general, and ICE in particular—one in which large-scale raids would become a major part of their public identity. The raid in New Bedford attracted even more attention largely because of its proximity to Boston, a city with a vocal progressive population. Activists in Boston were able to use their access to multimedia equipment and the Internet to make public the abuses detainees endured and the inhumane nature of the raid. The raid in Little Village was in the heart of the Latino community of a major city and thus struck a chord with people who may have thought that raids were restricted to rural meatpacking factories. The Postville operation seems to have been the apex of ICE's inventive tactics. The huge outcry with regard to the criminalization of migrants and the Congressional hearing on raids appears to have convinced ICE officials not to pursue criminal prosecution of undocumented workers. In raids since the Postville operation, ICE agents have not brought in the DOJ to prosecute workers.

The intensification of efforts to deport, detain, and terrify immigrants in the United States has not led to a mass exodus of undocumented immigrants. These large scale raids have, however, had the effect of drawing media attention and making it seem as though the government is doing what it can to crack down on undocumented migration. The cost of these raids is the devastation of communities, the tearing apart of families, and the promotion of a culture of fear and terror. The intensification of raids in recent years means that undocumented migrants experience a growing sense of fear of detention and deportation. Millions of U.S.-citizen spouses, children, and siblings of undocumented immigrants have to worry each day about the possibility that their loved ones and their breadwinners will be taken away from them (Pew Hispanic Center 2007).

This change of strategy to focus on interior enforcement has been done in the name of national security. These massive budget increases have been possible because the DHS presents its needs in the context of national security. Although there are no clear connections between protecting the nation from terrorism and removing workers from meatpacking plants, ICE has capitalized on fears of terrorism to request funding for workplace raids. In turn, these raids serve as media spectacles that make it seem as though ICE is doing its part to protect the nation.

The raid in Postville provides a case in point. ICE had warrants for nearly 700 people. They arrested fewer than 400. No efforts were made in the aftermath of the raid to find the remaining 300 people. ICE had the option of turning over those warrants to the local police department, but they did not. Had ICE perceived those undocumented migrants to be a threat to society, it seems reasonable that they would pursue the remaining 300 migrants, or at least allow the local police to do so. However, they did not (Peterson 2009). One could interpret their failure to follow up with the remaining warrants as an indication that the Postville raid was primarily a spectacle—meant to send a message, and not intended to "protect the nation from dangerous people."

Subsequent to the Postville raid in May 2008, ICE seems to have scaled back its worksite enforcement operations. As of this writing in March 2011, there have been no major worksite raids since the arrest of 28 workers in Bellingham, Washington in February 2009. The public outcry in the aftermath of the Postville and the other raids seems to have led ICE to pursue other strategies in recent years. Immigrant detention, in contrast, shows no signs of abating.

Immigrant Detention

People arrested during immigration raids often are placed in immigrant detention facilities. Noncitizens can also be placed in these facilities after being arrested by ICE agents, encountered by Border Patrol agents, or released from incarceration by state or local jails and prisons. The arrival of thousands of Cubans and Haitians in the early 1980s led to a surge in immigrant detention, reversing the policy enacted in 1954 to detain only migrants who were clearly dangerous (Dow 2004). Ellis Island, renowned as a dismal penitentiary for arriving migrants, was closed in 1954 when the INS announced that it would no longer detain migrants who were not clearly dangerous. The U.S. Attorney General, Herbert Brownell, Jr., declared on November 12, 1954:

> In all but a few cases, those aliens whose admissibility or deportation is under study will no longer be detained. Only those deemed likely to abscond or those whose freedom of movement could be adverse to the national security or the public safety will be detained. All others will be released on conditional parole

or bond or supervision, with reasonable restrictions to insure their availability when their presence is required by the Immigration and Naturalization Service (*New York Times,* 11/12/1954: Page 14).

Over the next three decades, relatively few immigrants were detained. However, racism infused the immigration debates from the beginning of the twentieth century to its end. In 1980, 125,000 Cubans and 15,000 Haitians arrived by sea to Miami. The Cubans were the infamous "Marielitos," poorer and darker than their compatriots who had arrived in the 1950s and 1960s. The Haitians, who were even darker and poorer, were not made to feel welcome by the local or federal governments. In response to the arrival on the shores of South Florida of a tide of brown and black migrants, the INS reversed its policy of thirty years of nondetention (Dow 2004). On July 1, 1981, the attorney general insisted in a Congressional hearing that migrants should be detained as they wait for their exclusion hearings. The following day, the INS announced its new detention policy, which mandated the detention of most Haitians and some Cubans—mainly those found to have had criminal records in Cuba. The decision to detain Haitian asylees was taken primarily to deter more Haitians from attempting to come to the United States to request asylum. Prior to 1981, Cubans and Haitians usually were paroled into the community and were given a date to come back to have their asylum cases heard. The mass detention of Haitians in prisons and camps caused some public outcry, yet the policy of detaining asylees has remained in place ever since. These changes in INS detention practices marked a new era in INS policy—that of a consistently expanding jail complex (Stewart 1986; Dow 2004).

Over the past thirty years, ICE has gone from a policy of presuming that noncitizens do not present a threat to society to a policy of assuming they do present a threat, and only releasing migrants who can prove otherwise. This has translated into a dramatic surge in the number of detainees. The first notable increase came with mass Cuban and Haitian immigration in the early 1980s. The second, more substantial, increase occurred after the passage of the Illegal Immigration Reform and Immigrant Responsibility Act of 1996 (IIRIRA) (Dow 2004; Welch 2002). This law required the detention of legal permanent residents convicted of an array of crimes and expanded the grounds on which asylum seekers were to be detained (Morawetz 2000). The third dramatic surge came with the creation of the DHS in 2003. The infusion of money into DHS has allowed it to enforce immigration laws more aggressively and to house more detainees. In 1973, the INS detained a daily average of 2,370 migrants. By 1980, this had gone up to 4,062. By 1994, the daily average was 5,532; it was about 20,000 in 2001; and, in 2008, ICE detained an average of 33,400 migrants a day (Dow 2004: 8–9; Immigration and Customs Enforcement 2008b; Kerwin and Lin 2009).

Some of the migrants detained by ICE are detained at ICE facilities, others at private prisons, and still others at county and state jails. People detained by ICE include asylum seekers, long-term permanent residents, and undocumented migrants (United Nations Human Rights Council 2008). More than two-thirds of ICE detainees are in county or local jails.[34] The time that immigrants spend in detention has also increased dramatically, from an average of four days in 1981 to an average of 54 days by 1994 (Welch 2002: 107). ICE reports indicate that the average time in detention had gone down to 37.6 days in 2007, due to an increase in expedited removals. However, snapshot data from January 25, 2009, reveal that of the 32,000 people in ICE custody on that day, the noncriminal detainees had been detained for an average of 65 days, as compared to 121 days on average for detainees with criminal convictions.[35] Lengthy stays in detention are particularly pernicious for people with medical issues. These issues often go unattended, primarily because detention is designed for short-term stays. Detention centers are not equipped with the necessary medical facilities (Seattle University School of Law 2008).

Francisco Castañeda was thirty-five years old when he entered ICE custody in March 2006, after spending four months in prison on a drug charge. He had come to the United States from El Salvador when he was ten years old. At the time of his detention, he had a fourteen-year-old U.S.-citizen daughter. While he was detained, Castañeda complained to ICE officials of painful lesions on his penis. He was sent to specialists, each of whom determined that he needed a biopsy to tell whether he had penile cancer. The U.S. Public Health Service and the Division of Immigration Health Services, however, denied him the biopsy, on the grounds that it was an elective procedure. Despite excessive bleeding, he was given only ibuprofen for pain. After suffering in custody for eleven months, he was released and went to the hospital. In February 2007, he was diagnosed with penile cancer and had nearly his entire penis removed. Although he received chemotherapy upon his release, Mr. Castañeda passed away on February 16, 2008, leaving his daughter fatherless (Patel and Jawetz 2007).[36] This is one example, albeit extreme, of the systematic denial of health care to immigrant detainees. I have chosen it for its impact, but many lesser examples of health care denial to immigrant detainees occur every day and contribute to not only health problems for the detainees and their families, but also added costs and administrative challenges to the enforcement agencies.

The United States detained mostly southern and eastern Europeans in the late nineteenth and early twentieth centuries. Today, most detainees hail from

Latin America and the Caribbean. As of January 2007, the countries that were most represented in ICE detention facilities were Mexico, El Salvador, Guatemala, Honduras, the Dominican Republic, and Haiti.[37] In a 2009 report, researchers found that 37 percent of detainees were from Mexico, 28 percent from Central America, 7 percent from the Caribbean, and 6 percent from South America—accounting for 78 percent of all 177 countries from which detainees come (Kerwin and Lin 2009). Although many migrants come from Europe and Asia, these migrants are much less likely to end up in detention facilities. One reason for this is a change in laws in 2004 that allows immigration inspectors to detain any undocumented migrant apprehended within 14 days of entry and 100 miles of the border. Because Latin Americans are more likely to enter across the southern border, they are more likely to be detained under these provisions (Seattle University School of Law 2008). Another reason for the preponderance of Latin Americans in detention centers is related to racial profiling of noncitizens (Aldana 2008). Although Asians account for 25 percent of undocumented migrants, they are less likely to be targets of immigration enforcement actions, likely for reasons detailed above where ICE agents have substantial discretionary power in arrests.

Detention Practices Today

Immigrant detention centers in the United States have come under severe criticism from human rights organizations, nongovernmental organizations (NGOs), the United Nations, and the inspector general. Some of the major concerns are the prevalence of physical and verbal abuse of detainees, inadequate medical care, insufficient food, lack of phone and library access, lack of access to religious counsel, overcrowding, and inadequate access to legal counsel. Many of these problems are compounded by the fact that some detainees remain in detention for several months.

In the United States, people charged with a criminal offense have the right to legal counsel, regardless of their ability to pay for it. People in immigrant detention facilities, however, do not have this right to legal counsel, as they face immigration charges, not criminal charges. Individuals who face immigration charges may obtain legal counsel, but the government doesn't provide it. Immigrant detention centers are holding cells for noncitizens awaiting trial or deportation. Because they have not been charged with a crime, they do not have the legal right to access to legal counsel. Many detainees, however, would benefit greatly from access to immigration lawyers who may be able to prevent them from being deported or allow them to be released from detention. Most detainees are unable to afford legal counsel. Those who are able to afford a lawyer or who are lucky enough to find a lawyer who will work *pro bono* often have difficulties being represented. In a recent report by the Seattle University School of Law (2008), researchers pointed to several barriers to legal counsel. First, there was inadequate access to private meeting rooms. Second, staff at the facility opened confidential legal correspondence sent to detainees. Third, lawyers often had to wait for hours to see detainees. Finally, detainees could be transferred without notice at any time. All of these factors present obstacles to providing detainees with effective legal counsel.

This lack of access to legal counsel results in people being deported who may have a good case for remaining in the United States. The deplorable conditions in these facilities combined with the lack of access to counsel may lead detainees who are eligible for asylum based on mistreatment in their country of origin, or permanent residence based on family ties in the United States, to agree to be deported. Faced with a choice between spending several months or years in a detention facility and agreeing to be deported, many migrants choose this latter option, even if they have a good case for remaining in the United States. The issues surrounding the process of deportation will be addressed more fully in the next chapter.

A 2006 Office of the Inspector General (OIG) study confirmed many of the complaints activists have been making for years with regard to detention facilities. According to the OIG's December 2006 report, the five facilities visited were out of compliance with ICE detention standards. For example, these standards mandate that detainees be given a physical exam within 14 days of their arrival. At the Corrections Corporation of America (CCA) San Diego facility, 11 of the 19 detainees they audited had not undergone this required physical exam. In addition, at three of the five detention centers they visited, 196 of 481 medical requests were not responded to in the required time frame (OIG 2006). These oversights have had grave consequences in recent years, including the death of 66 detainees between 2004 and 2007 (Bernstein 2008). A report released in July 2009 by the National Immigration Law Center and the ACLU, titled "A Broken System: Confidential Reports Reveal Failures in U.S. Immigrant Detention Centers," indicates that ICE has not improved the facilities in response to these complaints (Tumlin, Linton, and Natarajan 2009).

The lack of sufficient medical attention is corroborated by reports of immigrant advocates. For example, one detainee reported it took two months from the time he broke his nose at a detention facility for him to be taken to the local hospital. In another case, a woman from Liberia was detained at a CCA facility in Arizona from November 2005 to April 2006; although she complained of physical pain on several occasions to the staff at the facility, she was not taken to the hospital for several months, although the facility's records show that she likely required medical attention. When she was finally taken, the hospital doctors determined that she had a cyst the size of a five-month-old fetus and required immediate surgery. ICE then released her from detention on medical parole to avoid having to pay for the surgery (Patel and Jawetz 2007).

A report issued on March 29, 2010 revealed that mentally ill residents of the United States are often detained and deported. People who have been declared mentally incompetent to stand criminal trial in the United States have been processed by immigration judges and ordered deported. For example, a fifty-year-old legal permanent resident who had lived in the United States since 1974 was declared incompetent by a New York criminal court and ordered to serve ninety days in a mental institution. Before the order was implemented, he was transferred to an immigration detention facility, where he was not given proper medical treatment. This legal permanent resident was able to gain release and avoid deportation because of the active intervention of his mother and his criminal defense lawyer—but not without the stress of being detained and denied proper medication—which could have been devastating for someone such as him with severe schizophrenia (Texas Appleseed 2010).

In addition to these extreme abuses, detainees often live in unsanitary conditions with inadequate food and cleaning services. At the Hudson County Correction Center (HCCC) in Kearny, New Jersey, the OIG report found that clothes are washed only once or twice a week, and socks and undergarments are not exchanged on a daily basis. The report further found that at Berks County Prison (BCP) in Leesport, Pennsylvania, detainees are given only one uniform and must sit around in their undergarments for two to six hours when they send their uniform in for washing (Office of Inspector General 2006). In addition, detainees were not given sufficient outdoor recreation time; they were generally allowed outside only three days a week (Office of Inspector General 2006).

ICE has detention standards that mandate the way detention centers should be operated. However, a 2009 report by the National Immigration Law Center, based on a system-wide analysis of ICE's compliance with its own standards, reveals "substantial and pervasive violations of the government's minimum standards for conditions at immigration detention facilities" (Tumlin, Linton, and Natarajan 2009: 7). For example, the report cites a United Nations Human Rights Council (UNHCR) study that found that one facility had neither indoor nor outdoor recreation programs for detainees, even though ICE regulations mandate that detainees be provided with at least one hour of recreation each day, and that efforts be made to ensure that recreational activities be held outdoors. When ICE has reviewed its own facilities, it does not always hold them to their own standards. For example, ICE reviewers rated facilities with no outdoor programs as acceptable for the recreation standard (Tumlin, Linton, and Natarajan 2009).

ICE's violation of its own policies sometimes has deadly consequences, as seen in the case of Yusif Osman, who never received the mandatory entrance medical exam. Osman is one of eighty-three immigrant detainees who died in or soon after their detention between 2002 and 2007, thirty-two of whom were younger than forty (Priest and Goldstein 2008: A01). Yusif Osman, a native of Ghana and a legal permanent resident of the United States, was detained by immigration authorities for crossing the border with a conational who used a false identification card. Osman had gone to Mexico for a visit. On the way back, he gave a ride to another Ghanaian. Osman's passenger was using a fake identification to enter the United States, and Osman was arrested for transporting an undocumented person across the border. Upon entering into ICE custody in March 2006, Osman was not given the requisite entrance medical exam. As a result, it was not noted that he had a heart problem that required treatment. When he collapsed on the floor of his cell three months after being taken into custody, it took the staff nearly an hour to get to him. By that time, it was too late for thirty-four-year-old Osman, who died because his heart suddenly stopped. *The Washington Post* reports that his death likely could have been avoided with "timely treatment, perhaps as basic as an aspirin."

Children and Families in Detention

The abysmal conditions in which migrant detainees are held become even more abhorrent when we consider that many detainees are children. Migrant children who are asylum seekers, undocumented, or charged with crimes are held in juvenile facilities, shelters, adult jails and prisons, and newer family detention centers. In 1998, Human Rights Watch conducted an investigation of the Berks County Youth Detention Center, where many minor immigrant detainees were held.[38] At this facility, migrant children are detained in both a secure-detention facility, where children who have been charged with crimes are held, and in a shelter care facility where children who are in the custody of child welfare authorities are held. In the secure detention facility, migrant detainees comingle with children convicted of serious crimes. The Human Rights Watch report indicates that those children in the shelter care facility had few complaints, except for issues related to language barriers. In contrast, those children in the secure detention facility were much less satisfied with their conditions. Spanish and Chinese speaking juveniles, for example, reported that they were punished for speaking in their own languages, and disciplinary measures, such as doing pushups, for these perceived violations were frequent.[39]

According to this report, very few children had adequate legal counsel, since the government does not pay for attorneys for immigration cases. However, since the law does not permit local immigration judges to hear cases from children without a lawyer or a family member present, many children's cases were simply not heard, thus prolonging their detention. This situation is exacerbated both by the relative isolation of the facility and the transfers of children to other facilities without notification.[40]

The Human Rights Watch report also found that some children were detained unnecessarily. For example, a child from China was detained for one year at the Berks facility despite the fact that her uncle had agreed to take custody of her. She told the researchers that she cried every day that she was in secure detention. Also, four Pakistani children were held in secure detention for three months, although they each had relatives in New York with guardianship papers.[41]

The most notorious family detention center is the T. Don Hutto Center in Texas, a former prison operated by CCA. Hutto has come under the scrutiny of a number of journalists and human rights agencies, despite the fact that no reporters have been admitted to Hutto since a single-day group media tour in February 2007. Even Jorge Bustamante, the U.N. Special Rapporteur on the Human Rights of Migrants, was denied the opportunity to visit Hutto during his visit to the United States. Bustamante was scheduled to tour the facility in May 2007, as part of a fact-finding mission on migrants in the United States. However, just days before his scheduled visit, DHS announced that he would not be granted access, due to the fact that "Hutto was subject to 'pending litigation'" (Gupta and Graybill 2008: 27).

At Hutto, families were detained together but often slept in separate cells. Only very young children were allowed to sleep with their mothers, and fathers slept in separate quarters. In addition, children were not allowed to have stuffed animals, crayons, pencils, or pens in their cells. Moreover, if children woke up during the night upset or ill, only staff members could attend to them; their parents were not allowed to go to their rooms at night, nor were children allowed to leave their rooms (Talbot 2008).

Many detainees housed at the T. Don Hutto Center complained that they did not have adequate food. Families were given twenty to twenty-five minutes to eat. However, this included the time that they had to get their food and sit down. Thus, a pregnant woman with two children said that she often was hungry because she did not have enough time both to eat for herself and to feed her two young children. This was compounded by the fact that she was not allowed to take food out of the cafeteria to eat later. She also complained that only children were given milk; thus, despite her doctor's order to drink milk, she was unable to do so. This same woman shared a twin bed with her two children, as they had only a bunk bed and were scared to sleep alone.[42] According to an investigation carried out at Hutto by the Women's Commission for Refugee Women and Children and Lutheran Immigration and Refugee Service, women and children were often denied sufficient and appropriate medical attention. They found that detainees' complaints were ignored, that the pulling out of teeth was the only dental treatment available, and that potentially serious medical cases were ignored.

At the Hutto facility, children and adults were allowed one hour of recreation each day. This is the only time that children had access to age-appropriate toys, as they were not allowed to have toys in their rooms. One can imagine that small children grew anxious in these circumstances. When children misbehaved, the staff often threatened them with separation from their parents. The same report indicates that, at Hutto,

> staff members encourage parents to keep their children quiet and get children to behave by telling children and their parents that if the child does not do what they are told to do by staff they will be taken away. Nelly, a 9-year-old girl detained with her 3-year-old sister and her mother, who is applying for asylum, told us that if she misbehaved she would be separated from her mother.... All those we interviewed expressed frustration that children are punished for what is normal behavior for young children like running around, making noise, and climbing on the couches.

This disciplinarian approach is particularly disconcerting when we consider that families, especially asylum seekers, are often detained for several months. For these and other reasons, Michelle Brame, the author of the "Locking Up Family Values" report, recommends that the family detention facilities be closed and alternatives to detention be used in place of this. Alternatives to detention include placing migrants on house arrest and using ankle bracelets to keep track of migrants awaiting immigration trials. In response to complaints by immigration advocates and media attention to the T. Don Hutto Facility, in 2009, ICE decided to stop detaining families in the facility. In September 2009, they released the last family from Hutto and began the process of transforming the facility into a detention center for female detainees.[43]

Indefinite Detention

In early 2009, there were 4,154 people in ICE detention who had been detained for six months or longer. There were 1,312 who had been in ICE detention for more than one year (Kerwin and Lin 2009). Some of these detainees were fighting their cases; others were awaiting removal; still others had been ordered deported, but there was no country to which they could return. People in this latter group are referred to as *indefinite detainees*. Some of these people have been convicted of crimes in the United States and have served their sentences. Others have not been charged or convicted of crimes, such as asylum seekers who have not been granted refugee status. One example is Salim Y., a twenty-six-year-old Palestinian. He stowed away on a ship bound for the United States and sought asylum once he arrived. An immigration judge denied his petition for asylum in 2001. He was then placed in detention while awaiting deportation. Since Salim was born in Gaza and lived most of his life in a refugee camp in Libya, there is no country to which he can be deported—Israel does not recognize Palestinians born in Gaza as their citizens.[44] Salim Y. languished in detention for four years until a judge finally ruled that he was to be released, because there was no country to which he could be deported and because indefinite detention is not permitted under U.S. laws. In a more recent case, an entire Palestinian family was detained in Texas, because there was no country to which they could be returned. The family included Salaheddin Ibrahim, his pregnant wife, Hanan, and four of their five children.[45]

Farouk Abdel-Muhti spent two years in ICE detention, without ever being charged with a crime. Farouk was born in Palestine, and thus, like Salim Y., could not be deported. He was arrested for being undocumented and spent two gruesome years in county jails and immigrant detention centers prior to being released. Abdel-Muhti died of a heart attack two months after his release in 2004. He was fifty-seven years old when he died while giving a speech at the Ethical Society in Philadelphia. His early death was likely related to the lack of medical attention and poor conditions during his two-year stay in detention (Fernandes 2006).

People cannot be deported to countries with which the United States has no official diplomatic ties. These countries include Cambodia, Cuba, Iran, Iraq, Laos, Vietnam, former satellites of the Soviet Union, and Gaza. In a Supreme

Court decision in 2001, *Zadvydas v. Davis,* the Supreme Court mandated that immigrants who had been legally admitted to the United States could not be subjected to indefinite detention when their deportation was not foreseeable.

This case revolved around the situation of Kestutis Zadvydas, who had been born in a displaced persons camp in Germany in 1948 to parents believed to be Lithuanian. He came to the United States when he was eight years old with his parents and other family members and subsequently became a legal permanent resident. After being convicted of possession with intent to distribute cocaine and serving his sentence in prison, Zadvydas was ordered deported. However, Germany would not accept him because he was not a citizen, and Lithuania refused because he was unable to establish citizenship there. The INS also tried, to no avail, to deport him to his wife's country of origin, the Dominican Republic. Based on this case, the Supreme Court decided that detainees must be conditionally released if there is no significant likelihood that they will be deported in the foreseeable future. It is noteworthy that Mr. Zadvydas was chosen as the test case for indefinite detention, because the majority of the indefinite detainees were Cubans, and few were European. Perhaps the attorneys thought the judge would be more sympathetic to a white defendant.

The *Zadvydas v. Davis* (2001) case applied only to migrants who had been lawfully admitted to the United States.[46] This outcome did not bode well for those Cubans who came to the United States in 1980 and 1981 on the so-called "Mariel Boatlift." These Cubans had not been formally admitted into the United States. Instead, they were only paroled into the United States. This meant that, in legal terms, they were not considered to have been formally admitted, and therefore, the Zadvydas case did not apply to them. As a consequence, many Mariel Cubans spent decades in prison for relatively minor offenses. Omar Rodriguez, for example, spent two years in prison in Texas for possessing two ounces of marijuana. He was released in 1984, but found himself in jail soon after, again for possession of marijuana. The second time, he was sentenced to four months in prison, and, upon his release from prison, he was taken into INS custody. In 2004, twenty years after completing his sentence, he remained in INS detention (Dow 2004). In May 2004, the Tenth Circuit U.S. Court of Appeals heard the case of Guillermo Borges-Brindis, another Cuban who arrived in 1980 on the Mariel boatlift. In his first five years in the United States, Borges-Brindis was convicted of unlawfully possessing a weapon, assault and battery, selling a controlled substance, and first degree manslaughter. He was sentenced to prison, where he served time until 1991. Upon his release, the INS took him into custody and ordered him deported. Although he was still in custody thirteen years after having completed his sentence, the Court of Appeals found that he did not merit release, and denied his appeal.[47]

In 2005, indefinite detention came to the attention of the Supreme Court again. This time the Supreme Court decided in the *Clark v. Martinez* case that the provisions of Zadvydas should extend to all migrants in the United States. As a result of this decision, migrants can be detained indefinitely only if they pose an immediate threat to national security or to the safety of the community or any person.[48] Despite these Supreme Court rulings, some detainees continue to serve indefinite sentences for two reasons. Either a judge determines that they continue to be a threat to society, or they are lost in bureaucratic proceedings and do not have the opportunity to see a judge.

Attorneys from the Catholic Legal Immigration Network (CLINIC) conducted a study between March 2004 and September 2005 and found that there were still about twelve hundred indefinite detainees. And, in 2007, the ACLU and the Special Rapporteur Jorge Bustamante found that migrants continued to be found in indefinite detention. According to the CLINIC report, many migrants remain in detention because they are not given the mandatory local reviews every ninety days. And, if they have the ninety-day review but are not released, most detainees have to resort to filing suit to have their cases heard again, even though they are entitled to a review every ninety days.[49]

When the OIG of the Department of Homeland Security conducted its own investigation in 2007, it found that 20 percent of detainees were not released or reviewed within the mandatory ninety days. The OIG reviewed a selective sample of 210 files and found that 14 had not received the mandatory ninety-day review, and 3 had not received a review after 180 days. Overall, of the 8,6ninety noncitizens with final deportation orders in March 2006, 1,725 were still in detention in June 2006, and 428 remained in detention as of February 2007. Many of these people were from countries that did not cooperate with U.S. officials. For example, of the 246 people from China who were ordered deported, only 90 were deported within ninety days; 120 were deported within 180 days, and 32 remained in detention after 360 days. In the case of China, the detainees are not released because DHS determines these detainees will eventually be deported. Although the process can be lengthy for Chinese immigrants, the United States has diplomatic ties with China, and the deportations can be processed. In contrast, because the United States has no diplomatic ties with Cuba, Laos, Cambodia, or Vietnam, most noncitizens from these countries are released because DHS recognizes that they cannot actually be deported. Nevertheless, in 2007, eight

Vietnamese and two Cubans were not released after one year, and between 10 and 25 percent of the detainees from these countries remained in detention for more than the maximum allotted time of ninety days.[50]

Asylum Seekers

Asylum seekers, essentially, are people who flee persecution in their home country and seek protection in other countries. The right to seek and enjoy asylum is enshrined in Article 14 of the Universal Declaration of Human Rights (UDHR). In the United States, asylum-seekers must prove that they have a well-founded fear that, if returned to their home country, they will be persecuted based on their race, religion, nationality, membership in a particular social group, or political opinion. Noncitizens may apply for asylum at the port of entry, after arriving in the United States, or when they are facing deportation. In 2003, about a third of all asylum-seekers were granted asylum, with the remaining cases denied (Congressional Research Services 2005). There is quite a bit of contention around the issue of asylum-seeking. Immigration rights activists argue that asylum-seekers often have to leave their country quickly and thus are unable to produce evidence of their persecution. Detractors point out that asylum-seekers may be economic refugees or, in the worst case, potential terrorists.

Under the 1996 laws, applicants for asylum must convince the receiving border inspector that they have a credible fear of persecution. Otherwise, they face expedited deportation. This process has been criticized by refugee advocates, because border inspectors are not fully trained for the interview process. If refugees pass the credible fear of persecution test conducted by the border inspector, they are usually placed in detention while their applications are being processed. Some are detained for a few days, yet others are detained for years while awaiting trial. The UDHR states that "the right to seek and enjoy asylum is a basic human right; individuals must never be punished for seeking asylum." The DHS, however, maintains that detention is not punishment; it is a security measure to ensure that people report to their trial. In 2002, 9,260 of the 9,749 people who were found to have a credible fear of persecution were detained by the INS. Their average stay in detention was 43.5 days (Frelick 2005).

In many cases, after being detained for days, months, or years, an immigration judge determines that the asylum-seeker has a well-founded fear of persecution and is granted asylum. The fact that many petitioners are eventually granted asylum causes critics to question why asylum seekers are treated like criminals and housed in prison facilities, often along with people who have been convicted of crimes. Applicants for asylum face mandatory detention, often after having committed no crime.

Orbelina Brisuela and her son Fredy, age eleven, came to the United States to apply for asylum. A trained asylum officer found that they had a credible fear of persecution. They were ordered to be detained while they awaited their hearing. Despite the acknowledgement that they likely had experienced persecution, they faced further indignities at the hands of immigration agents. When they arrived at the detention facility, T. Don Hutto, a guard, interrogated them from 10 p.m. to 5 a.m. And Fredy was issued "torn, stained, and yellowed clothing and underwear upon his arrival" (ACLU 2007).

Many people who face persecution are denied asylum by border inspectors. In one case, a twenty-eight-year-old woman came to the United States from Albania, after having been gang-raped by armed gunmen. She feared facing such violence again and was stigmatized in her conservative community for having been raped. Her brother-in-law obtained a false passport for her, and she fled to the United States. The INS officials realized her passport was fake and ordered her deported when she arrived. She tried to apply for asylum but was reluctant to reveal all the details of having been gang-raped to the border inspector; therefore, she did not pass the credible fear test. Her case came to the attention of refugee rights' lawyers, and she successfully appealed her case. She was eventually allowed to return to the United States and was granted asylum (from Welch 2002: 88–89; source: ACLU).

For some asylum seekers, detention can be deadly. An elderly Haitian minister, Joseph Dantica, had been to the United States many times during his long life. In 2004, Dantica planned a trip to the United States to see his dying brother. He had his tourist visa and ticket ready and was awaiting the day of his departure. At the last minute, he was forced to flee from the church he had preached in for more than three decades. During that time in Haiti, UN troops and Haitian police were involved in an operation to root out local gangs. Dantica allowed United Nations troops to enter his church. Really, he had no choice, because they entered the premises with machine guns. However, when the UN troops shot local gang members from Dantica's premises, the gang leaders vowed that Dantica would pay for this (Danticat 2007).

Dantica found himself fleeing from his town, disguised as a woman so that the gang members would not recognize him. After several days of hiding out, the day of his departure finally came and Joseph Dantica and his son Maxo boarded a plane for Miami, where his niece lived (Danticat 2007). When Dantica arrived at the Miami airport, instead of showing his valid tourist visa, he told the CBP agent that he would like to apply for temporary asylum, because he feared for his life in Haiti. It is likely that he knew he would be staying longer than the 30 days his visa allowed and did not want to misrepresent himself to the agent (Danticat 2007). Unfortunately, Dantica's request for asylum meant that he was placed in detention at Miami's infamous Krome detention center (Fernandes 2006).

At Krome, the staff took Dantica's medicine and gave him replacements. On his second day there, Dantica began to experience stomach pains and complained to the officials. They initially dismissed his claims and denied his requests to see his family in Miami. The ninety-one-year-old Joseph Dantica began to have a seizure. Vomit shot out of his mouth and his eyes rolled back into his head. Dantica's lawyer was present and requested a humanitarian parole so that he could be taken to a hospital and be with his family. The medic from Krome responded that he thought that Dantica was faking. He nevertheless allowed Dantica to be taken to the hospital, in shackles (Danticat 2007).

Twenty-four hours after arriving in the emergency room, Joseph Dantica was seen by a physician. At 8:46 p.m., he was pronounced dead. His family's pleas to see him at Krome and at the hospital were denied, and Dantica died alone, five days after having arrived in the United States. The autopsy report showed that he "died from acute and chronic pancreatitis, ... for which he was never screened, tested, diagnosed, or treated while he was at Jackson Memorial Hospital" (Danticat 2007: 247).

Since September 11, 2001, asylum seekers are increasingly likely to be placed in detention. Asylum seekers are detained if they are unable to prove that they have community ties. Many are detained despite having such ties, as was Joseph Dantica, who had a niece in Miami. With the beginning of the war with Iraq, DHS initiated a program called Operation Liberty Shield, which requires mandatory detention for asylum seekers from thirty-three countries where Al Qaeda has been known to operate (Welch and Schuster 2005: 336). Although the DHS maintains that detention is not punishment, most detainees find it difficult to believe that being shackled, locked up, and treated without dignity is anything but punishment. As Dantica's case shows, detention can be an unforgettable punishment, for the detainees and their loved ones.

Protecting the Nation?

The high human cost of the surge in interior enforcement renders it necessary to consider the benefits of the enforcement regime. Why has this strategy been implemented? Looking through DHS documents for an explanation of why we have seen an increase in interior enforcement, the most frequently cited explanation is national security—the core of the DHS mission. The first priority of the DHS is to protect the nation from dangerous people. In Secretary Michael Chertoff's statement in support of the 2009 budget request, he stated:

> We will continue to protect our nation from dangerous people by strengthening our border security efforts and continuing our efforts to gain effective control of our borders. The Department's main priority is to prevent additional terrorist attacks against our country.

In this introductory statement, Secretary Chertoff confounds border security with terrorist prevention. He continues to do this in the statement. When he lists DHS's key accomplishments, the first accomplishment is "More Fencing at the Border." He lauds the fact that, by the end of 2008, U.S. CBP will have erected 670 miles of fencing along the border.

As Chertoff continues to praise DHS's accomplishments in terms of protecting the nation, he cites their "Record-Breaking Law Enforcement." He points out that ICE removed about 240,000 "illegal aliens, made 863 criminal arrests, and fined or seized more than $30 million following worksite investigations." In this statement, Chertoff is celebrating the fact that arrests in worksite enforcement operations increased ninefold between 2003 and 2008. Chertoff makes a direct connection between raids and national security. He cites the arrest and removal of 4,077 undocumented workers in worksite enforcement operations under the goal of protecting the nation from dangerous people.

There is no evidence to suggest that the undocumented workers removed from meatpacking plants are dangerous people. Moreover, the fact that most were removed on administrative and not criminal grounds is clear evidence that they had no criminal records. The vast resources that ICE has poured into these worksite enforcement operations has been possible due to the unwarranted conflation of national security with the removal of undocumented migrants. The same could be said for mandatory detention, especially the detention of asylum seekers.

Asylum seekers have to undergo lengthy investigations into their past. The in-depth nature of the probe into their lives makes asylum requests a highly unlikely route for potential terrorists to enter the country. The detention of children and families is also highly questionable as a strategy to protect the nation from dangerous people. Overall, it does not seem to be the case that the increase in interior enforcement of immigration laws is making the United States a safer place. It is clear, however, that these actions are causing harm to immigrants, their families, and their communities.

It may be the case that DHS officials are well aware that home and worksite raids are not making the United States a safer place, yet they use this rhetoric strategically to request budgetary allocations from Congress. Members of Congress may also be aware of the ineffectiveness of these strategies in terms of fighting terrorism but are unwilling to vote against anything that promotes fighting terrorism. Perhaps this is the best we can expect from bureaucrats and lawmakers in the current context of the war on terror. In that case, it is up to the citizenry to insist on the implementation of measures that actually enhance national security, not that simply claim to do so. It is also up to the citizenry to speak up against these sorts of policies that do little to make the country safer but do worlds of harm to communities and families.

To gain a full picture of the effects of the current enforcement regime, it's important to look at another aspect of interior enforcement—the rise in deportations, particularly the deportation of long-term residents of the United States. The stories and data in the next chapter shed further light on the dire human consequences that are the result of the existing enforcement regime.

CHAPTER 3

RACISM AND THE CONSEQUENCES OF U.S. IMMIGRATON POLICY

Vern fled an abusive family situation in Guatemala when he was ten years old. He set out alone for the United States but ended up in Mexico, where he spent ten years working at a wholesale market in Mexico City. In 1991, when he was twenty years old, Vern finally achieved his goal of traveling to the United States. Once in the United States, he applied for political asylum. The Immigration and Naturalization Service (INS) issued him a work permit while his case was being reviewed, and he began to work in a frozen food processing plant in Ohio. He met a Honduran woman, Maria, also applying for political asylum, and they began to date. Years went by, and each year, they received work permits from the INS that allowed them to continue working and to remain legally in the United States. Confident their cases eventually would be resolved, Vern and Maria married and had their first child in 1996.

In 1998, Vern received a notice that he should leave the United States; his asylum application had been denied. Vern was devastated; he had established a life in Ohio and had few ties to Guatemala. He decided to stay, hoping that his wife's application would be approved and that she could apply for him to legalize his status. Vern thought he had a good chance of obtaining legalization and decided that his best bet was to remain in the United States. Vern was counting on two things happening: 1) that he would not be among the less than 3 percent of undocumented migrants apprehended by immigration officials; and 2) that his wife's temporary legal status would eventually be legalized and he, too, could obtain legalization. Vern and Maria had another child together and set down roots in Ohio. Vern rose up the ranks in the food processing plant, eventually becoming supervisor. Maria also worked there, but she worked on the line and earned less.

Vern and his family had a comfortable life, but Vern lived in fear that immigration agents would come for him. To avoid this, he did everything he could to stay out of trouble with the police; he never drank, avoided making traffic violations, and abided the laws at all times. He learned English, took his kids on outings every weekend, and tried to blend in as much as possible. Although Vern was undocumented, he lived as a "model citizen."

It wasn't enough. One Sunday morning, two immigration agents came to Vern's house and arrested him in front of his children, ages twelve and nine. The immigration agents were part of a Fugitive Operation Team that was designed to find *fugitive aliens*—people like Vern who had ignored their deportation orders. Vern was put into detention, and, eight days later, he was in Guatemala, the country he had left nearly three decades before.

From 1991, when Vern applied for asylum until 1998, when his application was denied, Vern lived legally in the United States. Vern's unlawful conduct consisted of his failure to leave after being issued a deportation order in 1998. More than a decade later, Vern was apprehended in his home by immigration agents and forcibly removed from the United States. He was not given the opportunity to explain to a judge that he had not abided by his deportation order because he had already formed a family in the United States and that his family depended on him to meet their daily needs. He also was not given the chance to explain that he had worked at the same job for sixteen years, that he had never had trouble with the law, that his two children were Americans, or that his wife was very close to attaining legal status, which could ensure his own legal status.

After being arrested by immigration agents, Vern was not given a hearing; he was simply deported. Deportation is "regulatory, not punitive, so constitutional provisions for due process and other rights of criminals [are] not applied" (Warner 2005: 64). It seems excessive to deny judicial review to a person such as Vern who had lived in the United States for over more than a decade, had U.S.-citizen children, and had few, if any, ties to another country. To deny Vern judicial review of his deportation order was to ignore the notions of due process and constitutional protections that are so important to the United States. It also ignored his human right to form a family and to be with his family.

Vern's story is one of many examples of the consequences of U.S. immigration policies for U.S. families. Since 1996, about 1.6 million U.S. citizens have been separated from their parents, spouses, and children as a result of punitive immigration laws (Human Rights Watch 2007). Deportations have denied the human rights of citizens and noncitizens—specifically the right to form a family and the right to judicial review. These rights are enshrined in the Universal Declaration of Human Rights (UDHR). A discussion that takes into account the stories and data on the role systemic racism plays in the deportation process will allow us to reflect on how U.S. immigration laws and policies consistently diminish the human rights of the citizens and noncitizens they affect.

Deportation and Racism Today

Most undocumented migrants are not deported. There are approximately eleven million undocumented people in the United States. In 2008 less than 3 percent—about three hundred thousand of them-—were deported from the United States. The Department of Homeland Security (DHS) has an internal goal of deporting four hundred thousand people a year. If they reached their goal, and if there were no new undocumented migration, it would take DHS thirty years to deport all eleven million undocumented migrants. However, given the fact that people continue to cross the border undetected and to overstay their visas on a regular basis, the reality is that DHS will never remove all undocumented migrants. DHS officials are well aware of this, so they target certain people to deport. Their mandate from Congress is to target the most dangerous migrants. Exactly who is being targeted by immigration enforcement agents is a question worth exploring further.

The following analyses will show that, despite DHS's claims that they target the "worst of the worst," the reality is that the main targets of immigration policy enforcement are Afro-Caribbean small-time drug peddlers and Latino undocumented workers. Instead of securing the nation, as the DHS claims, immigration agents use racial profiling to deport as many people as possible. Deporting meatpacking workers and drug users does not make America any less susceptible to terrorist attacks. Instead, these tactics tear apart families and prevent immigrants from applying for legalization or citizenship even when they qualify. In this chapter, we will take a close look at who is being deported and why.

First, let's consider who is *not* being deported: people from countries the U.S. government associates with terrorism. Given that DHS claims to be making the nation safer through deportation, it is remarkable that the agency almost never deports people to countries that the U.S. Department of State identifies as sponsoring terrorism: Iran, Iraq, Syria, Libya, Cuba, North Korea, and Sudan. In 2007, for example, 319,382 people were deported. Among these were 49 Iranians, 27 Iraqis, 40 Syrians, 76 Cubans, and 13 Sudanese. (Data were not available for Libya and North Korea.) Instead, deportees are most often nationals of countries with which the United States has amicable relations: our allies in the Western Hemisphere.[1]

The United States also is not deporting people to the countries that send the most immigrants. As I've outlined earlier, the five countries of origin of most legal permanent residents in the United States are China, India, Mexico, the Philippines, and Vietnam. With the notable exception of Mexico, these are not the countries to which we send most deportees. Asians are unlikely to be apprehended and deported. In 2009, 393,289 people were deported. Among these were 5,507 Asians.[2] In 2007, there were about 230,000 undocumented South Koreans in the United States. Only 417 Koreans were deported from the United States in 2007. In that same year, there were about 280,000 undocumented Hondurans in the United States. Yet only 29,737 Hondurans were deported. In 2009, of the 393,289 people deported, 376,958 (96 percent) were Latin Americans (U.S. Department of Homeland Security 2010b).

The top five countries of origin of deportees in 2009 were Mexico, Guatemala, Honduras, El Salvador, and the Dominican Republic. These five countries alone accounted for 92 percent of all people deported in 2009. Table 3-1 lists the top ten countries to which deportees were sent in 2009; these ten countries represent 95.21 percent of people deported in that year. These data call attention to a glaring fact: though Asians are prominent among immigrants overall, it is actually Latin Americans and Caribbeans who are overrepresented among deportees. In addition, although punitive immigration policies are carried out in the name of the War on Terror, the primary targets are not people usually associated with terrorism. Why are Latin Americans the near-exclusive targets of U.S. immigration policies?

Much of this has to do with stereotypes: in much of the U.S. public perception, "Mexicanness" is equated with illegality. The association of Mexicans with undocumented status renders Mexicans much more likely to be questioned about their legal status than Asians and Europeans. In light of similarities between Mexicans and Central Americans, the presumption of illegality also often applies to Central Americans. As a corollary, undocumented Asians and Europeans are much less likely to be presumed to be undocumented, even though they make up nearly a quarter of all undocumented migrants (Passel 2006).

Findings such as this and those to be presented make it clear that racism plays a role in the selection of migrants for deportation. Legal scholar Kevin Johnson (2004) argues that, because the majority of immigrants that come to the United States each year are people of color, the differential treatment of noncitizens in

Table 3-1 Top Ten Countries to Which Deportees Were Sent: 2009

Country	Total	Percent	Cumulative Percent
Mexico	282,666	71.87%	71.87%
Guatemala	29,182	7.42%	79.29%
Honduras	26,849	6.83%	86.12%
El Salvador	20,406	5.19%	91.31%
Dominican Republic	3,464	0.88%	92.19%
Brazil	3,407	0.87%	93.05%
Colombia	2,443	0.62%	93.68%
Ecuador	2,303	0.59%	94.26%
Nicaragua	2,098	0.53%	94.79%
Jamaica	1,615	0.41%	95.21%
Total # of Deportees	393,289		

Data Source: DHS OIS. Table 38. ALIENS REMOVED BY CRIMINAL STATUS AND REGION AND COUNTRY OF NATIONALITY: FISCAL YEARS 2000 TO 2009.

U.S. legal practices amounts to racial discrimination. I extend Johnson's analysis by demonstrating that not only are noncitizens in general consistently denied basic human rights, but also that black and Latino noncitizens are more likely to be targets of immigration law enforcement than white or Asian noncitizens.

This analysis draws from sociologist Eduardo Bonilla-Silva's (2004) suggestion that some immigrants may be moving into an "honorary white" group. This group does not fully benefit from white privilege, but is not as disadvantaged as African-Americans. Although I agree with Johnson that all noncitizens are disadvantaged by our legal system, my analyses show that noncitizens from Latin America and the Caribbean are more likely to be victims of punitive immigration policies than are noncitizens from Europe or Asia, even when we take into account their relative proportions in the population. As Bonilla-Silva points out, dark-skinned Latinos in the United States are disadvantaged in ways that East Asians are not. The reasons for this are closely related to stereotypes of black men as criminals and of Mexicans and Central Americans as undocumented, particularly as undocumented border-crossers. There are also stereotypes about East Asians. These stereotypes, however, are less likely to be related to illegality or criminality.

The differential treatment of black and Latino immigrants in the United States is a reflection of systemic racism in U.S. society. Joe Feagin (2000: 31) defines *systemic racism* as "a diverse assortment of racist practices; the unjustly gained economic and political power of whites; the continuing resource inequalities; and the white-racist ideologies and attitudes created to preserve white advantage and power." He further contends that "every major aspect of life is shaped to some degree by the core racist realities." The system of deportation and detention of immigrants is no exception: it is clearly shaped by the "core racist realities" of the United States. As Melvin Oliver and Thomas Shapiro (2006) explain, it is not necessary for laws to use explicitly racial language to reproduce racial inequalities. Insofar as laws, policies, and institutions create inequitable outcomes in their implementation, they can be considered part of the structural racism that has pervaded U.S. society since its inception (Feagin 2000).

Over the past hundred years or so, U.S. immigration policy has changed several times. More often than not, these changes have been to the disadvantage of people defined as nonwhite. One of the first large-scale exclusionary laws of the United States was the Chinese Exclusion Act of 1882, which forbade the entrance of Chinese into the United States. This was followed by the Quota laws of the 1920s, which restricted the entry of people not from northern Europe (Johnson 2004; de Genova 2005). Present-day laws are different in two ways:

1. The excluded groups are no longer Southern and Eastern Europeans, Jews, or Asians, but Latin American and Caribbean nationals.
2. The laws do not express an overt racial bias yet have similar racially unequal consequences. The manner in which immigration policy is enacted today ensures that black and Latino immigrants are more often subject to detention and removal than white and Asian immigrants.

The changes in immigration policy over the course of the twentieth century are the result of a complex, and often contradictory, set of geopolitical interests and varying nativist sentiments. In the early twentieth century, the U.S. government enacted a series of laws that effectively ended Asian immigration and, furthermore, denied citizenship to people of Asian descent living in the United States. During World War II, 120,000 Japanese were placed in internment camps in the name of national security. However, in the context of the Cold War in the second half of the twentieth century, the United States began to implement laws that allowed for Asian migration. The 1965 laws lifted the ban on Asian migration. Later laws welcomed refugees from countries under Communist influence, including Vietnam and Cambodia (Ngai 2004). The restrictive laws passed in 1986 and 1996 were deliberated in the context of nativism often directed specifically at the influx of Mexican immigrants in the United States. The 1996 laws have led to the deportation of millions of Latin American and Caribbean immigrants over the past two decades.

Deportation of Undocumented Migrants

Noncitizens in the United States can be deported on criminal or noncriminal grounds. In fiscal year (FY) 2009, 128,345 people were deported on criminal grounds and 264,944 on noncriminal grounds. People deported on noncriminal grounds are noncitizens who lack the proper documentation to be in the United States or who have violated the terms of their visas. People deported on criminal grounds are those who been convicted of a crime that renders them deportable. The former group of people is known as *undocumented migrants* or *illegal aliens*. The second group is referred to as *criminal aliens* by DHS. Latin Americans are more likely to be deported for being out of status than Europeans or Asians because of stereotypes about what an undocumented migrant looks like. Caribbean and Latin American nationals are more likely to be deported on criminal grounds than Europeans or Asians because of stereotypes about black and Latino criminality.[3]

When we take into account the relative proportions in the population of undocumented migrants, Asians are much less likely to be deported than Latin American and Caribbean nationals. Figure 3-1 provides a visual representation of deportees from the top ten countries of origin of undocumented migrants in 2009, as compared to their numbers among the undocumented.

This graph shows that undocumented Hondurans have an 8 percent chance of being deported, and Guatemalans have a 6 percent chance as compared to less than 1 percent for Korean, Filipino, Indian, and Chinese undocumented immigrants.[4] All undocumented immigrants have committed the same infraction: unlawful presence in the United States.

Undocumented Latin Americans are likely targets because they have been construed as the quintessential "illegals." At times it seems as though "Mexican" and "illegal" are virtually interchangeable. Because Latin Americans often are portrayed as being undocumented, they end up also being more likely to be apprehended by immigration authorities. Although there have been some immigration raids in Chinatowns across the United States, and the occasional Israeli or Ukrainian immigrant is caught up in immigration enforcement actions, the majority of immigration raids have been aimed at Mexican and Central American immigrants. Because of stereotypes of Latin Americans as undocumented migrants, they are more likely to be targeted in enforcement efforts and thus more likely to end up in deportation proceedings.

The targeting of people who look Mexican in immigration enforcement actions is not only customary practice among immigration agents, but it also has been sanctioned by the courts. Law professors Chin and Johnson explain:

Figure 3-1 Ratio of Undocumented Migrants to Deportees: 2009

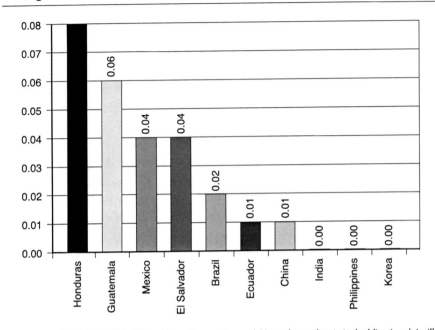

Data Source: DHS OIS: Table 38 and http://www.dhs.gov/xlibrary/assets/statistics/publications/ois_ill_pe_2009.pdf.

In a 1975 case regarding the Border Patrol's power to stop vehicles near the U.S.-Mexico border and question the occupants about their citizenship and immigration status, *United States v. Brignoni-Ponce,* the high court ruled that the 'likelihood that any given person of Mexican ancestry is an alien is high enough to make Mexican appearance a relevant factor.' In 1982, the Arizona Supreme Court agreed, ruling in *State v. Graciano* that 'enforcement of immigration laws often involves a relevant consideration of ethnic factors.'[5]

The 1975 court decision *United States v. Brignoni-Ponce* "authorized the Border Patrol to rely on 'Mexican appearance'" when deciding whom to interrogate (Johnson 2004: 30). This means that, today, "race-based enforcement generally continues unabated, unreported, and unremedied" (32). This profiling occurs despite the fact that the majority of Mexicans are not undocumented; many more are citizens or legal permanent residents (Passel 2006). This profiling has wide-ranging effects; a recent survey found that 57 percent of Latinos in the United States worry they or someone they know may be deported (Lopez and Minushkin 2008).

In April 2010, Governor Jan Brewer of Arizona signed into law Senate Bill (SB) 1070—a law likely to lead to even more racial profiling. This law made undocumented migration a crime of trespassing in the State of Arizona—the punishment for which includes a fine and jail time. In U.S. law, being undocumented is not a crime, and deportation is not considered punishment; it is a civil penalty. Because deportation is not punishment, it is imposed with few procedural protections and is outside the purview of most Constitutional protections (Kanstroom 2000). For this reason, immigration agents can detain people without establishing reasonable suspicion, and noncitizens are not afforded counsel in deportation proceedings. In Arizona, if the Supreme Court rules that SB 1070 is indeed Constitutional, police officers will be trained to enforce immigration laws and will turn suspected undocumented migrants over to federal immigration agents to be deported. Many critics have argued that racial profiling will be inevitable in Arizona when police officers are obliged to check the immigration status of people they suspect to be undocumented.[6] A May 2010 poll of 1079 adults nationwide revealed that only 15 percent thought that this law would not affect some racial or ethnic groups more than others.[7]

Analyses of the rates of deportation of people of different nationalities make it clear that racial profiling is already a fundamental part of current immigration policy enforcement. Based on the population estimates of undocumented people in the United States in 2007, I found Latin American and Caribbean nationals were more likely to be deported than Asians or Europeans. For example, 8 percent of undocumented Hondurans were deported, compared to less than 1 percent of undocumented Koreans, Filipinos, Chinese, and Indians. In 2007, there were slightly more undocumented Chinese and Filipinos in the United States than Hondurans. However, nearly 25,000 Hondurans were deported for being out-of-status, as compared to 408 Filipinos and 766 Chinese.

The Honduran case is so exceptional that it is worthwhile to look at it individually. I cannot fully explain the reason so many Hondurans are deported, but I suspect it is related in part to where Hondurans live. Hondurans are more likely to live in the South than other Hispanics; 54 percent of Hondurans live in the South, compared to 35 percent of all Hispanics. Furthermore, whereas most Hispanics who live in the South live in Texas, Hondurans are more likely to live in Florida or Louisiana. Eighteen percent of Hondurans live in Florida, compared to 8 percent of all Hispanics. Further, 6 percent of all Hondurans live in Louisiana, compared to less than 1 percent of all Hispanics.[8] It may be the case that Hondurans are targeted in Florida, because five different police jurisdictions in Florida cooperate with Immigration and Customs Enforcement

(ICE) agents, and Border Patrol agents are active in the state.[9] Hondurans' visibility in Louisiana, where relatively few Latinos live, may also be part of the explanation. Another potential explanation is that many Hondurans have applied for Temporary Protection Status (TPS) and thus are more likely to be in DHS databases. This could lead to more deportations of Hondurans. To be sure, however, a more comprehensive analysis of where and how Hondurans are encountered by immigration agents is needed.

The data currently available do not make it clear where and how Hondurans are deported. Nevertheless, we can come to some tentative conclusions using the available data from DHS. In 2008, Customs and Border Patrol (CBP) apprehended 723,840 people, and non-CBP immigration agents apprehended 67,728 people. The people who CBP apprehends may be people entering the country illegally. Others may be people found within 100 miles of U.S. borders, which include places such as San Diego, California, Tucson, Arizona, Buffalo New York, Miami, Florida, and New Orleans, Louisiana. Some of the people who CBP agents apprehend are sent to their countries of origin without being recorded as being deported, because they are permitted to withdraw their applications for admission. These people do not show up in the deportation numbers, which explains why there were nearly 800,000 apprehensions in 2008, yet only 350,000 deportations. Others apply for asylum and are placed in the appropriate proceedings. Still others are deported as *expedited removals,* which means they do not see an immigration judge but do show up in DHS records as deportees. Still others are allowed a hearing before a judge, after which they may or may not be deported. Expedited removals accounted for one-third of all removals in 2008.[10]

Let me explain what all this means for Hondurans. First, Hondurans may be more likely to be deported because of their concentration in Miami and New Orleans, which have active Border Patrol Sectors. Second, Hondurans are susceptible to apprehension by non-CBP agents. In 2008, 4,438 Hondurans were apprehended by non-CBP immigration agents. These were Hondurans living inside the United States, not Hondurans attempting to cross the border. In contrast, 936 Chinese were apprehended by non-CBP agents. There were an estimated 220,000 undocumented Chinese living in the United States in 2008, compared to an estimated 300,000 Hondurans. Thus, if we take a narrow approach and consider only non-CBP apprehensions, we can make a conservative statement that Hondurans are 3.5 times more likely to be apprehended by non-CBP immigration agents in the United States than Chinese, based on their numbers among the undocumented.[11] This is still a significant discrepancy. This exploration into the situation of Hondurans points to two important facts. The first is that DHS needs to provide more complete and accurate data to be able to determine the extent to which racial profiling is occurring within the agency. The second is that, regardless of exactly how it occurs, the consequences are clear: Latin Americans and Caribbeans are disproportionately targeted in immigration enforcement, and this disparity needs to be addressed.

Deportation of "Criminal Aliens"

A top priority for ICE has been to target the "worst of the worst" in the illegal population—criminal aliens incarcerated in U.S. prisons and jails; those who may pose a threat to national security or public safety.[12] Reports from ICE assure us that they are ensuring national security and public safety by deporting criminals. In 2008, the Homeland Security Committee allocated $180 million to the Criminal Alien Program to ensure that incarcerated noncitizens are deported.[13] However, a report from the University of California at Berkeley Law School finds that ICE "is not following Congress' mandate to focus resources on the deportation of immigrants with serious criminal histories."[14] Instead, it is encouraging local police to engage in racial profiling to arrest and deport people who engage in minor infractions of the law, such as kicking over traffic cones or public urination.

Under the Criminal Alien Program, local police have the authority to call ICE to check the status of anyone they suspect to be undocumented. For example, in 2006, ICE began a partnership with the city of Irving, Texas, that enabled ICE to investigate the immigration status of people held at the Irving Jail. Under this partnership, if Irving police arrest someone they suspect to be undocumented, they contact ICE to determine their immigration status. Of course, police officers can't tell someone's immigration status just by looking at them. In fact, in September 2007, of the 269 people that Irving police officers referred to ICE, only 186 were actually arrested by ICE. The others were lawfully present in the United States.[15]

Researchers at the UC Berkeley Law School found that 96 percent of the people held under the Criminal Alien Program in Irving were Hispanic. Moreover, police were more likely to arrest Hispanics for minor offenses once the city began to participate in the Criminal Alien Program. Most of the people detained under the Criminal Alien Program in Irving, Texas, were arrested for misdemeanors; only 2 percent were charged with felonies. The Berkeley report provides "compelling evidence that the Criminal Alien Program tacitly encourages local police to arrest Hispanics for petty offenses." This study of one city in Texas resonates with research I have been doing with deportees in Jamaica, Guatemala, the Dominican Republic, and Brazil. Deportees I have spoken with consistently tell me that they were stopped by police for a minor offense and subsequently placed in deportation proceedings.

Walter is one example. A citizen of the Dominican Republic, Walter took a boat to Puerto Rico when he was 15 and attempted to enter the United States illegally. However, he was caught and deported. When he was 19, Walter decided to try to migrate again. This time he went through Mexico and made it to New York City. Two years later, Walter met and married a U.S. citizen and obtained legalization in 1998 through family reunification laws. He intended to make his life in the United States; he worked at JFK airport to support his wife and their two children. In 2004, Walter was stopped by police officers for a traffic violation. When the officer checked Walter's immigration status, he discovered Walter had an immigration hold. It turns out that Walter had an order to appear at immigration court because immigration investigators had figured out that Walter had failed to mention on his application for legalization that he had been deported from Puerto Rico when he was 15. This accusation of immigration fraud resulted in Walter's residency being rescinded—six years after he was granted residency. Walter spent four years fighting his case, but in 2008 he lost and was deported to the Dominican Republic—as a criminal alien. His crime: immigration fraud. One out of six people deported on criminal grounds are deported for immigration crimes such as this (U.S. Department of Homeland Security 2010b). Walter did omit crucial information from his application for legalization, but does this make him among the "worst of the worst"?

More than one million people have been deported on criminal grounds since the passage of the 1996 laws. 94 percent of these deportees are from just ten countries: Mexico, Honduras, El Salvador, Dominican Republic, Guatemala, Colombia, Jamaica, Canada, Brazil, and Haiti.[16] Many of these deportees are people who, like Walter, were stopped by police officers and handed over to immigration agents. In my ongoing research with deportees in Guatemala and Jamaica, I have found that Jamaicans often end up being deported through their involvement with the criminal justice system. For example, a Jamaican citizen named Elias who had lived in the United States for more than thirty years was charged with possession of crack cocaine, spent eighteen months in prison, and then was ordered deported.

In contrast to the Jamaicans, many Guatemalan deportees I talked to reported that they were deported after being stopped by police, who then turned them over to immigration authorities without charging them with a crime. Both are subject to racial profiling, but this process works differently for Jamaicans than for Guatemalans. Jamaicans are more likely to be targeted by police as suspects in drug crimes in places such as Brooklyn or Queens. Guatemalans are more likely to be suspected to be undocumented and turned over to immigration by police officers who cooperate with immigration agents in places such as Orange County, California.

The deportation of people convicted of crimes involves cooperation between criminal law enforcement agents and immigration law enforcement agents. Any noncitizen in the United States can be deported after being convicted of a criminal offense. *Criminal deportees* thus include tourists, students, undocumented migrants, asylees, legal permanent residents, and other temporary and permanent visa holders who have been convicted of a criminal offense. *Asylees* are people who have been granted political asylum because of danger to their life in their home country. *Legal permanent residents* are people who have gone through the immigration process and have been issued what is commonly known as a *green card*. Many asylees and legal permanent residents have spent a large part of their life in the United States.

Human Rights Watch reports that just under 10 percent of the 897,099 people deported on criminal grounds between April 1, 1997 and August 1, 2007—87,844—were legal permanent residents of the United States, and about 20 percent—179,038—were legally present in the United States as either legal permanent residents, asylees, parolees, or on a temporary visa. The records, unfortunately, provide limited data on the crimes for which deportees were convicted; 44 percent of the cases had no crime data at all. The limited data available, however, indicate that 19 percent of people deported on criminal grounds were deported for nonviolent criminal immigration offenses—and 71 percent of these for illegal entry. According to ICE's own reports, 30 percent of criminal deportees in FY 2009 were deported for drug offenses, 16 percent for traffic offenses, and 16 percent for immigration offenses. ICE reports indicate that relatively few people were deported for violent offenses: 7 percent for assault, 2.5 percent for robbery, and 2 percent for sexual assault (U.S. Department of Homeland Security 2010b).

The majority of criminal deportees have been long-term residents of the United States; half of the people deported between 1997 and 2006 on criminal grounds had spent more than fourteen years in the United States (Transnational Records Access Clearinghouse 2007). The fact that increasing numbers of deportees are people who have been in the United States for extended periods of time means that deportations affect more people in the United States, and the effects are more widespread. For example, if a migrant farm worker comes to the United States to work for six months and is deported after three months, the impact of his deportation is felt primarily by him and his family in Mexico. The principal effect of this deportation is the loss of the wages for the farm worker and the loss of labor to the farm owner. This is quite distinct from the deportation of a person who has been in the United States for two decades, has children in the United States, and has strong community ties. His deportation entails much more than the loss of wages. His children lose a father, his wife a husband, and his community members a valuable and productive member.

Most undocumented migrants are not deported, and neither are most legal permanent residents who commit crimes. To be deported for committing a crime, a noncitizen first has to be caught, then charged and sentenced, and finally placed in deportation proceedings. Noncitizens can be deported for crimes such as shoplifting and drug use. Most of these minor crimes go undetected by law enforcement agents. Because some people face deportation for these legal violations, it is useful to think about who is being targeted by law enforcement agents. There are about 12 million legal permanent residents in the United States (U.S. Department of Homeland Security 2006). Between 1997 and 2007, 87,844 legal permanent residents were deported—less than 1 percent of this population (Human Rights Watch 2009). It is reasonable to assume that more than 1 percent of this population actually committed crimes. For example, studies have shown that nearly one-third of high school students in the United States have shoplifted, and the same proportion has used illegal drugs.[17] More than 40 percent of all people in the United States have used illegal drugs at some point in their lives.[18] Most citizens and noncitizens who commit minor crimes are not arrested, charged, or sentenced for these crimes. Thus, it is crucial to consider which segment of the noncitizen population is most likely to be deported for engaging in criminal activity.

It is well established in criminological scholarship that blacks and Latinos are more often the targets of law enforcement than whites or Asians (Feagin 2000; Western 2007; Petit and Western 2004). The criminal justice system systematically disadvantages black and Latino men. Even though black and white men have similar levels of criminal activity, black men are seven times more likely than white men to be imprisoned, and Latinos are four times as likely (Collins 2004; Feagin 2000; Western 2007). In the case of drug offenses, the data are particularly striking. In the United States, black men are sent to prison on drug charges thirteen times the rate of white men, yet five times as many whites use illegal drugs as blacks. Although whites are much more prevalent among users, blacks are much more likely to end up incarcerated.[19] These data are important for understanding deportations, because about a third of all deportees are deported for drug charges, and most criminal deportees are men. Notably, in the Dominican Republic, local government officials reported to me that 80 percent of criminal deportees are deported on drug charges.

In the United States, blacks and Latinos are more likely to be incarcerated than whites or Asians, and this is particularly pronounced for men. In 2005, 8.1 percent of black males aged twenty-five to twenty-nine were in prison, compared to 2.6 percent of Hispanic males and about 1.1 percent of white males in the same age group (U.S. Department of Justice 2006). Asians are less likely to be incarcerated than whites.[20] The more frequent incarceration of black and Latino men is a result of heavy policing of black and Latino neighborhoods, racial profiling by police officers, discriminatory laws, and discriminating judges. All of these factors work together to render it more likely that black men will be found behind bars than in college or the military (Gilmore 2007; Western 2007; Feagin 2000).

Racism in the criminal justice system has severe implications for black and Latino/a immigrants. Many Jamaicans, Dominicans, and Haitians are phenotypically indistinguishable from African-Americans and often experience the same set of resource deprivations and racist ideologies and practices that lead to the mass incarceration of black men. Immigrants from Latin America often live in Latino neighborhoods that are heavily policed. This means that immigrants of African and Latin American descent are more likely to be jailed and eventually deported than immigrants of European or Asian descent who are not subject to the same set of prejudices and discriminatory actions as blacks and Latinos/as. Whereas the immigrant population includes many whites and Asians, blacks and Latinos have an almost exclusive presence among detainees and deportees (Dow 2004).

Data on the noncitizen population in 2000 from the U.S. Census[21] along with data from the DHS allow us to explore the probability of deportation for noncitizens from various nationalities. The 2000 Census data breaks down the foreign-born population into citizens and noncitizens. Thus, we can look at the likelihood that someone who was a noncitizen in 2000 would be deported in 2007, broken down by country of origin. Figure 3-2 shows the likelihood that a noncitizen residing in the United States in 2009 would be deported for engaging in criminal activity. There is a clear trend in these data; people from Latin America and the Caribbean are much more likely to be deported on criminal grounds than people from Asia or Europe.[22] For example, in 2007, Hondurans were eight hundred times more likely to be deported on criminal grounds than Japanese, relative to their proportions in the noncitizen population. In that same year, Mexicans were twenty-eight times more likely to be deported on criminal grounds than Filipinos, and forty-nine times more likely than Indians, relative to their proportions in the noncitizen population.

One possible explanation for these disparities is that Latin American and Caribbean nationals are committing more crimes. This is possible; however, the proportional differences are too great for this to be a complete explanation. There is no reason to believe that one national origin group would be 28 or 49 times more likely to commit crimes than another national origin group, much less 800 times more likely! In fact, the data discussed next indicates otherwise.

A study, based on self-reported drug use, found that Mexican immigrants between the ages of 12 and 17 were about 33 percent more likely to use illicit drugs than were Asian youth (Gfroerer and Tan 2003). This age group is not representative of all immigrants, but it is an important sample because about a third of all criminal deportees are deported on drug charges (see Table 3-2).

Figure 3-2 Ratio of 2000 Noncitizen Population to 2009 Criminal Deportees

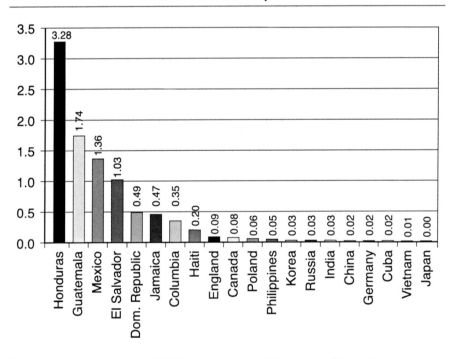

Note: All countries had more than 200,000 Noncitizens; Top 20 Countries of Origin of Noncitizens. Data Sources: U.S. Census. DHS OIS: Table 38 D.

Table 3-2 Crimes for Which People Were Deported: 2009

Crime category	Number Deported	Percent of total
Drugs	37,993	29.60%
Traffic Offenses	20,367	15.87%
Immigration	19,807	15.43%
Assault	9,436	7.35%
Larceny	4,228	3.29%
Burglary	3,795	2.96%
Robbery	3,252	2.53%
Fraudulent Activities	2,903	2.26%
Sexual Assault	2,792	2.18%
Family Offenses	2,611	2.03%
Other	21,161	16.49%
Total	128,345	100.00%

Data Source: DHS OIS: http://www.dhs.gov/xlibrary/assets/statistics/publications/enforcement_ar_2009.pdf.

Although self-reported drug use is not always reliable, there is no reason to believe that Mexicans are more likely than Asians to misreport their drug usage.

Another study, conducted by the Office of National Drug Control Policy, breaks down self-reported drug use by national origin.[23] According to this study, Koreans were 1.8 times more likely to have used illicit drugs than Salvadorans. Yet, Salvadorans were 34 times more likely to face deportation. This study also found that Jamaicans were 3 times more likely to have used illicit drugs than Indians, yet Indians were 5 times more likely to have used drugs other than marijuana than Jamaicans. Jamaicans were 24 times more likely to have been deported than Indians. Self-reported use of drugs other than marijuana is significant because possession of small amounts of marijuana usually is not grounds for deportation, whereas possession of a small amount of crack or cocaine can be grounds for deportation. These findings provide support for the "honorary white" thesis, insofar as Asian and European immigrants are considerably less likely than Latin American immigrants to find themselves in removal proceedings for having violated criminal laws, even though according to self reports, they have used drugs in some cases more frequently than their Latin American counterparts.

Consequences of Deportation

As we have seen, deportation laws disproportionately affect people of Latin American and Caribbean origin. Another striking aspect of deportation law is the lack of judicial review of deportation cases. In Chapter 1, "Roots of Immigration to the United States," I described two laws passed in 1996: the Anti-Terrorism and Effective Death Penalty Act (AEDPA) and the Illegal Immigration Reform and Immigrant Responsibility Act of 1996 (IIRIRA). Under these laws, legal permanent residents face automatic deportation if they have been convicted of "aggravated felonies." Deportation is automatic insofar as people convicted of aggravated felonies do not have the right to judicial review of their cases. Judges cannot take into account their family ties in the United States or whether they have ties to their country of origin. Judges have no discretion once a determination is made that a crime is an aggravated felony. Because of the limited options for cancelling deportation orders, many people with strong ties to the United States have been deported.

Deportees Uprooted from Their Homes in the United States

Between 1998 and 2007, more than 2 million people were deported from the United States. More than 100,000 of these deportees had U.S.-citizen children (Office of Inspector General, Department of Homeland Security 2009). Deportations have been on the rise since the passage of the 1996 immigration laws. There were 50,924 deportations in 1995 and 208,521 in 2005, a fourfold increase in ten years (Dougherty, Wilson, and Wu 2006). In FY 2008, nearly 350,000 people were deported—more than 50 percent more than were deported in the entire period between 1981 and 1990. Many of the people who have been deported have been legal permanent residents. Among deportees are people who have spent nearly their whole lives in the United States and who face deportation for relatively minor offenses.[24]

Moreover, the majority of people who are deported are people of color. This means that the devastating effects of the deportation of long-term residents of the United States are felt more strongly in communities where people of color predominate. As discussed in Chapter 2, "The Department of Homeland Security and the Immigration Enforcement Regime of the Twenty-First Century," worksite enforcement operations and other immigration raids create a context of fear in many immigrant communities. This further exacerbates preexisting inequalities between whites and nonwhites in the United States. Many people who are deported have committed fairly minor crimes, and the punishment of permanent separation from their loved ones seems overly severe.

In the U.S. legal tradition, deportation is not punishment, yet it often amounts to banishment from the only country people have known, for relatively minor legal infractions. Xuan Wilson, for example, came to the United States when she was four years old. In 1989, she was convicted of writing a forged check for $19.83. Because this minor offense was considered a crime of moral turpitude, Wilson was ordered deported in 2003 (Cook 2003). Mary Anne Gehris came to the United States from Germany as an infant. In 1988, she was involved in an altercation in which she pulled the hair of another woman. She was charged and convicted of battery and received a one-year suspended sentence; she did not have to serve time. However, since she was a noncitizen, she faced mandatory deportation, without judicial review (Morawetz 2000). Gehris was fortunate to have found advocates for her cause. She was granted a pardon from the governor, which meant that she was not deported to a country she barely knew for a relatively minor offense (Welch 2002).

Families of deportees suffer greatly as well. In 1997, Jesus Collado, a forty-three-year-old restaurant manager and legal resident of the United States, went to the Dominican Republic for a two-week vacation with his wife and children. When he returned, the border inspector checked the INS records and found that Collado had been convicted of a criminal offense in 1974. Collado had been convicted of statutory rape for having consensual sex with his fifteen-year-old girlfriend when he was nineteen. Because of the retroactive nature of the 1996 laws, Collado faced mandatory detention and deportation without judicial review (Welch 2002). His family faced losing their father, husband, and provider. Many times, the consequences for family members left behind can be devastating. Gerardo Mosquera, a native of Colombia, was deported for a $10 marijuana sale in 1989, although he had been a legal resident for twenty-nine years. He left behind his U.S.-citizen wife and children. Mosquera's seventeen-year-old son committed suicide after he left, in part because of his depression over losing his father (Master 2003).

In some cases, criminal aliens have no idea they have committed crimes that render them deportable. Emma Mendez de Hays faced deportation for translating a conversation for her Spanish-speaking cousin in 1990. Mendez de Hays answered the phone in her home, and the caller asked for her cousin. Her cousin, who did not speak English well, told her to tell him she would help him the next day. Mendez de Hays relayed the message and hung up. It turned out the caller was an undercover narcotics officer, and Mendez de Hays was found guilty of using a communication device to facilitate the distribution of cocaine. She did not serve time for this offense and thought the whole incident was behind her when, in 1996, she returned from a visit to Italy with her fiancé. INS officials immediately detained her and placed her in deportation proceedings for her 1990 guilty plea. She spent two years in INS detention while she fought her case through appeals. She finally won when a U.S. Supreme Court decision invalidated some retroactive deportation orders (Cook 2003). Notably, Mendez de Hays did not avoid deportation because of her family ties in the United States or her lack of ties in Colombia. She won because the court determined that, in this case, the law could not be applied retroactively.

Catherine Caza came to the United States when she was three years old. She was ordered deported at the age of forty in 1997, for a crime she had committed seventeen years prior. In 1980, Caza was taking amphetamine pills prescribed by her doctor. Her boyfriend convinced her to sell him twenty-one of them. He turned out to be an undercover police officer. In court, she pled guilty and was placed on probation for five years. The 1996 laws rendered her ineligible for a waiver for deportation, and, despite the nature of her offense, the thirty-seven years she had spent in the United States, and her seven-year-old U.S.-citizen daughter, the judge had no choice but to order her to be deported (Master 2003).

The deportation of people for relatively minor crimes—shoplifting, small drug sales, and forged checks—is surprising. The disproportionate severity of the consequences of deportation is exacerbated by the fact that many of these people have spent nearly all their lives here. Many learned to shoplift or resorted to selling drugs because of their environment in the United States. When a child born in Thailand and adopted by U.S. parents is convicted of forging checks and stealing a car, we cannot blame his country of origin for his criminal activity. John Gaul, the adopted child of U.S.-citizen parents, was deported to Thailand at age nineteen, after having served time for these felonies (Master 2003). What is the logic behind this exile? As the 1953 Presidential Commission charged with reviewing deportation orders pointed out, "Each of the aliens is a product of our society. Their formative years were spent in the United States, which is the only home they have ever known. The countries of origin which they left . . . certainly are not responsible for their criminal ways" (quoted in Morawetz 2000: 1961).

The fact that judges are not allowed to take family ties into account in aggravated felony cases means that immigrant advocates do not have the chance to make the case that people who spend their formative years in the United States should not be deported. The fact that a person was born in Thailand or Brazil should not render her removable from the United States. When a Brazilian adoptee who has spent nearly his entire life in the United States is arrested for shoplifting, his crime has nothing to do with the fact that he was born in Brazil, and everything to do with what he has learned in the United States. Cases such as those listed earlier make it evident that not only are illegal aliens deportable, but permanent and other legal residents of the United States are deportable as well. For example, a person who has been in the United States for fifteen years but was convicted of having jumped a turnstile in a subway ten years ago is also deportable. Of course, the DHS cannot hope to find all such people, but legal permanent residents who have prior convictions are potentially deportable. Those who have been convicted of aggravated felonies and crimes of moral turpitude cannot apply for U.S. citizenship or leave the country, for fear that their criminal record will be discovered and that they will be detained and deported. Their homes also could be raided at any time, as National Fugitive Operations Program agents could discover their criminal record and raid their homes. For example, Alberto, a Jamaican deportee, told me that his home was raided in 2007 and he was deported in 2008 on the basis of a 1984 conviction.

What Happens to Deportees When They Reach Their Country of Origin?

Deepa Fernandes (2006) reports that people who are deported to Haiti are often incarcerated for undefined periods of time in the National Penitentiary in Haiti. Her description of the National Penitentiary, where there were more than one hundred deportees during her visit at the end of 2005, is appalling.

> Haitian jails fail every standard of human decency. If your relative does not bring you food, chances are you will go hungry. There is no drinking water, just what your relative brings you. Inmates are packed like sardines into cells. There are no beds, just a few filthy mattresses in each cell. Inmates either sleep on the hard floor or share the mattress. Each cell has one bucket in the corner that is used by all the cellmates as the toilet. Often the bucket overflows, and days pass before it is emptied and cleaned (104).

Fernandes (2006) discusses the case of Marc, a Haitian who had been deported from the United States for "smoking a joint" (28). Upon landing in Haiti, he was immediately locked up at the National Penitentiary. There, he was beaten by prison guards, and his arm was broken. Since he was not provided with medical treatment, his arm became deformed. Marc had spent most of his life in the United States and was a legal permanent resident. He had only one relative in Haiti, an uncle, and barely spoke Haitian Creole. Nevertheless, he will never be able to return to the United States. His case is similar to Wilber's. Wilber had lived in the United States since he was eight years old. He was a legal permanent resident and had three U.S.-citizen children, as well as a wife who was a U.S.

citizen. Wilber was convicted of domestic violence and served eighteen months in prison. This conviction rendered him deportable, and after five months in detention, he was deported to Haiti. There, he was taken directly to the National Penitentiary, where he was denied food and had to bribe the guards to avoid being brutalized. He was able to get out when his wife came to Haiti and bribed the prison guards. Unwilling to endure any more time in Haiti, and barred permanently from the United States, he moved to Canada, where his wife and children are able to visit him (Fernandes 2006).

In the January 2010 earthquake in Haiti, the National Penitentiary was destroyed, and all the prisoners escaped (Goodman 2010). In addition, DHS put a temporary stop to deportations to Haiti in the aftermath of the earthquake. For a time, Haitians who faced deportation either remained in detention or were released. However, barely a year after the devastating earthquake, deportations to Haiti resumed.[25]

Based on my research with deportees in Jamaica, nearly all are financially stricken. Those who spent the most time in the United States have the most difficulty readjusting. For example, O'Ryan moved to the United States when he was six years old, to join his mother and grandmother who had gone a few years before. He went as a legal permanent resident, first to the Bronx, and then to Brooklyn. In elementary school, the other kids teased him at first, because of his accent. "It took me years to learn how to talk like this," he told me with a strong New York accent.

O'Ryan graduated with honors from his junior high school and made it into John Dewey, a competitive high school in Brooklyn. However, most of his friends weren't attending school, and he slowly stopped going to school. After dropping out of high school, O'Ryan earned his GED and enrolled in Mercy College, where he was studying computer programming. He tried to stay out of trouble though, because he hated the look on his mother's face whenever she heard he was getting into trouble.

When he was twenty-three years old, O'Ryan was found driving a car with illegal drugs inside and was given the punishment of eighteen months in boot camp. On the day of O'Ryan's graduation from boot camp, his mother, his girlfriend, and his newly born daughter came to the graduation. O'Ryan saw his daughter for the first time. He was expecting to go home with them and start his life again. But, immigration agents were waiting for him and told him he was going to be deported.

O'Ryan had been in the country for nearly twenty years and had no family he knew in Jamaica. O'Ryan qualified for citizenship, and, in fact, had applied when his green card expired in 1996. His mother and cousin applied at the same time. His mother's citizenship went through, and then his cousin's. So, he went to check on his citizenship. The citizenship office told him he needed to redo his fingerprints. He finally received the letter saying he should go to the swearing-in ceremony in 2001, five years later.

Unfortunately, O'Ryan had been arrested a few weeks earlier and was in jail when his letter arrived. So, at the age of twenty-five, O'Ryan was deported to a country he barely knew. His grandmother's sister agreed to take him in, and he went to her house to live. Back in Jamaica, it was hard to find work. He has found work occasionally, but never a permanent position. He also has trouble making friends in the small town where his aunt lives. He feels like he really has no one in Jamaica, except for his great-aunt.

When I spoke with O'Ryan in the summer of 2009, he was thirty-two years old and had been in Jamaica for seven years. He had recently found a job and was earning $50 a week, barely enough to pay for his food and transportation. His mother was sending him money when she could and coming to visit every year. It is hard for O'Ryan not to dwell on the "what ifs." What if his citizenship application had been processed just a few months earlier? What if he didn't get into an argument with his boss? What if he didn't answer his phone that day to go pick up his friend? What if there wasn't a road block that evening? What if his mother didn't choose to move to Brooklyn when they migrated from Jamaica?

The deportees I met in Jamaica who had spent most of their lives in the United States have seen their dreams shattered. They are paying a dear price for their crimes. O'Ryan, for example, says he understands he made mistakes, but he finds it difficult to see it as fair that he should pay for those mistakes for the rest of his life. He doesn't see a future for himself in Jamaica, where he feels like a foreigner.

Many deportees are people who have grown up in the United States. Readjustment to a new country is often quite difficult. When I met Katy in Guatemala, she had been back to the country where she was born for nine years, yet still had trouble adjusting. When she reminisced on her life in the United States, she had many fond memories: "My last Christmas in the U.S., I couldn't even think of anything to ask for; I had everything." Katy lived with her parents and her sister in a spacious house in suburban Louisiana. Her parents fled political turmoil in Guatemala when she was two years old; her father was a witness to a political assassination and was forced to leave the country. In the United States, they were able to achieve the American dream. They had a house, several cars, and two daughters headed for success. Katy's father had his own business painting cars, her mother was a housewife, and Katy was a typical American teenager. On weekends, she went out with her friends to the mall or the movies. Tears streamed down her face when she thought of all she had lost—of the life she once lived.

Katy was fifteen years old when immigration agents told her family they had a week to leave the country because her father's application for political asylum was denied. She was finishing up middle school, and her sister was enrolled in college. This was their worst nightmare. When the immigration agents arrived to carry out the deportation order, they handcuffed Katy, who was waiting at the school bus stop. "It was in front of everybody," she told me. Katy's father and sister were taken to a county jail, and Katy and her mother were allowed to stay at a friend's house for their last four days in the country. Although Katy had been in the United States for thirteen years, and her father had been in the United States since before she was born, they had not successfully legalized their status and were deported.

They were fortunate that they had a place to live in Guatemala; Katy's grandmother had passed away and left them a house. However, it was a simple dwelling, with adobe walls, a tin roof, and the bathroom outside on the patio. It is already difficult to be an adolescent, and Katy did not deal well with this fall from riches to rags. She fell into a deep depression and barely left the house for more than a year. Unable to read or write Spanish, she never went back to school.

In the United States, Katy excelled in school, was popular with her friends, and never got into trouble. She had dreams of becoming a veterinarian, and her sister was already studying to be a doctor. When they were deported to Guatemala, her dreams were shattered. When I spoke with Katy, she had been in Guatemala for nine years. The wounds from this experience were deep, and Katy shed tears for most of the interview. Just thinking about what happened to her and her family was too much to bear.

Deportations and Human Rights Violations

These stories of deportees are troubling. In addition, the punitive deportation laws of the United States are in violation of a variety of international treaties and covenants. Article 13 of the International Covenant on Civil and Political Rights (ICCPR) specifies that noncitizens should be allowed to "submit the reasons against [their] expulsion," yet immigrants who are convicted of aggravated felonies have no opportunity to present evidence of their ties to the United States in their deportation hearings. The 1996 laws only permit them to argue that their crime should not be classified as an aggravated felony. Potential deportees are not permitted to present other reasons against their deportation.

For example, Suwan was deported to Cambodia after living in the United States as a refugee with his wife and two young children. His crime was two counts of indecent exposure. In immigration proceedings, this is considered an aggravated felony. Suwan's crime was that he had urinated outdoors at the construction site where he worked, because there was no toilet available. Suwan's deportation was mandatory; the judge did not have the opportunity to consider whether his crime was serious enough to warrant deportation to a country from which he had been awarded asylum. Once the judge determined that the crime was indeed an aggravated felony, the severity of the crime itself was not considered. The judge also could not take into consideration the impact of his deportation on his family or the consequence of his being deported to a country from which he had been granted asylum. Suwan was denied his right to a fair hearing and ordered deported, due to the absence of judicial review of these cases (Capps et al. 2007).

In addition, deportations without due process violate people's rights to form a family, as codified in the UDHR; the International Covenant on Economic, Social, and Cultural Rights (ICESCR); and the ICCPR. In this latter convention, which the United States has ratified, Article 10 stipulates that "the family is the natural and fundamental group unit of society and is entitled to protection by society and the State." In many deportation cases, however, judges are not allowed to take into consideration the extent to which family members, even those who are U.S. citizens, will be affected by the deportation of a spouse, father, mother, brother, or sister.

In some cases, judges are not allowed to consider family ties. In other cases, undocumented migrants are given no opportunity to have their case heard by a judge. In August 2009, I went to the military airport in Guatemala City, where, on average, one planeload of deportees from the United States arrives each day. On that day, one of the deported passengers was an indigenous Guatemalan woman who had lived for sixteen years in the United States and who had three children who were U.S. citizens. She had crossed the border without inspection in 1993 and had lived in the United States without legal documentation since she arrived. In July 2009, she was arrested in Florida and placed in immigration detention. Her husband, a legal permanent resident, paid an immigration lawyer $3,000 to fight her case. Unfortunately, the woman was deported before having the opportunity to go to trial and ask for cancellation of removal. In light of the length of her stay in the United States, her husband's legal status, and her children's citizenship, she may have been granted a cancellation of removal. She told me her lawyer told her not to sign any documents, so she had not signed anything. In the airport in Guatemala, she was confused and lost and did not understand how she had been deported. She had no family in Guatemala and nowhere to go. Her parents had passed away, and she had no brothers or sisters. This woman had not benefited from the right to a trial and had been denied the right to be with her family.

Racism and Immigration Policies

Current immigration laws, practices, and policies violate the human rights of citizens and noncitizens, reproduce racism, and create a climate of fear and repression. In this way, these laws affect all people in the United States by further enhancing the extent to which our society is riddled with racism and repression. The general climate of strict enforcement of immigration laws in the post-9/11 era has further exacerbated the situation. A recent nationally representative survey of Hispanics found that nearly one in ten Latinos had been stopped by authorities and asked about their immigration status. It is thus no wonder that the majority of those Latinos surveyed said that they worry about deportation (Lopez and Minushkin 2008). These numbers indicate that the racial profiling of Latinos is widespread and that Latinos are targeted in immigration enforcement efforts (Aldana 2008).

The fact that the majority of noncitizens who have their human rights violated are people of color is consistent with other patterns of systemic racism in this country. The systematic mistreatment of immigrant detainees and the mass removal of noncitizens from this country are consistent with the general denial of full citizenship and rights to people of color in the United States. It is important to document these human rights violations and to analyze them from an antiracist standpoint. This point of view allows us to see that the racism embedded in immigration policy is not isolated, but a foreseeable by-product of a society that systematically denies the dignity and humanity of people of color. The criminalization of black men leads to the deportation of a disproportionate number of Dominicans and Jamaicans. The stereotype of Mexicans and of those who look Mexican as "illegals" leads to the targeting of Mexicans and Central Americans in immigration enforcement efforts.

These practices and policies are not simply isolating and removing immigrants of color; the immigrants are also leaving behind their families who are, in most cases, also people of color. Those children, spouses, and parents who witness their loved ones being mistreated and banished are also victims of this systematic denial of human rights. In light of patterns of segregation, whole communities of Mexicans and Mexican Americans are growing up seeing the sort of structural racism we are familiar with in terms of the distribution of resources. They're also seeing their mothers, fathers, brothers, sisters, neighbors, and community leaders being told that they have no right to be here, and, in many cases, being forcibly removed from their communities. We must not take lightly the sort of message that these policies and practices are sending to these future generations of Americans. Just as African-American children often grow up knowing that blacks are more likely to be locked up, Mexicans and other Latin American and Caribbean people grow up knowing that people like them are being expelled from this country—at the rate of nearly one thousand people a day. This chapter has dealt with the consequences of deportation for deportees. The next chapter explores the consequences of the threat of deportation for families in the United States.

CHAPTER 4

THE IMPOSSIBLE CHOICE

FAMILY VERSUS CITIZENSHIP IN U.S. IMMIGRATION POLICIES

In the spring of 2008, I spoke with Melissa, a native-born U.S. citizen who faced a difficult choice. She had fallen in love with and married a Brazilian man, Sergio. Sergio had violated the terms of his visa by overstaying his tourist visa. This infraction alone would not have been a problem. However, it became a big issue when Sergio reentered the United States after overstaying and didn't remain outside of the country for the requisite period. Sergio was not aware of the requirement that he remain outside of the country after overstaying his tourist visa and thought all was well, especially because the border agents had allowed him to reenter without advising him of this problem. Nevertheless, because of these violations of the Immigration and Nationality Act (INA), the Department of Homeland Security (DHS) ordered Sergio to be deported when he applied for legalization. Sergio's deportation order forced Melissa to choose between abandoning her U.S. citizenship to be with her husband or staying in the United States and dissolving her union with Sergio, because he was now permanently ineligible for admission to the United States based on his immigration violations.

As this example shows, Melissa has been affected severely by immigration policy, although she is not an immigrant. When I spoke with her, she was flustered and found it hard to reconcile the fact that her status as a U.S. citizen did not entitle her to live in the United States with her spouse. She had tried every legal maneuver possible, but the law did not provide for Sergio's legalization. Sergio had to leave the United States and could never return legally. Melissa told me that she planned to annul the marriage. She was not willing to give up her right to remain in the United States; she chose to sacrifice her marriage.

Melissa's case is similar to thousands of U.S. citizens who are married to undocumented or out-of-status immigrants. Many of these immigrants were brought here as small children. Others, like Sergio, were unaware of their visa violations. Although many pundits imagine that ridding the country of undocumented immigrants will be beneficial to all citizens, the deportation of immigrants frequently has an adverse impact on their citizen spouses or children.

As we've already established, to some extent, immigration policies in the United States have had negative consequences for citizens, families, and communities. People who are not U.S. citizens and are thus subject to deportation often have U.S.-citizen spouses and children. In many cases, they also have extended family members who are U.S. citizens, and they live in communities with citizens. Some have been in the country for a few days, but others have settled here and have been here for decades. Thus, policies that affect noncitizens have clear consequences for citizens.

As we move into the second decade of the twenty-first century, the U.S. Congress has not been able to reach an agreement on comprehensive immigration reform. The two houses have only been able to agree that more enforcement is needed. For example, they have passed laws such as the Secure Fence Act, which is designed to reinforce the southern border, and they have appropriated funds for the DHS to increase both border and interior enforcement. Meanwhile, legislatures in states such as Arizona, Colorado, Oklahoma, and Tennessee have passed laws designed to make life more difficult for undocumented people within their states. Over the past few years, most of the laws passed by individual states and the Federal government have been punitive. They are in keeping with the previous set of laws passed by Congress in 1996 that have led to the deportation of more than one million noncitizens and the detention of many more.

These laws have been designed either to get rid of or to make life more difficult for noncitizens, without taking into account the effect these laws also have on citizens. Noncitizens are our mothers, fathers, sisters, brothers, wives, husbands, sons, daughters, uncles, aunts, cousins, and fellow community members. Because families are made both by blood and by choice, any citizen can be affected by immigration policies. Two clear examples are adoption and marriage. As I described in Chapter 3, "Racism and the Consequences of U.S. Immigration Policy," adopted children of U.S. citizens have been deported to their country of birth because of the 1996 laws, specifically IIRIRA, which made deportation mandatory for people charged with certain crimes. For some adopted children, youthful indiscretion has meant being severed from the only families they have known. Their parents must live with grief and guilt for not taking the steps to naturalize their children. In other cases, plans to form a life together have been foiled when the undocumented fiancés and spouses of U.S. citizens learn that they have no way to legalize their status, which comes as punishment for having committed the civil infraction of crossing the border without permission.

Citizenship and Human Rights

According to the 14th amendment of the U.S. Constitution, all persons born or naturalized in the United States are citizens. Jacqueline Bhabha (2004: 93) points out that "citizenship is the legal correlate of territorial belonging. It signifies official recognition of a particularly close relationship between person and country." This relationship entails the right to participate in politics as well as the right not to be banished from one's country of citizenship.

The rights awarded by U.S. citizenship are few: the right to live in this country and the right to vote. The right to vote can be taken away in all but two states if one is incarcerated. In twelve states, if one has a felony conviction, he or she may be permanently barred from voting.[1] The *only* citizenship right that is inalienable, then, is the right to territorial belonging. Although inalienable, your right to territorial belonging is greatly diminished if your family does not share this right. As Jastram (Migration Policy Institute Migration Information Source 2003: 1) points out, a "family's right to live together is protected by international human rights and humanitarian law. There is universal consensus that, as the fundamental unit of society, the family is entitled to respect, protection, assistance and support." In many cases, people are forced to choose between exercising their only inalienable right as U.S. citizens—that of living in the United States—and one of their most fundamental human rights—the right to family unity. Citizens must choose between their family and their country when their spouses do not share their right to be here and are ineligible for citizenship or even lawful presence in the United States.

Although U.S. law does not provide for the right to family unity, the right to live with one's family *is* protected under international human rights treaties. The U.S. government has ratified the International Covenant on Civil and Political Rights (ICCPR). The ICCPR was inspired by the U.S. Constitution and stresses the importance of equality, freedom from discrimination, religious freedom, and the right of free association. Although the United States has ratified the ICCPR, it has not ratified the optional protocol that allows the Human Rights Committee of the United Nations to consider complaints against states.

Thus, although the United States is in violation of this treaty, its provisions are unenforceable (Blau and Moncada 2005). Despite the fact that the provisions are not enforceable in the United States, it is worth paying attention to the extent to which the United States complies with the ICCPR. The United States has ratified this treaty, and it is one of the treaties that is most in line with our fundamental values as a nation.

Many deportation cases don't consider a noncitizen's status as a spouse of a U.S. citizen. The ease with which the spouse of a U.S. citizen can be deported is in violation of provisions of the ICCPR, which emphasize the importance of family unity. For example, Article 10 of the ICCPR stipulates that "the family is the natural and fundamental group unit of society and is entitled to protection by society and the State." In many deportation cases, however, judges are not allowed to take into consideration the extent to which family members—even those who are U.S. citizens—will be affected by the deportation of a spouse, father, mother, brother, or sister. Current laws force citizens to choose between self-deportation and family dissolution.

The deportation of a family member violates U.S. citizens' rights to family unity and infringes on the right to full citizenship. Full citizenship entails feeling a sense of belonging and involves the realization of civil, political, social, and cultural rights. This includes not merely the right to vote or to hold elected office, but also the right to feel as if one is part of the nation, and the right to be a full member of society (Jenson 2001; Marshall 1950; Pakulski 1997). This sense of belonging is impinged upon when one's spouse, parent, or child is forcibly removed from this country.

Being a full citizen means being what Rosaldo (1994) calls a *first-class citizen,* as opposed to a *second-class citizen.* Democracies have long existed with first-, second-, and third-class citizens. Wallerstein (2003) argues that the very concept of citizen required the creation of a hierarchy of citizens. Nevertheless, current theorists of citizenship propose that political, social, and cultural inequalities are detrimental to the realization of a democratic society (Jenson 2001; Richardson 1998; Pakulski 1997). This democratic society is understood as one in which all people (or at least all adult citizens) have equal access to the rights and responsibilities that go along with being a full member of a society.

Immigration policies that lead to family separations force people to choose between their legal citizenship right to territorial belonging and their human right to form a family. This tension between human rights and citizenship rights requires U.S. citizens to decide between two rights that should be inalienable. If the U.S. Constitution grants U.S. citizens territorial belonging and the Universal

Declaration of Human Rights (UDHR) and the ICCPR grant all people the right to family unity, it is unconscionable that people should be forced to choose between their family and their country.

Immigration policies directly and indirectly affect millions of citizens. Policies that force family separations and the removal of community members impinge on many citizens' sense of belonging to this country. Children that grow up in immigrant communities witness their parents, cousins, uncles, neighbors, and friends being taken away by immigration authorities. The knowledge that members of your community are constantly subject to the threat of deportation diminishes one's own sense of belonging to the country. If, for example, you grow up in Chicago thinking of yourself as a Mexican, as many U.S.-born children of Mexicans do, and you know that many Mexicans are subject to removal, this knowledge is likely to weaken your sense of belonging to the country. In this way, deportations encroach upon children of immigrants' full citizenship in the United States.

U.S. Citizens Married to Undocumented Immigrants

Many people in the United States find it surprising that the spouse of a U.S. citizen can be deported. We saw in the previous chapter that immigrants convicted of crimes can be deported, notwithstanding their familial ties in the United States. In this chapter, we will see that noncitizens who have not committed crimes also are ineligible for legalization when they have entered the country illegally.

In collaboration with *Latinos Progresando,* a not-for-profit legal services provider and community-based organization in Chicago, I conducted interviews with nine couples, most of whom were their clients. The people I interviewed were couples: U.S. citizens married or engaged to undocumented immigrants from Mexico. In each case, the undocumented immigrant married to a U.S. citizen was ineligible for citizenship or legalization because of provisions in section 245(i) of the INA.

In 1994, Congress passed the Commerce, Justice, State (CJS) Appropriations Act, which added a temporary subsection (i) to section 245 of the INA. Under this act, undocumented migrants who were present in the United States could apply for legalization. Previous to this act, these migrants would have had to leave the United States to apply for admission to the United States. This change allowed families to stay together while their immigration paperwork was being processed. This temporary subsection was set to expire on October 1, 1997. Prior to expiring, it was extended, first until 1998 and then until April 30, 2001.

These provisions have been debated in Congress several times since 2001, but as of yet, this subsection has not been reenacted.[2]

The legalization provisions in section 245 (i) gained importance when the Illegal Immigration Reform and Immigrant Responsibility (IIRIRA) was passed in 1996. IIRIRA contained a provision that indicated that a person who is unlawfully present in the United States for more than one year would be inadmissible for ten years. This meant that people who were able to legalize without leaving the country did not face this ten-year bar. Once 245 (i) expired and prospective legal permanent residents had to leave the country, they often found themselves subject to the "ten-year-bar," upon attempting to reenter the country.[3]

Because 245 (i) has not been renewed, individuals who enter the United States without inspection and then remain unlawfully present for more than one year must return to their country of origin and remain there for ten years before becoming eligible for immigration benefits. Some of the people I introduce in the following sections found themselves in this situation, in which the undocumented partner faced the ten-year bar. The INA further stipulates that people who enter without inspection, stay for more than one year, leave, and then reenter the United States illegally, without waiting the mandatory ten years, are subject to a permanent bar. Many of my interviewees found themselves in this situation, as they had returned to Mexico to visit family or to attend funerals or other important events. Mexicans in this latter group have no options for legalization under current laws, despite being married to U.S. citizens and having children who are U.S. citizens.

The threats of being subject to a ten-year bar or permanent bar are elements of how immigration law affects the lives of many couples. To have materials that would be useful in a campaign to change this subsection of immigration law, the leaders at *Latinos Progresando*, a not-for-profit legal services provider and community-based organization in Chicago, asked me to conduct interviews with their clients who were ineligible for legalization, and we agreed that I could also use the materials in my own research. The interviews lasted between forty and ninety minutes and focused on gaining an understanding of how immigration policies affected their lives. I conducted the interviews in both Spanish and English, and I have translated the excerpts presented here. I introduce each of the couples I interviewed to put a human face on these social, political, and legal issues.

Fermín and Margarita

Fermín is in his early thirties. He came to the United States from Durango, Mexico, when he was just seventeen. In Mexico, he finished primary school.

When he arrived in Chicago, he got a job in maintenance and has worked at that same job ever since. He would like to be a supervisor at his job, but he tells me his legal status prevents him from being promoted in his company. He jokes that once he gets his papers, he is sure to become a business partner. For now, the company he works for doesn't even give him regular raises. He does, however, have health insurance and pays into social security. He is not sure if he will be able to collect when he retires, though, because for the past fifteen years, he has been using a social security number that is not his.

Fermín's wife, Margarita, looks younger than her forty-some years. She grew up in Chicago's West Town but says she never got involved in the gang violence that was endemic in her neighborhood. Her parents are from San Antonio, Texas, but came to Chicago when she was very young. Margarita dropped out of high school and has worked at a series of low-wage jobs. Presently, she works in a nursing home and supplements her income with a part-time job at Burger King. Most weeks she works seven days a week.

When I asked Fermín about the town he is from, he said he barely remembers. He imagines it must have changed in the fifteen years he has been here in the States. He supposed his home town is likely not as ugly as it was when he left. Fermín came to the United States because all his brothers and sisters were already here, and he wanted to help out his parents who remained in Mexico. He was the last one to come and now, most of his siblings are legal permanent residents. He, however, came too late to qualify for the 1986 amnesty.

Fermín and Margarita met six years ago. They became friends, then lovers, and moved in together four years ago. They currently have been married for sixteen months. They don't have children together, but Margarita's youngest daughter and her young son live with them. Margarita and Fermín are the godparents, and Fermín considers the toddler to be his own grandson.

Fermín and Margarita got married so they could spend their lives together, but the current law states that, for Fermín to be in the country legally, he first would have to return to Mexico for ten years. Fermín and Margarita bought a house together two years ago, and they both need to work full-time to pay the mortgage and other bills. Like many low-income families, they are struggling to make a comfortable life for themselves. With careful budgeting, they have been able to do that, but without Fermín's income, this would be impossible.

Both Fermín and Margarita have their whole families in the United States. Margarita was born in the United States, as were her parents. Although she has Mexican heritage, she has no connection to Mexico. She has never been to Mexico and speaks more Spanglish than Spanish. Fermín spent the first seventeen years of his life in Mexico, but all his brothers and sisters are here in the United States. His father recently passed away. His mother has a visa to come to the United States, and thus spends a lot of time here. He said he wouldn't die of starvation if he were sent back to Mexico, but he would have to make a whole new life there. He would lose the life he has worked hard to make here in the United States. Margarita doesn't feel she can abandon her children and grandchildren to uproot and go to Mexico, so they have decided to stay together and hope that immigration officials don't catch Fermín.

Fermín said he tries not to think about the fact that he could be detained and deported at any moment. However, he sometimes can't help thinking about Margarita's grandchildren, especially the younger ones. He feels like he is their grandfather and treasures the time they spend together. A smile came across both of their faces whenever they talked about the grandchildren. Fermín tries to teach them Spanish and about life in general. During the interview, Fermín pulled out his cell phone and played a recording of Margarita's two-year-old granddaughter singing in Spanish and English.

"I don't know if I deserve to be here legally or not—only God knows. I can only hope," said Fermín. Later, he changed his mind. "I can say that I deserve to be here, because any time I have a ticket or something, I pay right away.... They can't say I live off of the government, because I have never lived off of the government. They can't say I am a burden on the government, because I am not. I pay my taxes.... And, now with the economic stimulus, everyone is going to get it, except for us, who don't have social security numbers."

Leticia and Rolando

Leticia, a stay-at-home mom, and Rolando, a factory worker, are in their early thirties. They have two sons: one thirteen, and the other nearly two years old. They met in high school at a soccer game, when they were each sixteen. Their high school romance got serious. Leticia became pregnant with their older son when they were both just seventeen.

Leticia's teenage pregnancy meant that both of them left school before finishing the twelfth grade. Rolando went to work to support their young family. Leticia dedicated herself to caring for their infant son, Ricardo. When Ricardo was old enough to go to preschool, Leticia got a job in customer service. She'd like to get a job in a nonprofit, doing something that would allow her to give back to her community, but she feels that without further schooling and with a toddler to care for, she will have to put that off for now.

Rolando has been working in the same factory for nine years and said his job is more or less secure. He'd like to be a mechanic or something to do with fixing things, but he doesn't want to take the risk of leaving his job and learning a new trade. With two children, he doesn't want to take any financial risks.

Leticia's parents brought her to Chicago from Puebla, Mexico, when she was eighteen months old. She doesn't remember crossing the border, but she knows that she came over illegally with her mother and older sister. Her father was already in the United States. Leticia and her parents were able to obtain legalization and subsequent citizenship through the 1986 amnesty. Because Leticia is a U.S. citizen, she can travel freely back and forth between here and Mexico. She has been back to her place of birth and describes it as a small town with not much more than a few houses.

Rolando was born in Mexico City, where he spent the first half of his life. When he was fourteen, his father left for the United States. Upon seeing that they could make a better living in the United States, his parents decided to move the whole family to the United States. When Rolando's father sent for his wife and children, Rolando did not want to come. Like most teenagers, he did not want to leave his friends behind and start his life over again. However, because he was not old enough to make those sorts of decisions for himself, he came with his mother and sister. When they got to Chicago, Rolando's parents enrolled him in high school. Rolando didn't like it when he got here and still doesn't like it that much. But because his wife and children are from the United States, he has decided to stay here.

Rolando and Leticia did not get married until 2003, several years after their first son was born. Rolando did not want Leticia to think that he was with her just for the papers, so he did not opt to formalize their union. Leticia tried to convince him, because she knew that the 245 (i) provision of the LIFE Act, which would allow Rolando to regularize his status, was going to expire in 2001. But, Rolando said, they were still young and not sure of what they wanted to do. Now, however, he regrets that decision and wants to regularize his status. Currently, Rolando does not qualify for any of the legalization options available. Despite being married to a U.S. citizen and having two U.S.-citizen children, the fact that Rolando crossed the border without inspection fifteen years ago and has since returned to Mexico leaves him with no options.

What further exacerbates their situation is that Rolando was deported in 1998 and reentered subsequently. This makes it even more difficult for him to legalize his status. Rolando was deported after being picked up by local police officers. He and his brother were pulling up to an auto parts store when two officers approached them and asked if they had driver's licenses. Even though Rolando was not driving, both of them were taken to the police station. The police officers told them that they were going to be deported, and they were transferred to an Immigration and Naturalization Service (INS) detention center. After two weeks in the detention center, Rolando decided that he could not take being imprisoned anymore and signed a voluntary departure, which meant that he agreed to self-deport. Leticia bought him his airline ticket, and he was able to go to Mexico. Rolando's brother remained in the detention center for six weeks before he was taken to Mexico on a U.S. Marshall plane. Both of them have since returned to the United States, although Rolando reports that crossing over has become more difficult in recent years.

Getting to the United States without permission is difficult, and living here without papers is not easy either. For example, Rolando and Leticia would like to travel together. They have been thinking of taking their son to Disney World for several years now, but they are worried that Rolando could be deported if they tried to get on an airplane. They also would like to travel to Mexico so their children can see Rolando's parents. Even travel around Chicago is complicated, because Rolando has not been able to renew his driver's license. They have also been saving up to buy a house. However, because Rolando has been working with a false social security number, he doesn't have a credit history. Furthermore, Leticia is not working now, so they can't take out a loan to buy a home.

Leticia would not mind going to Mexico City; she likes it there. She wouldn't mind moving there for one year, or even up to three years. But the idea of staying in Mexico permanently is a different story. Rolando doesn't think he or Leticia have many employment options in Mexico, given their lack of education. Also, they have to think about their children, especially Ricardo, who is thirteen and has spent his whole life here. Like most parents, they want to give their children the best opportunities possible. They see better options for their children in the United States.

It is in the best interest of Leticia and her children—all U.S. citizens—to remain in the United States, and for Rolando to remain in the States with them. Rolando is the primary breadwinner, and his deportation would be financially and emotionally devastating for this family. However, immigration laws stipulate that Rolando must be deported. If found, Rolando will be deported as a criminal alien, because he reentered the United States after being deported. His crime: crossing the border so that he could be with and provide for his family. It is hard not to see the irony here. Illegal reentry is a victimless crime. If Rolando is punished for this crime, the victims will be Leticia and their children.

Lorena and Alfredo

Both Lorena and Alfredo are in their early twenties. They have been married for six years and are making plans for their future. For now, they have decided to put off having children, in part because Alfredo has not been able to legalize his immigration status. They have had to put other things on hold as well, such as finding ways to make Alfredo's business grow and allowing Lorena to start her own business. She would like to open up a Laundromat that has a restaurant attached—"Something big," she said.

Lorena was born in Chicago near Humboldt Park and was home-schooled. Once she completed high school, she went to college for a few years. Today she works as an administrative assistant. Alfredo was born in Guerrero, Mexico, in a fairly large town. His mother decided to come to the United States after having separated from her abusive husband. She came over in 1996 and left her children with her mother. After two years working in the laundry of a hospital, she was able to bring Alfredo and his siblings. Alfredo was thirteen when his mother brought him here.

Lorena and Alfredo have been married since March 2005. Lorena's family is from Zacatecas, and Alfredo's family is from Guerrero, Mexico. One day they would like to travel to Mexico together to see where each other's families are from. However, due to Alfredo's legal status, they have to content themselves with traveling within the United States for now. They do manage to get around though; last summer they drove all the way from Chicago to Miami. They enjoyed the road trip but would like to have the option of flying. Alfredo, however, cannot board a plane because of his lack of an official state ID.

Alfredo has a small company that does body shop work for local car dealers. He has a few dealers that he works with on a regular basis. Sometimes his lack of a valid driver's license prohibits him from getting work from new dealers.

Because Alfredo has been here for more than one year unlawfully and because he crossed the border illegally, he would have to go back to Mexico for ten years to qualify for legalization. Lorena thinks it is unfair that the law leaves them with no other option. She pointed out that this is tantamount to not permitting marriages between U.S. citizens and undocumented people.

She has a good point. In many ways, this restrictive legislation is similar to anti-miscegenation laws that, up until the 1960s, forbade blacks and whites from marrying in some states. Now people are allowed to get married, but the law does not permit the undocumented spouses of U.S. citizens to remain in the United States. Just as interracial couples had to go to Canada to get married, undocumented people and their spouses have to leave the United States to live together legally.

For now, Lorena and Alfredo have decided to stay here. Alfredo's lack of a driver's license makes his daily life difficult, both in terms of finances and stress. Each time he sees a police officer, his heart rate goes up. Lorena has to worry each day about what might happen to Alfredo. They deal with this challenge, however, and continue to work toward their future here.

I asked Lorena and Alfredo what they thought would happen were Alfredo to be ordered to go to Mexico for ten years. They both agreed that they would go together, and Alfredo says that they might end up staying there. They would try their luck setting up a business in Guerrero. Lorena has been to Mexico, although only for a couple of weeks on vacation. She said she would accompany her husband but pointed out that they would have to leave debts here. Also, as small business owners, Lorena sees their leaving as a loss to the U.S. economy and questioned the logic behind this. Were they to leave, Alfredo would lose his business. Lorena pointed out that Alfredo is not taking jobs from anyone. In fact, he has employees. He doesn't, however, have health insurance. Lorena has insurance through her job but said that the cost for including Alfredo is prohibitive.

Lorena and Alfredo's case is not as heart-wrenching as those cases where small children are involved or ailing family members are at risk. However, it sheds light on the way that current immigration policies are putting a serious damper on the future not only of undocumented youth, but on this country in general. Lorena and Alfredo are intelligent, innovative, determined, and have great potential. They are exactly the kind of young people this country needs to remain prosperous in the global economy. The way the current laws are structured, however, this young couple is at risk of either becoming embittered or simply leaving and taking their great ambitions to Mexico, where their dreams may or may not be realized.

Mario and Giselda

Mario is in his mid thirties and speaks with confidence about his job, concern for his son, and affection for his wife, Giselda. Giselda is in her early forties and is a fair-skinned woman with long black hair and piercing dark eyes whose eloquence belies her humble origins.

Mario was born in Nayarit, Mexico, a fairly large city, where he finished college prep school. He came to the United States with his sister when he was seventeen, with the hope of going to college. He fantasized about being recruited by the

NBA. Armed with the green card of a friend who bears a strong resemblance, Mario was able to cross the border in Tijuana. From there, he rode in the trunk of a car to Los Angeles. In California, he wasn't able to further his studies as he had planned, but had to work to support himself.

Giselda works as a presser in a dry cleaning factory. The work is hard, and she comes home tired. She pointed out that her low level of schooling, limited English ability, and lack of other experience prevents her from getting a better job. In the small town Giselda is from, in Zacatecas, Mexico, there are only a few houses and a one-room schoolhouse. The teacher herself had only completed the third grade. Thus, Giselda attended school for a year and a half and barely learned to read.

Once in the United States, because Giselda had to work and care for her young children, she was never able to complete her schooling, and she didn't have the opportunity to learn much English. She eventually separated from her spouse and later met Mario. Giselda has been in the United States for nearly thirty years, has become a U.S. citizen, and said she can't imagine returning to Mexico.

Giselda and Mario met in California and have been together seven years. Giselda worked in the building across the street from Mario, and they saw each other each afternoon as they left work. Although at first they just exchanged glances and then casual greetings, they eventually got to know each other and fell in love. They lived together for a while in California, but hearing that there were better jobs in Chicago, they decided to move with their then-newborn son.

Their son is now five years old and is in preschool in Elgin, Illinois. Despite their busy work schedules, both try to go to the school meetings as often as they can. Giselda also has a daughter in high school who takes dance classes and stays after school to get help with her homework, because Giselda's limited education doesn't allow her to be of much assistance. On Sundays, Giselda and Mario go to church, go out to eat, shop, visit family, or go to the park with their young son.

Mario and Giselda came to *Latinos Progresando* to find out if, because Giselda is a U.S. citizen and Mario is undocumented, they could change Mario's legal status. Giselda crossed the desert to come to the United States with her former spouse in 1981 and thus was eligible for the 1986 amnesty, despite having crossed the border without inspection. After getting permanent resident status, Giselda was able to become a U.S. citizen. The same options are not available to Mario because of the penalty provisions in 245(i) section of the INA. Because Mario crossed the border without inspection, if they apply for legalization now, he would have to go back to Mexico for ten years as a penalty for having crossed the border illegally.

If immigration agents were to arrest, detain, or deport Mario, his family would risk losing everything. Mario makes significantly more income as a welder than Giselda does as a presser. In addition, years of low-wage work and a divorce have left Giselda with a bad credit history. For this reason, their house and car are in Mario's name. Without Mario's salary, Giselda and her children would soon be homeless and without transportation to get to work or school. This is why they want to legalize Mario's status, to not have to live with the fear that they will lose everything.

I asked Mario what would happen if he had to go back to Mexico for ten years, as the law stipulates. He responded that he wouldn't be able to stay in Mexico for ten years. Although he would be able to find a job with his skills, it would not be enough to support his family in the United States. If they went to Mexico as a family, they would most likely have to live in poverty. Giselda said that she can't go back to Mexico after twenty-nine years here; she has grown children who were born here and are now well established. Moreover, Giselda recently became a grandmother and wants to continue seeing her daughter and granddaughter. Giselda and Mario both have lived in the United States for longer than they lived in Mexico.

Melanie and Oscar

Melanie and Oscar recently moved to Chicago, where Melanie is doing her practicum for her Master's degree in sustainable development. I visited them in their tidy, sparsely decorated apartment in the Pilsen neighborhood of Chicago. Like many young newlyweds, they are carving out a space for themselves and making plans for their future.

The daughter of two schoolteachers, Melanie was born in Fort Wayne, Indiana, where she attended a religious private school and lived in a primarily white middle class world. Bored with small-town life, she began to travel around the world at eighteen. When she returned from her travels and studies eight years later, she was pleased to find that Fort Wayne had changed. Fort Wayne had become a destination for refugees and migrant workers from all over the world, with people from Burma, Somalia, Afghanistan, and Mexico making it their home.

When I met Melanie, she was thirty-two years old and working on her thesis while volunteering with a community-based organization called *Mujeres Latinas en Acción*, as part of her practicum. She was happy with her placement in Chicago, because it allowed her to merge her interests in reproductive health and sustainable development. As a student at the School for International Training in

Vermont, Melanie was able to live abroad for extended periods of time. Melanie has lived in a long list of places and loves to travel.

Oscar was born in a small town about four hours from Mexico City. He said the town has no more than thirty houses and, although it has a primary school, he had to go to another town to attend high school. His parents, like most townspeople, were farmers. They had a piece of land where they planted corn, wheat, and beans. They were initially able to eke out a living from that land, but things got difficult in the early 1990s, in part because of the devaluation of the peso. At that point, his father went to Mexico City to work. With the signing of North American Free Trade Agreement (NAFTA) in 1994, it was no longer profitable to even plant corn. In 1995, at the age of fourteen, Oscar had to leave school and go to work in Mexico City.

Like most men in their town, Oscar's older brother came to the United States in search of work, while Oscar went to Mexico City. Things were going well for his older brother in the United States, so Oscar decided to make the trip north. Oscar crossed the border with a group of nearly one hundred people. He said they walked a few hours and were in the United States. Oscar planned to finish school when he got here, but he found out he was unable to when he arrived in Fort Wayne, Indiana.

Oscar and Melanie met in Fort Wayne, Indiana in 2002. Oscar had been living there for several years, and Melanie was working in a community-based organization that provided services to refugees and immigrants. A few months after meeting, they began dating and, in late 2006, Oscar and Melanie got married.

Soon after they were married, Melanie began her studies at the School for International Training in Vermont. Oscar stayed behind in Fort Wayne. However, once Melanie finished her coursework, she was able to move to Chicago to do her practicum, and Oscar moved to Chicago with her. Thus, a year after being married, they were finally able to make a home together.

This young couple with bright prospects is unsure of their future. Because Oscar crossed the border without inspection, his marriage to a U.S. citizen does not make him eligible for legal permanent residence at this time. Moreover, Oscar has been in the United States for twelve years and has gone back to Mexico on several occasions to visit his parents. His having returned to Mexico and illegally reentered the United States further makes him ineligible for any sort of legalization options.

Oscar's legal status has increasingly become a burden for this couple. When Oscar first arrived, he was able to find a job, buy a car, obtain car insurance, and get a driver's license. Yet, in Indiana, the state purged the records in 2007 and cancelled the driver's licenses of everyone who did not have a valid social security number. This caused their insurance company to cancel their insurance policy. They even canceled Melanie's policy, which means that in Chicago, the couple must rely on public transportation to get around.

Melanie told me that she often finds herself worrying about whether Oscar will come home, especially if he is a little late in arriving. She also was unsure about sharing information with regard to Oscar's legal status with her friends and family and often has to tell half-truths. Melanie has not abandoned her wanderlust. She has left the country a few times during their relationship and has had to go alone. This past summer she went to Peru, but Oscar was unable to accompany her. She even went alone to Mexico, Oscar's country of origin. This summer, Melanie's brother is planning his wedding, and Melanie will go alone; they fear Oscar could be deported if he were to get on an airplane.

When I asked Melanie if she would go to Mexico with Oscar were he to be deported, she said that of course she would. Melanie actually finds the idea of moving to Mexico to be attractive. However, she pointed out that, even if they moved to Mexico, she would want to be able to bring her whole family, including Oscar, to visit her family here. Furthermore, she considers the fact that she would not be able to do that to be a violation of her human rights. If, for example, something were to happen to her parents, Melanie would have to come to the United States alone and be without the support of her husband in the moment when she would need him most.

Melanie also lamented the climate of fear and hate that is growing in the United States. Although the racism against Latinos doesn't affect her directly, it does affect her indirectly through her marriage and close friendships with Latinos and Latinas. She doesn't want to live in a society marked by racism and hate.

I spoke to Melanie three years after the initial interview—in January 2011. When we spoke, she and Oscar were living in Mexico and had recently had their first child. They had decided that Oscar's undocumented status was preventing them from living life as they wished in the United States, and Melanie opted for exile from the United States. They applied for Oscar's legalization and may return someday, if he is granted legalization. Under current laws, his chances are slim.

Pablo and Maia

Pablo and Maia are an attractive couple—the kind that elicits smiles on the streets. Pablo is soft-spoken and careful with his words. Maia has passion for what she does and what she believes in. They both speak lovingly of Maia's son,

Dante, who is ten years old. Pablo has been a father figure for him since he was two. Both are proud of Dante's accomplishments: his place on the honor roll, his skill at playing the violin and the drum, and his feats on the soccer field.

When we met, Maia was nearly thirty and was in graduate school, while working as a case manager for high-risk pregnant mothers. Her favorite aspect of her job is that she can help women who are facing the same difficulties she encountered as a young single mother. Maia was born in Holland, Michigan, which she describes as primarily white, but with substantial Latino, African-American, and Asian populations. It is a segregated town, and Maia and her family lived in the part where all the other black families lived, called Little Harlem. Her parents worked in the local factories and did not earn very much. Maia's great-grandfather was one of the first black settlers there and set up a station on the underground railroad in Holland.

Pablo is the same age as Maia. He grew up in Mexico City with his mother and three siblings. Pablo and Maia now both live in Kalamazoo, Michigan. Pablo works as a supervisor at a construction supply company. He dreams about going back to school and becoming an immigration lawyer to help people who find themselves in situations similar to his own, as an undocumented Mexican. Pablo finished high school in Mexico but has not been able to further his education here.

As a cook in a restaurant in Mexico City, Pablo's mother struggled with her wages to raise three children. Once her children were finished with school, she decided to come to the United States to save up enough money to open her own restaurant. Pablo accompanied her, since he already had one sister in the United States, and his other sister was planning to make the trip as well. In 1998, when Pablo was twenty years old, they set out for the United States. Neither Pablo nor his mother or sister had permission to enter the United States. They entered illegally at the border near San Diego. Pablo planned to stay for two years.

Pablo didn't like it in California. He had to work hard and had few opportunities to learn to speak English. After moving to Michigan in 2000 and being in the United States for ten years, he has grown accustomed to life in Michigan and does not want to return to Mexico. He likes the opportunities the United States has to offer, and he likes where he lives in Kalamazoo, Michigan. In addition, he plans to marry Maia.

Maia and Pablo met at one of the few salsa clubs in Kalamazoo. Pablo asked Maia to dance, and they danced a few numbers together. They didn't exchange information at first, but a month or so later, they saw each other again. This time, Pablo asked Maia for her number and she gave it to him. That was in 2000, and eight years later, they are still together.

The current immigration laws have negative effects both on their daily life and on their long-term plans. As for their daily life, Pablo and Maia have to live with the fear that Pablo will be deported. He told me that Michigan recently passed a law that prevents him from getting a license because he does not have a valid social security number. The license he now has will expire in one year. He is aware that he could be detained and deported, and he does not like living with the fear that this could happen at any time. He also is aware that he could be fired from his job at any time because of his status.

There are a lot of things Pablo and Maia would like to do and can't because of Pablo's status. Pablo wants to go back to school, and Maia would love to support him. Pablo helped Maia get through school by taking care of Dante. She wishes she could do the same for him. They also would love to travel together out of the country, but they know Pablo would be deported upon their return.

They also told me that they can't even get married, because a law was recently passed in Michigan that requires a social security number to obtain a marriage license. If they do find a way to get married, the current law stipulates that Pablo will have to go to Mexico for at least ten years, because he has lived here illegally for more than a year. In addition, Pablo would likely be permanently barred from entering the United States, because he has entered illegally more than once. Under the current laws, Pablo and Maia are not allowed to live here in the United States together.

Pablo and Maia would be happy to go to Mexico for a year. Maia said she likes the idea of taking Dante there for one year. However, the idea of going for ten years or permanently is not so appealing. It would be hard, because Dante is close to his father, who lives in Michigan. Also, Dante is at the top of his class in Kalamazoo, and Maia is not sure that Dante would be afforded the same educational opportunities in Mexico. "It would be nice to have a choice," though, said Maia.

Maia connected the plight of immigrants to the history of African-Americans:

> I would like to see the United States take a step back and see what is happening. It is like time repeating itself all over again. You know, it's okay to be in the kitchen, but it's not okay to come out of it. And, so I would like for them just to be fair. Until it affects them, until they have a niece or a daughter who meets someone and this happens to them, I know a lot of people aren't moved by it. I would just like for them to be fair, and just think that, the United States hasn't done a lot of things right, and we haven't been right to people just in

general, the way we treat people, and it's time for us to change that. We learned from 9/11 that people are mad at us because of things we are doing. It is time for us to treat people better, and I think this would be a good way to show it.

Fatima and Antonio

Fatima is thirty years old, graduated from Loyola with a BA, and now works as a family therapist, counseling families whose children are in juvenile detention. She likes being able to help people, to give them hope, and to figure out ways to make their life better. Her husband, Antonio, paints houses for a living. He would like to go back to school, to learn a trade such as an electrician, or maybe open a business.

Fatima was born in Mexico City and has been back to visit nearly every year since she first came here when she was four years old. Fatima's father passed away when she was two, leaving her mother a widow with three children. Her mother decided that it would be easier for her to raise her children in the United States. She was able to obtain visas, and they came to the United States on an airplane. Eventually, the whole family obtained citizenship.

Antonio was born in Michoacan, Mexico, in a small town. His father, an agricultural worker, was attacked by a bull when Antonio was thirteen. This accident left him an invalid, and Antonio and his brother left school to go to Mexico City to work. They found work in a car wash and stayed there for six years. When Antonio was in Mexico City, a woman from his town in Michoacan asked him to accompany her to cross over to the United States. Antonio arrived in Dallas and eight months later, decided to come to Chicago. In Chicago, he spent several months working as a day laborer until he found a more stable job as a painter. He has been in that job now for four years. Now he works seven days a week most weeks, often ten to twelve hours a day.

Not too long after Antonio found his current job, he met Fatima. Neither of them went out much, but by chance, they met when they were both out dancing. They exchanged numbers, became friends, and then began dating. Eventually they moved in together and got married. When I spoke with them in May 2008, they had a two-and-a-half-year-old son.

Fatima and Antonio came to *Latinos Progresando* to see if there was anything they could do to legalize Antonio's status. Antonio has been living here illegally since he crossed the border in 2003. Fatima said she wanted to know if there were any options, because she is constantly stressed out. She often worries about Antonio. When he goes to work, she worries about whether or not there will be a raid, or if he will be stopped on his way to work. This stress is clearly wearing on her, as her voice broke and her eyes welled up with tears as she talked to me.

Tears began to fall profusely as Fatima told me that it hurts her deeply that Antonio wants to see his parents and his parents want to see him, but he can't go back to Mexico. Fatima even feels as if it is partly her fault that Antonio can't see his parents. *"A veces, yo siento que es un poco de mi culpa. Maybe, si no me hubieses conocido, no te detuviera nada aquí."* "Sometimes, I feel like it is a little my fault. Maybe, if you hadn't met me, nothing would keep you here."

When their son was born, Fatima became ill. She continues to suffer from an immune disorder and admits that she worries that she may not survive her next hospitalization. The doctors are not sure exactly what her illness is, and she goes in regularly for tests. When she became seriously ill, she had to be transferred to a Level IV hospital. She is concerned that she would not find the appropriate medical care in Mexico, and that moving there would mean that she would be going only to die. Then, she pointed out, "What would become of my son?" Her voice broke as she told me that she wishes she could be sure that her son would be okay if the unthinkable were to happen—if she were to pass away. This is one of their most pressing reasons to obtain legalization for Antonio.

Antonio said he wishes he could visit his parents. He pointed out that he could easily go to Mexico. But, he is not willing to risk being unable to return, since his wife and son are here and he does not want to leave them alone. They also are aware that if Antonio goes back to Mexico, it further complicates their options for legalization. Therefore, it is not a risk they are willing to take, even though it saddens him that he can't visit his parents.

Fatima said that before she found herself in this situation, she did not live life every day in fear. Now, each day, she finds herself asking herself whether her husband will come home. Knowing that he can be arrested, detained, and deported any time is hard to deal with. Fatima said in some ways, she wouldn't mind moving to Mexico, but she feels like she has given so much to the United States. She also has her student loans to pay off. Fatima went to Loyola, a fairly expensive private university. They also have to think about their son's future. She feels like their options would be limited in Mexico. She was worried that she would not be able to find the appropriate medical care in Mexico. For starters, she wouldn't have medical insurance, and she fears she would not be able to afford her expensive prescriptions in Mexico.

It is also possible that Antonio could be deported and would be unable to return. I asked Fatima what would happen in that situation. She said that, apart from breaking apart her family, she would suffer financially. They recently purchased a home near Midway Airport. Without Antonio's income, she would have to sell the house. Fatima has plans to return to school to get her MA in counseling, and she would not be able to do that. Most of all, she would be emotionally devastated. Having a loving partner has enabled her to withstand life's challenges—her own illness, her aging mother's ailments, and her son's all-too-frequent visits to the doctor.

Fatima pointed out that the laws do not just affect Antonio, who is here illegally, but they also deeply affect her and her son, both of whom are U.S. citizens. As a family therapist, Fatima is well aware of the pernicious effects of family separation on children. She asked why the government would want to separate families when we are well aware of the consequences of family separation. In her work, she has to counsel children who have turned to juvenile delinquency, in part because their parents are divorced. She does not want her child to grow up in a single-parent family.

Tears welled up again in Fatima's eyes when she asked if she, her son, and her husband were not humans. The importance of this family remaining together brought tears to my eyes as well. It is clear that the stress of Antonio potentially being deported is taking its toll on Fatima. It is hard for her to come to terms with why her own government would not want for a loving family such as theirs to stay together. Fatima said that she would be able to deal with the loss of a loved one through death, because one can reconcile that as God's will. But, she said it would hurt even more if her own government were to take away her husband, the father of her son.

Meredith and Alex

Meredith and Alex live in a quiet neighborhood just south of Chicago. They recently purchased a home and were fixing it up when I met them. After having made several renovations to the inside, the warm summer months had allowed them to begin beautifying the outside of the house.

Meredith is in her early thirties. She grew up in a middle class neighborhood on the south side of Chicago and attended a public school that was primarily black, but also had some Latinos and whites. Alex is in his late twenties. He was born in Leon, Mexico, a fairly large city in Guanajato. Many people from his neighborhood have emigrated. Alex came to the United States illegally in 2001, with an older friend. Alex's brother had been in the United States for four years already and agreed to pay for his passage. His roots go back further, though, as

Alex's grandfather had been to the United States as a *bracero* (a temporary farm laborer) in the mid-twentieth century.

Meredith and Alex work together at a bar not too far from where they live. Meredith is a bartender, and Alex is a bar back (a bartender's assistant). In addition, Alex works as an electrician during the day, and Meredith is enrolled in graduate school, where she is working on her PhD. Alex finished high school in Mexico. He also studied electricity and enjoys exercising his profession here. He picked up the second job to earn more money. Meredith and Alex met at work about five years ago. They started going out in 2005 and were married in 2008.

Alex and Meredith have consulted a number of lawyers and other advocates to find out if Alex can legalize his status, due to his marriage with Meredith. The first two lawyers told them that they were not eligible for immigration benefits. The third lawyer told them that they should apply for Alex's papers, but there was a risk involved. Because Alex has never been apprehended by immigration authorities and has not returned to Mexico, he faces the ten-year bar on reentry to the United States. However, he and Meredith may be eligible for a waiver. To obtain this waiver, Alex needs to apply for admission in Ciudad Juarez, Mexico. They cannot be sure, however, that Alex will be granted the waiver when he applies for admission; the office in Juarez grants about 75 percent of these waivers and denies the other 25 percent. In any event, they filed the family petition the day after they were married and are considering taking the risk.

Meredith and Alex think they have a good chance of getting the waiver, because Alex has not gotten into trouble with the law apart from being arrested four times for driving without a license. His legal status prevents him from obtaining one. It also works in his favor that he has not returned to Mexico since he has been here.

For now, Alex continues his life here as best he can. He faces certain challenges, though. In Chicago, the local police do not cooperate with immigration authorities. Thus, although Alex has been arrested for driving without a license several times, the police have never turned him over to immigration authorities. However, he does face severe fines. Each time he has been arrested for driving without a license, he has been set back more than a thousand dollars. Meredith pointed out that being undocumented also means that Alex can't get into a union job that would provide better pay and benefits. Their house and car are only in her name. She said that, overall, they have a good life, but there is always that underlying fear. When she hears on the radio that there has been a raid somewhere, she can't help but be worried that something might have happened to Alex. In addition, she feels as if she has to be prepared to move to Mexico at any time.

I asked Meredith if she would be able to pay for the house were Alex to be deported. She said that she would not stay here if Alex were to be deported. She pointed out that she might be able to financially, but she is not willing to be separated from her husband. "The house is both of ours," she said. Alex added that they would lose everything they have worked for if he were to be deported. "We would have to make very difficult decisions," said Meredith.

Alex said that it would not be easy were they to move to Mexico. They would suffer financially, at least initially. Furthermore, it would be hard on any couple, especially if they have children. If they were to go to Mexico, they would go to Leon where Alex's parents live. Meredith said she would likely be able to find a job in tourism and Alex in a factory. But the pay would be minimal. Alex's father, for example, works ten hours a day, six days a week, and earns about $100 a week, which is barely enough to feed his family. He depends on Alex's and his brother's remittances to supplement his income. Of course, as Meredith pointed out, she would first have to arrange a work permit in Mexico.

When I spoke with Meredith in February 2011, she told me that she and Alex had recently had a baby. The new addition to their family will make moving to Mexico even more challenging. She also told me that she had finished her PhD and gotten a job as a professor. It would be a very difficult decision for Meredith to leave her university position, after working for many years to get where she is. Nevertheless, Meredith refuses to be separated from her family.

Sarah and Aron

Sarah and Aron plan to get married soon. Until then, they are enjoying life as a young couple in Chicago. They are thinking of having children, but they want to make sure that Aron can stay in the United States before they take that step.

Sarah recently completed two bachelor's degrees from the University of Illinois at Chicago (UIC)—one in nursing, and another in social work. When I met her, she had only had her nursing license for a few days and was looking for work. She had decided to take up nursing after working as a social worker, because she wanted more practical, useful skills that would allow her to contribute to the community. Ideally, she hoped to find a job that would allow her to use both degrees—something that permits her to work toward a more healthy community overall.

Aron began his studies at the Universidad Nacional Autonoma de Mexico (UNAM) in fine arts. He completed five years of his eight-year degree in classical music. He came to the United States with the hope of finishing his degree, but he has not been able to reengage his studies. For now, he gives private music lessons. Since he was young, Aron has been enamored with classical music and decided to make a career out of it.

Sarah was born in a small town in Wisconsin; her high school class had fifty students in it. Sarah did not want to pursue farming for a living, so she decided to leave upon graduation from high school. She began her university studies at the University of Wisconsin at Madison but later decided she wanted to move to Chicago, where she enrolled in UIC.

Aron is from a vibrant lower-middle class neighborhood in Mexico City, where most people do not migrate to the United States. Aron has been in the United States for only two years. He found himself unable to continue his studies in Mexico for financial reasons and decided to come to the United States to find a way to make enough money to continue his education. He made it clear to me that the only reason he wants to make money is to be able to finish his degree, not just to have more money. His sister and mother had been in the United States for about a year before he came, and he decided to come join them.

Aron crossed over through Sonora in June 2006. Many of the people who crossed over with him returned, due to the difficulty of the trip. Aron did not attempt to cross through the desert, which would have been difficult. Instead, he came through the city. The Border Patrol found him twice, but he got through the third time and made his way to Chicago to reunite with his sister and mother. He has not been back to Mexico since.

When he was in Mexico, Aron imagined the United States would offer him many opportunities to earn money and to study. What surprised him most is, having everything he could want—a car, a house, furniture, clothes, food—doesn't offer him as much satisfaction as he anticipated. As he put it, "When you have all of that stuff, you don't know what to do. To me, the idea of having a car was something big. When you actually have one, though, nothing really changes." In addition to his realization that material items are not fulfilling, Aron has found that here in the United States, he doesn't have the option of continuing his schooling. He is determined, however, to find a way to reach his goals.

In the meantime, Aron has been finding fulfillment in other areas. As part of a community organization, *Arte y Realidad,* he began to provide free guitar classes to Latino youth in the Pilsen neighborhood of Chicago. He then branched off and started giving low-cost group classes to community members.

Aron met Sarah shortly after he arrived. Aron had befriended one of Sarah's roommates, and they met at Sarah's house in Pilsen. Sarah plays the piano, and they share an interest in classical music. One evening, Aron was planning to go to a concert, and he invited Sarah. A few months later, they became serious. Several months after that, they decided to get married. They had been engaged for about six months when I spoke with them in June 2008.

Sarah also works for a community organization that installs public radio stations in communities in Latin America. Community leaders contact them, and Sarah and other team members go to the community to install the radio and to teach them how to develop their own broadcasts. Recently, Sarah went to Nicaragua to take some equipment to a community that had a radio station, but the equipment had become broken. Sarah told me that her trips to this community were part of her motivation to become a nurse. The radio is operated by a women's health group, and she is inspired by their work.

Sarah and Aron came to *Latinos Progresando* to find out what their options for legalization were, if they were to get married. The legal services counselor told them that Aron faced the possibility of having to return to Mexico for ten years, were they to apply for his legalization on the basis of their marriage. They have the possibility for appeal, but there are no guarantees, and they have to be ready for Aron to return to Mexico if the appeal is not granted. They have been to other lawyers for consultations, and the other lawyers have told them more or less the same information. If they decide to go through with the process, they will need a lawyer. For that, they need to save thousands of dollars.

For now, Aron is living without authorization in the United States, and it affects most aspects of his life. Aron told me that he sees a strong distinction, a chasm, between people who have social security numbers and those who don't. His lack of a social security number due to his legal status affects him in countless ways. For example, when they drive, Sarah has to be behind the wheel. While Sarah has been able to visit Aron's family in Mexico, he can't go. Sarah said she enjoyed meeting them, but it was weird to meet them without Aron present. Sarah can come and go to Mexico as she pleases, but Aron can't. Sarah said that Aron's lack of rights has made her cognizant of the immense privileges that come along with legal status. At the same time, if Aron were to be deported, it would affect Sarah's life tremendously. She is careful to have some savings, in case of such an emergency.

Aron would like to travel around the United States to participate in concerts, but his worries about being arrested by immigration agents keep him from traveling as much as he would like. Although it is risky for Aron to drive, he does get behind the wheel sometimes to help his mother or sister out with a ride somewhere. In Chicago's brutal winters, getting across the city on public transportation can be trying. Aron has been stopped by the police, but he has been fortunate enough to have been released with just a warning from the officer.

Aron's legal status keeps him from studying in Chicago, as the out-of-state tuition is out of the couple's reach. Aron has looked into continuing his studies to get his Bachelor of Fine Arts, but can't afford it at this point.

If Aron were ordered to leave the United States for ten years, it would be difficult for them to get by in Mexico. If Aron were to reenter the United States illegally, he could be permanently barred. Aron also is not ready to return to Mexico, because he has not yet reached the goals he set for himself in the United States. Thus, he said that, were he to be deported or ordered to leave for ten years, he would likely move to another country, perhaps Cuba. It might be difficult for Sarah to enter Cuba, but she said she would try and perhaps study medicine there. If Sarah and Aron are forced to leave the United States, they will have to find another country whose immigration laws will permit them to live together.

Sarah said she doesn't mind living abroad. However, she doesn't feel completely prepared just yet. She first would like to have the chance to practice nursing here in the United States so she would be in a better position to take those skills abroad. Once she feels ready, she wouldn't mind working abroad. Sarah and Aron both want to be ready to leave the United States if and when the time comes. And, they hope that they will be able to make the decision themselves, as opposed to having it made for them.

Aron pointed out that, were he to be deported to Mexico now, he wouldn't have anywhere to go. His mother and sister are here. He also doesn't have enough savings to last long in Mexico. What Aron earns teaching music is barely enough to survive on, so saving is difficult for him.

When I asked them how they would like for the laws to change, Aron responded that he thinks it is important to change more than simply Section 245(i), because his family is also here, and they have no options for legalization. Aron has a sister who has a U.S.-citizen son with another Mexican. Aron lamented that since she can't travel to Mexico, his nephew may never know Mexico. He said there needs to be a comprehensive immigration reform. Sarah agrees. She points out that a change in Section 245(i) would be designed to help citizens married to undocumented immigrants, but that others deserve rights as well. Immigrants come here to work and should be granted legalization.

In closing, Aron asked me if it would be a good idea for them to travel by airplane to California. Aron had received an invitation to perform at an event in California, and they wanted to know how much of a risk it would be to travel by plane. I told them it would be a great risk, because the airport is considered a border zone and Aron could be arrested by immigration agents in the airport. There also would be a risk associated with traveling by Amtrak or Greyhound, because immigration agents have targeted these companies also. They could drive, but it would be a thirty-hour trip. And Sarah would have to be in the driver's seat for the entire trip.

The Impossible Choice

Each of the U.S.-citizen women whose story I have told above faces a situation in which the laws of the United States do not permit them to live in this country with their families intact. For now, they have decided to wait it out and hope that the laws will change. Some of these couples have brighter prospects than others. Meredith recently earned her doctorate and is embarking on a successful career as a university professor. Since Alex has never returned to Mexico, and thus only violated immigration laws once, they have a fairly good chance of obtaining a waiver when their immigration appointment comes up. If, however, their waiver is denied, Meredith will face the choice of dissolving her family or giving up her citizenship rights. If she chooses to move to Mexico, when she comes to the United States to visit her parents, Alex will have to remain behind.

In contrast, Melanie and Oscar have much worse prospects for legalization. Melanie also recently earned a professional degree, and her skills could be an asset to this country. However, Oscar crossed the border several times without permission, which renders his chances for being granted a waiver extremely minimal. Melanie has decided that she will choose her family unity over her citizenship rights, and she and Oscar have moved to Mexico while his immigration case is pending.

Fatima's case is different, for although she has indicated that her family unity is more important, she is not sure she or her son will receive the medical care they need in Mexico. She finds the idea that Antonio could be deported to be extraordinarily stressful and almost regrets having put her family in this situation. If their spouses are deported, each of these women will have to choose between their country and their family.

The women have two options:

1. Do nothing and hope that immigration agents don't find their spouses.
2. Apply for immigration benefits for their husbands, on the basis of their marriage.

If the women choose option 1, they have to live with the fear that their husbands will be deported. If they choose option 2, they have to take a trip to Ciudad Juarez for their immigration appointment. If their husbands are denied the immigration benefit, they will not be allowed to return with their wives to the United States.

If their husbands are deported or denied immigration benefits, these women will have to choose between remaining together as a family and exercising their right not to be banished from their country of citizenship. In addition, living with the idea that their husbands could be excluded at any moment infringes on these women's sense of belonging to this country. It is difficult to feel as if one is a full-fledged member of society when one could be denied the right to live in this country as a family. Fatima has lived here since she was two years old and finds it difficult to reconcile her feeling that she is part of this country with the fact that immigration agents could deport her husband at any point. Maia is familiar with the injustices brought upon African-Americans in pre–Civil Rights America. She finds it appalling that this country continues to deny fundamental rights to certain sectors of society. Each of these women experiences a diminishing of her citizenship rights through the knowledge that her family life could be ruptured at any time.

Family unity is allegedly at the core of immigration policy. The family unit is the microcosm of the nation. Despite this, another important aspect of U.S. society—the rule of law—has taken precedent. Of course, there must be a balance between the rule of law and family unity. People convicted of murder, for example, are denied their right to family unity while in prison. Once they serve their time, however, they are free to pursue their family life. People who commit the infraction of crossing the border twice are not given the same consideration. As these stories show, not only do border crossers suffer for this, but so do their families.

Gendered Effects of Immigration Policy

In Chapter 3, I pointed out that nearly all deportees are men. Yet, it is clear that, although mostly men are deported, women also experience the consequences of deportation. The consequences of immigration policy are gendered; men and women experience them differently. The way that immigration law is enforced means that men are more likely to be deported and women are more likely to be left behind. The DHS does not issue statistics on deportees by gender. However, based on my conversations with officials who receive deportees in four countries, it is safe to say that at least three-quarters of all deportees are men.

When I set out to do the research for this chapter, it was not my intention to only interview women. However, all the contacts that *Latinos Progresando* gave me and all the people I was able to interview turned out to be U.S.-citizen women with undocumented partners. The reason I was more likely to find U.S.-citizen women with undocumented partners is that women who migrate to the United States illegally are more likely than men to migrate to join a partner who often is also undocumented. Because women are migrating to join a partner, they are less likely to marry a U.S. citizen. We saw this in the story of Giselda, who migrated to join her husband. By the time she divorced him, she already had her legal permanent residency.

Christiane Harzig[4] points out that U.S. immigration policy is gendered insofar as family reunification is the most important factor in immigration admission. Often, this has meant that male labor migrants travel to the United States as sojourners, and, eventually family reunification policies allow them to bring their wives and children. A University of Notre Dame report on Mexicans in Chicago informs us that 85 percent of Mexican men in Chicago traveled there to find work, as compared to only 39 percent of women. In contrast, 59 percent of women indicated they moved to Chicago to be with relatives, as compared to 53 percent of the men in the survey.[5] The higher numbers of Mexican men who migrated to find work lend support to the argument that Mexican men are more likely than women to travel as labor migrants, whereas women are more likely than men to join their spouses who have migrated. Migration policies that treat labor migrants differently from those who migrate to reunite with their families thus would have disparate impacts on men and women. With regard to the cases discussed in this chapter, the key policy here is one that places limits on the immigration benefits associated with marriage to U.S. citizens. If U.S.-citizen women are more likely to marry undocumented men than vice versa, this policy would have a gendered impact.

Mass deportation thus has different effects on men and women in the United States. Men are more likely to be apprehended by immigration agents—either through their involvement with the criminal justice system or being subject to immigration raids and checkpoints. Women are more likely to find themselves raising children without the help of a deported father. The consequences of mass deportation are similar to those of mass incarceration. Both remove (mostly) men from communities and deprive children of their parents. Both put economic and emotional strain on families. Both are racially stratified—blacks and Latinos are more likely than whites or Asians to be incarcerated and to be deported (Western 2007). As we will see in the next chapter, there are striking similarities between immigration policy and criminal justice policy in terms of their racially disproportionate impacts, ineffectiveness, and perceived political benefits.

We have seen women who must contemplate what will happen to them and their families if Immigration and Customs Enforcement (ICE) decides to target their undocumented partner. Is it fair to say that these women should not have chosen undocumented immigrants for their life partners? Should they have researched immigration laws before falling in love? Were they simply foolish to imagine that their country would allow them to live in peace with their husbands? Can you imagine yourself going to an immigration lawyer to find out if your chosen life partner is eligible for legalization? If you are told he is not, what are you supposed to do? These are hard questions, and the agony each of these families faces is a clear indication that there is something fundamentally wrong with having to choose between your country and your family.

CHAPTER 5

THE IMMIGRATION INDUSTRIAL COMPLEX

WHO PROFITS FROM IMMIGRATION POLICIES DESTINED TO FAIL?

In previous chapters, we learned how immigration policy is detrimental to immigrant communities as well as to citizens. We have seen that the inability of many migrants to remain legally in the United States is cause for social concern, yet the policies that have been implemented have done little to alleviate challenges associated with undocumented migration. Why haven't policy makers come up with better solutions to the current crisis? A discussion of the immigration industrial complex will help address this key question.

The *immigration industrial complex* refers to the public and private sector interests in the criminalization and marginalization of undocumented migration, immigration law enforcement, and "anti-illegal" rhetoric. This concept is based on the idea that there exists a convergence of interests that drives the United States government to pass and then avidly enforce a set of immigration policies that consistently have failed to achieve their stated goals. The profit potential is at the root of this human rights crisis, yet political power plays a significant role. In this chapter, I explain how the failure of immigration policy is due to a confluence of powerful interests that prevent the passage of laws that would ameliorate the situation of undocumented migrants and their families.

The Failure of Immigration Policy

The majority of immigration policies implemented in the late twentieth century and debated in Congress in the early twenty-first century have been more effective at making life difficult for immigrants than at achieving any long-term solutions that could benefit both citizens and noncitizens. None of these measures provide a real solution to the crisis of deaths at the border or to the crisis of a large marginalized population in the United States. They fail to take into account the impossibility of sealing the 7,000 miles of borders that encircle the United States. They often ignore the motivations for migration explained in the first chapter, particularly the fact that U.S.-based corporations, the military, and the CIA have engaged in activities that have created migration flows and attracted migrants to the United States. In addition, they do not account for the dependence of many employers on the temporary workforce that migration policy and industry practices have created. Nearly all the proposed measures enhance the marginalization of some sectors of the migrant population.

As discussed in Chapter 1, "Roots of Immigration to the United States," our country has depended on immigrants for centuries, and U.S.-based legislators, corporations, and employers are largely responsible for migration flows. This complicity almost never forms part of the legislative debate. I have also explained, in Chapter 2, "The Department of Homeland Security and the Immigration Enforcement Regime of the Twenty-First Century," the wide array of problems generated by the surge in interior enforcement. The escalation of interior enforcement has been tremendously expensive and ineffective. In the 2006 raid on the Swift meatpacking plants, ICE agents arrested nearly 1,300 workers. This operation took months to plan and implement and cost millions of dollars. Even if ICE were capable of carrying out a similar operation every day, it would take nearly thirty years to remove the seven million undocumented workers from this country in this fashion. In short, immigration raids are not a viable solution, unless your goal is to tear apart families, destroy businesses, and create a marginalized and fearful population.

The problems associated with the detention and deportation of undocumented immigrants discussed in Chapters 2 and 3, "Racism and the Consequences of U.S. Immigration Policy," are similar. We are currently stretching our resources with the average daily detention of 30,000 immigrants, costing taxpayers nearly $3 million per day. Even if we were to increase the number of detainees tenfold, we would barely be up to 5 percent of the current undocumented immigrant population. Not only do we not have the detention facilities; we also do not have the lawyers to give those detainees due process, the judges to charge them, or the vehicles to transport 12 million people out of the country. Many deportees, especially Mexicans, simply return to the United States. They return because of extensive family ties in the United States and because they know there are jobs available.

Punitive immigration policies are implemented and proposed despite substantial research that demonstrates that harsh immigration policies fail to achieve their stated goals (Cornelius and Rosenblum 2005; Golash-Boza and Parker 2007; Massey, Durand, and Malone 2002). The militarization of the border merely pushes migrants and would-be migrants to more remote areas to cross the border, putting their lives in danger. On average, one person dies each day attempting to cross the border. In fiscal year (FY) 2005, 472 bodies of perished migrants were encountered in the harsh terrain of the United States/Mexico border. The bodies of other deceased migrants were likely not found.[1] Because of the increased difficulty in crossing the southern border in recent years, migrants must go to more remote places to cross. This enhances their vulnerability to gang violence, their chances of being sexually assaulted, their need to rely on smugglers, and the probability of their being injured or dying. Human rights researchers have found that as many as 70 percent of women crossing the border face sexual assault, and that some women take birth control pills before crossing, knowing that being raped is a likely possibility.[2]

There have been numerous studies that demonstrate the inefficacy of tough immigration laws, but these results have fallen on deaf ears in Congress. For example, in a testimony prepared for the House Judiciary Committee in August 2006, Professor Wayne Cornelius presented evidence that increasing border enforcement does not discourage unauthorized migration. Cornelius (2006) argued that

> tightened border enforcement since 1993 has not stopped nor even discouraged unauthorized migrants from entering the United States. Even if apprehended, the vast majority (92–97%) keep trying until they succeed. Neither the higher probability of being apprehended by the Border Patrol, nor the sharply increased danger of clandestine entry through deserts and mountainous terrain, has discouraged potential migrants from leaving home.... With clandestine border crossing an increasingly expensive and risky business, U.S. border enforcement policy has unintentionally encouraged undocumented migrants to remain in the United States for longer periods and settle permanently in this country in much larger numbers.

Despite mounting evidence that increased border enforcement does not reduce illegal entries into the United States, the only immigration legislation to be passed in the wake of the massive immigrants' rights marches in 2006 focused exclusively on border enforcement. Shortly after Cornelius presented his convincing data in August 2006, the Secure Fence Act passed the House on September 14, 2006, and the Senate on September 29, 2006, with few dissenting votes in either body. The Secure Fence Act authorized the building of a 700-mile barrier at the southern border of the United States. Congress has yet to appropriate the billions of dollars needed to erect this barrier, which is likely to lead to more migrant deaths, as migrants are pushed into more remote regions of the borderlands (Cornelius 2006; Anguiano Téllez 2007).

Vast increases in the budget for border and interior immigration law enforcement have not led to decreases in the population of undocumented immigrants. The Department of Homeland Security continues to enact, albeit with greater force, the same strategies that its predecessor, the INS, used, despite evidence that these strategies are ineffective. Congress continues to appropriate billions of dollars to enhance the Border Patrol and to carry out more deportations. These tactics make the lives of immigrants more difficult, but they do little to address the challenges presented by the presence of a large undocumented population.

The Roots of the Immigration Industrial Complex

The War on Terror has translated into a War on Immigrants. That's because of the fusion of national security with immigration law enforcement and the consequent allocation of funds to enforce immigration policy. This is not new: undocumented migrants have been targets of harsh immigration policies in ebbs and flows since the passage of Immigration Reform and Control Act (IRCA) in 1986. Despite the limited efficacy of the immigration enforcement actions of the late 1980s and early 1990s, enforcement returned with new vigor in 2003. Scholars predicted the failure of these measures (Donato, Durand, and Massey 1992; Calavita 1989), yet few critics have considered why Congress has passed laws that are destined to fail and why Congress has appropriated billions of dollars to the Department of Homeland Security (DHS) to implement these laws. As Wayne Cornelius (2005: 15) puts it: "Why does the United States' ten-year-old set of policies for controlling unauthorised immigration persist, long past the point when it became apparent that they are not working?" Cornelius briefly answers his own question by pointing to the political capital to be gained from being tough on immigration, the conflation of the War on Terror with immigration policy, and the "insatiable appetite for immigrant labour—much of it low-skilled—which is not satisfied by existing laws and policies" (16).

In these concluding lines, Cornelius (2005) is hinting at a coalescence of interests in these failed policies. This idea of a confluence of interests, or convergence of agendas, resonates with the concept of an industrial complex. Scholars of migration have invoked this concept in their discussions of a "security-industrial complex" (Mills 2004; Koerner 2002); the "border-industrial complex" (Akers Chacón 2006); and the "immigration-industrial complex" (Fernandes 2006; Koulish 2007). Each has invoked this concept of an industrial complex, yet mostly in passing; none has taken full advantage of the complexity of this framework. However, it is beneficial to take these analyses one step further by considering and applying the extensive work done in the areas of the prison and military industrial complexes (MICs) to an explanation of the workings of the immigration industrial complex. I have chosen the term *immigration industrial complex* following the lead of Robert Koulish and Deepa Fernandes, from the three available, because it is the best suited for a consideration of how profit potential influences certain facets of immigration policy. In particular, the border is included in the framework of immigration policy, and immigration is only part of national security.

Legal scholars, historians, and journalists have devoted their attention to the profit potential of immigration law enforcement. This body of work points to the great profits to be made from the current enforcement regime and the dubious connections between fighting terrorism and arresting undocumented migrants. Brendan I. Koerner, for example, wrote in *Mother Jones* in 2002: "Because federal expenditures on homeland security are projected to rise dramatically in the coming years—and because every aspect of civilian life, from food distribution to public transit, could be affected—a wide range of industries ultimately stands to benefit." Deepa Fernandes (2006) argues that "enforcing immigration policy has become the latest way to make a quick buck" (169). Robert Koulish (2007) contends that "catching aliens is a lucrative business made all the more so by exploiting already blurred distinctions between immigration and national security." Justin Akers Chacón (2006) maintains that "border enforcement has become a profitable enterprise" and that "this unprecedented investment in border enforcement has spawned the term 'border-industrial complex' to denote the changing nature of immigration enforcement" (Akers Chacón 2006: 222–223). In this chapter, I expand on their work by engaging more fully with the literature on the MIC and the prison industrial complex to understand who benefits from immigration law enforcement, and, in turn, to help us understand better how the immigration industrial complex works.

What Is the Military Industrial Complex?

On his final night as president of the United States, in 1961, Dwight Eisenhower warned the American public of the dangers of the creation of a "permanent armaments industry of vast proportions" (Eisenhower 1961). Eisenhower urged Americans to be wary of the potential for the "unwarranted influence" of the "military industrial complex." These predictions turned out to be prescient; the U.S. arms industry continued to grow and became heavily influential in the arms race in the coming decades.

In the 1960s and 1970s, the concept of a MIC dominated much of the critical discussion of U.S. foreign and domestic policies. The basic idea behind this concept is that there are close relationships between the corporate elite, bureaucrats, and politicians, and these actors work together to ensure that state military investments serve the interests of capital (Moskos 1972; Cobb 1976). Although there was general agreement that such a complex existed, there were disputes with regard to who benefited from it and how it actually worked. Much of this discussion centered on the "self-serving accommodation between corporate elites, government bureaucrats, and the military hierarchy" (Moskos 1972: 499). Many sociologists used the framework provided by C. Wright Mills in *The Power Elite* to gain insight into how these actors came together to work in their own interest. As Moskos (1972) points out, this was not generally a Marxist analysis, insofar as the focus was not on the "economic relations of classes to the means of production," but on the way elite bureaucrats used their power and position to their advantage (502). The justifications for the build-up of the military industrial complex were largely due to an external threat—the specter of Communism. In contrast, the justification for the prison industrial complex was based on an internal threat—the fear of crime.

What Is the Prison Industrial Complex?

In the early 1990s, writers began to explore the idea of a prison industrial complex (PIC), drawing from scholarly analyses of the military industrial complex. In 1995, Mike Davis mentioned the PIC in a *Nation* article about the rise of prisons in California. These ideas were expanded on and taken to a national level by Eric Schlosser and Angela Davis in 1998, and then by a great many other thinkers in the past decade.

The PIC refers to the vast network of prisons, jails, courts, police officers, and other elements that purport to reduce the amount of criminal activity in our society. The PIC is a "self-perpetuating machine": the enormous investment in prisons, jails, and law enforcement combined with the perceived political benefits of crime control have led to policies ensuring that more people are sentenced to prison, thereby creating the need for more prison beds (Brewer and Heitzeg 2008: 637). A core feature of the idea of a PIC is that prisons are not built solely to house criminals, but that a confluence of interests has led to the building of more prisons, the enactment of harsher laws, and the mass incarceration of poor people. Those constituencies with interests in mass incarceration include the media, private contractors, politicians, state bureaucracies, and private prisons (Davis 1998; Gilmore 2007; Schlosser 1998; Do Valle, Huang, and Spira 2006).

The PIC has come into being because it serves the interests of powerful groups in our society. Politicians have used a tough-on-crime approach to gain votes. The mass media have highlighted local crime to attract viewers (Chermak 1994). Rural areas have turned to building prisons to boost local economic development; more than two-thirds of the prisons built in California between 1982 and 1998 were built on formerly irrigated agricultural land that was out of production (Gilmore 2007: 105–106). Finally, private prisons have cashed in on growing rates of incarceration (Brewer and Heitzeg 2008; Schlosser 1998; Do Valle, Huang, and Spira 2006). For these reasons, not because of excessive rates of criminality, we now have more than two million people behind bars in the United States, which is greater than ten times as many as we did prior to the 1970s. Mass incarceration of poor people has generated profits for private prisons and political capital for politicians, yet it has not made this country safer (Hattery and Smith 2006).

The Failure of Crime-Prevention Policy

The parallels between crime-prevention and immigration policies are striking. Despite substantial evidence that being tough on crime does not lead to safer communities, policies have hardly changed in response to this research.[3] In 1998, Angela Davis pointed out that, "Mass incarceration is not a solution to unemployment, nor is it a solution to the vast array of social problems that are hidden away in a rapidly growing network of prisons and jails. However, the great majority of people have been tricked into believing in the efficacy of imprisonment, even though the historical record clearly demonstrates that prisons do not work" (Davis 1998: 3).

The United States has many more people in prison and much longer sentence terms than other Western countries. In the United States, nearly 1 in every 100 people is in prison, which is six to twelve times more than the rates in other Western democracies (Tonry 1999)[4]. This is despite the fact that victimization surveys show that violent and property crime rates are about the same as in other countries. The only sort of crime for which the United States has a higher rate than other countries is gun violence (Tonry 1999). The high rates of incarceration in the United States are not due to higher rates of crime, but to policies designed to "get tough" on crime and drugs. These policies do not serve to reduce crime; rather, they represent "a shift toward a more exclusionary and punitive approach to the regulation of social marginality" (Beckett and Western 2001: 55). Moreover, despite the fact that crime rates have declined in recent years, incarceration rates have continued to increase (Mauer 2001).

Incarceration has a limited impact on crime rates. First, it is just one of many factors that influence crime rates; changes in the economy, fluctuations in the drug market, and community-level responses often have more pronounced effects on crime rates. Second, there are diminishing returns to incarceration; incarcerating repeat violent offenders takes these people off the street and thus reduces crime on the streets, whereas incarcerating nonviolent offenders has a minimal effect on crime rates[5] (King, Mauer, and Young 2005). Despite this, the incarceration of nonviolent offenders has skyrocketed in recent decades.

Notwithstanding the low efficacy of imprisoning nonviolent offenders, this is the segment of the prison population that has grown the fastest. Between 1970 and 2000, incarceration rates in the United States increased fivefold. Much of this increase was due to legislation designed to fight drugs. As such, drug offenders represent "the most substantial source of growth in incarceration in recent decades, rising from 40,000 persons in prison and jail in 1980 to 450,000 today" (King, Mauer, and Young 2005: 6). The irony of this is that the incarceration of drug offenders is a highly ineffective way to reduce the number of illegal drugs sold in the United States. When street-level drug sellers are incarcerated, they are quickly replaced by other sellers, because what drives the drug market is demand for drugs (King, Mauer, and Young 2005).

One can also gather evidence from large-scale trends to show that increased incarceration does not decrease crime rates. Between 1998 and 2003, some states greatly increased the number of people they sent to prison, whereas other states did not. The average decrease in crime rates in these states, however, was similar. The states with higher increases in incarceration did not experience more substantial declines in their crime rates (King, Mauer, and Young 2005). Despite the lack of evidence that increased incarceration rates lead to decreased crimes (Lynch 1999), we continue to build prisons and imprison more people (Gilmore

2007). Politicians who invest money in the criminal justice system can claim to their constituents that they are serious about law enforcement. This strategy creates the impression that they have crime victims' interests at heart and has become essential for winning electoral campaigns (Simon 2007). In a similar fashion, politicians who vote in favor of immigration law enforcement can allege that they are in favor of efforts to improve national security.

Immigration Industrial Complex: Fear, Interests, and Other-ization

The discord between rhetoric and reality when it comes to immigration policy points to the importance of using a framework similar to that of the prison and the military industrial complexes to understand the immigration industrial complex. The MIC relies on a fear of war; the PIC relies on a fear of crime; and the immigration industrial complex relies on a fear of foreigners. These respective complexes share three major features:

1. A rhetoric of fear
2. The confluence of powerful interests
3. A discourse of other-ization

Media pundits target undocumented migrants to promote fear, whereas industries such as meatpacking profit from the presence of a marginalized and temporary workforce. Politicians play on fear of immigration to win votes, while voting on immigration policy that is profitable for certain interests in the private sector. This confluence of interests in turn explains why the United States has yet to come up with a viable solution to the "problem" of undocumented migration just as we have yet to solve the drug "problem."

The Media and Fear-Mongering

A key element of the PIC is fear of crime, which is exacerbated by media reports on crime. This fear of crime creates a situation where communities accept the militarization of their neighborhoods, and citizens vote for candidates who promise to be tough on crime. Local news outlets often focus on local violent crimes to attract viewers who want to see sensationalist news (Chermak 1994). This focus on local crime gives the false impression that violent crime is endemic; people who watch local news are more likely to be fearful of crime (Romer,

Jamieson, and Aday 2003). In a similar fashion, national news networks have homed in on illegal immigration to attract viewers and have spread misinformation in the process.

News reporters, media pundits, and outspoken "anti-illegal" advocates instill fear in the hearts of people in the United States that our country is being overrun by "hordes" of "invaders" who wish to carry out the "*reconquista*" of the Southwest United States (Buchanan 2006; Huntington 2004). This fear in turn creates a situation in which people accept the increased militarization of both the border and the interior of the United States.

The Media Matters Action Network published a report on the representation of undocumented immigrants on cable news networks, appropriately titled: *Fear and Loathing in Prime Time: Immigration Myths and Cable News.* This report revealed that three shows—*The O'Reilly Factor, Lou Dobbs Tonight,* and *Glenn Beck*—consistently propagate myths about undocumented immigrants. These myths include the alleged criminality of undocumented immigrants, the falsehood that undocumented immigrants don't pay taxes, and the myth that Mexicans plan to carry out a *reconquista* of the United States (Waldman et al. 2008).

All these myths have been addressed by scholarly research. Extensive research by Rubén Rumbaut and his colleagues has demonstrated that immigrants are less likely to commit crimes than the native born; the incarceration rate of the native born was four times the rate of the foreign born in 2006 (Rumbaut et al. 2006). More than half of undocumented workers pay payroll taxes, and everyone pays property and sales taxes (White House 2005). The idea of a *reconquista* is perhaps the domain of a marginalized few, but certainly not the sentiment of most Mexican-Americans (Chavez 2006).

Lou Dobbs in particular is obsessed with the topic of illegal immigration; 70 percent of his shows in 2007 involved a discussion of illegal immigration. With these three shows—*The O'Reilly Factor, Lou Dobbs Tonight,* and *Glenn Beck*—on the air, viewers are consistently exposed to myths about illegal immigration. In the three shows combined, 402 of the shows in 2007 discussed illegal immigration, an average of more than one per day (Waldman et al. 2008).

Perhaps most controversial is these three shows' sensationalist discussion of crime. Discussion of crime took place in 189 of their shows in 2007, an average of more than once every other day. What's more, these hosts misrepresent the criminality of undocumented people. For example, on October 5, 2006, Lou Dobbs said, "Just about a third of the prison population in this country is estimated to be illegal aliens." This is a gross misrepresentation of the reality; less than 6 percent of prisoners are foreign-born, and only some of those are undocumented immigrants. The remaining are naturalized citizens, permanent legal residents, and other visa holders. Glenn Beck put flame to this fire by saying on his show on September 4, 2007, "Every undocumented worker is an illegal immigrant, a criminal, and a drain on our dwindling resources" (Waldman et al. 2008).

The constant propagation of hate-filled rhetoric dehumanizes undocumented migrants and renders them appropriate targets for law enforcement activities. One way this can be seen is in polls Lou Dobbs conducts on his show. On his March 5, 2007, show, Dobbs reported, "Ninety-eight percent of you [viewers] voted that illegal immigration, failed border security, and sanctuary laws are contributing to the rise in gang violence in this country" (Waldman et al. 2008). By consistently presenting undocumented migrants as criminals and dehumanizing them by referring to them as "illegals," these popular media pundits make viewers more likely to favor police action to rid the country of undocumented migrants.

Industry Profits from Undocumented Workers and Immigration Law Enforcement

The presence of undocumented migrants provides media pundits with a target for social discontent. Yet, undocumented workers provide a vital labor force in the United States. Moreover, certain sectors of the labor market depend heavily on undocumented migrants for labor. The undocumented labor force constitutes nearly 5 percent of the civilian labor force in the United States. This includes 29 percent of all agricultural workers, 29 percent of all roofers, 22 percent of all maids and housekeepers, and 27 percent of all people working in food processing (Passel 2006). This high concentration of undocumented migrants in certain sectors means that removing large numbers of undocumented migrants would lead to severe labor shortages in these industries. There is already some evidence that the rise in deportations and increase in border enforcement have negatively affected farm owners across the country. Severe labor shortages have led to the loss of crops, as well as the transfer of production to Mexico.[6] This loss of production, in turn, has ripple costs across the rest of the economy.

Nicholas de Genova (2005) argues that immigration policy in the United States is not designed to deter immigration, but serves to create a deportable migrant labor force. De Genova introduces the concept of "deportability" to describe the condition of undocumented migrants—deportability ensures that some migrants will be deported, but the overwhelming majority will remain, albeit in a socially marginal and vulnerable state (2005). Gilberto Rosas (2006) expands upon the arguments made by De Genova and introduces the concept of "policeability." By this, he means that the militarization of the border has created subjects that are deemed "worthy of dying in the treacherous geographies of the border, or subject to militarized policing, or vigilante actions, or daily forms of surveillance" (413). These concepts of policeability and deportability are useful for understanding the migrant condition and for exploring how the creation of disposable and marginal workers is not only detrimental to migrants, but also advantageous to employers. Punitive immigration policies not only create marginalized subjects, but also are beneficial to employers in certain sectors of the labor market insofar as they create a disposable workforce. The meatpacking industry is a prime example of this.

A quarter of all workers in food processing are undocumented migrants. Over the past two decades, the industry itself has evolved to accommodate a transient, marginalized workforce. A brief discussion of the way that meat is processed in the United States will make it clear that an undocumented workforce is the best suited for work in meatpacking plants in the Midwest. Furthermore, it is evident there is a benefit to the owners of meatpacking plants that undocumented workers are not eligible for legalization in the United States.

As depicted in Upton Sinclair's *The Jungle* (1985 [1906]), the meatpacking industry has been characterized by grueling conditions for at least a century and has historically used immigrants as its primary source of labor. These two characteristics have changed little in the past hundred years. What *has* changed is that, starting in the 1980s, meatpacking companies began to move their plants away from urban centers and closer to rural areas where livestock abound, especially near small towns in Kansas, Nebraska, Texas, and Colorado. Along with this move, meatpackers changed the way they cut meats. Whereas previously skilled and semi-skilled butchers would cut up the cattle, now the carcasses are moved along a powered chain where each worker is responsible for a specific operation on the carcasses. This new way of processing meat has resulted in a deskilling of the workforce as well as an increase in the rate of production. Plants now process much more meat at a much faster rate than they did just twenty years ago. This efficiency has also led to extremely high rates of turnover and injury in the meatpacking industry. Turnover rates are as high as 100 percent in some plants, and incidences of carpal tunnel syndrome increased 264 percent between 1980 and 1988 (Gabriel 2006; Champlin and Hake 2006).

When Human Rights Watch conducted a study of the meatpacking industry, they found that workers who tried to form trade unions and bargain collectively were "spied on, harassed, pressured, threatened, suspended, fired, deported, or otherwise victimized for their exercise of the right to freedom of association."[7]

They also found that many companies took advantage of workers' immigration status and lack of knowledge of their rights as workers in the United States to deny them these rights. Overall, they found the meatpacking industry to be characterized by unsafe working conditions, high rates of injury, and constant abuses from superiors. The changes in the way meat is processed have generated great profits for the largest meat processing firms, while putting smaller firms out of business. It may seem odd that the large meat processing companies moved out of cities with relatively high rates of unemployment to small towns with low unemployment, even given the advantages of being closer to the raw materials— the cattle. From a supply and demand perspective, it would seem that companies would have to pay higher wages to attract workers to areas with low levels of unemployment. The solution to this potential problem is that meat processing is designed in such a manner that workers can be easily trained to process meat at high rates of speed. This in turn causes high rates of injury and turnover. Thus, the meatpacking companies do not need a large, stable workforce, but rather a temporary workforce that is mobile and is willing to work for a few months and then move on. Temporary undocumented migrants are in fact an ideal workforce.

The town of Lexington, Nebraska, provides an example of this trend. Iowa Beef Processors (IBP) opened a large meat processing factory in Lexington in 1990, when the local unemployment rate was about 3 percent. When IBP opened its doors, 81 percent of the people hired were non-Hispanic, and Lexington and the surrounding areas had a low Hispanic population. Two years later, 57 percent of the new hires were Hispanic. Nearly all of these new hires had come from other states to work at IBP. The turnover rate at IBP was about 12 percent per month during its first four years, meaning that the entire workforce was replaced every nine months. While the average length of employment at IBP was eight months, the average employment at Cornland, a smaller plant in Lexington that was put out of business by the competition from IBP, had been thirty-three months (Gouveia and Stull 1997). The exceedingly high turnover rates and harsh working conditions make marginalized undocumented workers an ideal workforce for meatpacking plants. Undocumented migrants are ideal candidates for jobs with high turnover rates, because they are less likely to stay in the community once they are no longer employed there. Also, the marginalization of undocumented workers makes it difficult for them to fight for better working conditions.

Meatpacking industries profit from the *presence* of undocumented workers, insofar as they constitute a vulnerable workforce. A wide range of government contractors, however, directly benefit from immigration law *enforcement* through the profit potential. One sector that has profited from increased immigration enforcement has been the business of privately run immigrant detention centers.

The Corrections Corporation of America (CCA) is one of the main beneficiaries of the increase in immigrant detainees. CCA has a long history of profiting off of incarceration. It won its first government contract in 1984 to run an immigrant detention center in Houston. The company was inching along for the next decade, when it finally began to see substantial profits in the late 1990s. Its annual revenue shot up from $50 million in the early 1990s to $462 million in 1997. By 1998, its stock prices hit $44.00. CCA was doing so well that, at the end of the twentieth century, the company began to build speculative prisons—"excess prison space for inmates who did not yet exist" (Wood 2007: 232). These prisons were built with the expectation that the prison population would continue to grow. When rates of incarceration leveled off at the beginning of the twenty-first century, CCA faced serious problems. Its stock values fell from $44 dollars in 1998 to a mere 18 cents in December 2000. By 2001, CCA had 8,500 empty beds and was more than a billion dollars in debt (Wood 2007). Its rival, Wackenhut, also saw its stock lose a third of its value between 1998 and 2001 (Berestein 2008).

At the end of the twentieth century, the two leading private prison companies—CCA and Wackenhut—faced serious financial troubles. They had reinvested their immense profits in new prisons that were now sitting empty. The increased need for prison beds for immigrant detainees became their saving grace. On the verge of bankruptcy in 2000, CCA was awarded two contracts that allowed it to fill two empty prisons it had built speculatively—one in California City and another in Cibola County, New Mexico (Mattera, Khan, and Nathan 2003). It filled those prisons with immigrant detainees.

With these new contracts, CCA has been able to regain its financial footing. Its stock prices have fluctuated substantially but have generally improved since its low point at the end of 2000. CCA stock reached a new high of $32.40 in May 2007 and stood at about 27 dollars in May 2008. According to financial expert Eric Cheshier (2008), spring 2008 was a good time to buy CCA stock because their prospects for growth were quite positive. As of this writing, in April 2011, Google finance reports CCA stocks to be at $24.01 a share.

Many of CCA's earlier troubles stemmed from their inability to manage higher security prisons and from states cutting back funding for prisons. Thus, CCA began to set its sights on the federal government. By 2002, 32 percent of CCA's revenues came from federal agencies (Mattera, Khan, and Nathan 2003). In the post-9/11 context, the Federal Bureau of Prisons is giving even more contracts to private prison companies. Whereas there were about 15,000 federal inmates in private prisons in 2000, by 2004, there were 24,768. (Wood 2007: 233).

Much of the success of CCA is due to its lobbying efforts and political connections, combined with increased rates of detention for immigrants. Its federal lobbying expenses increased from $410,000 to $3 million between 2000 and 2004, and these efforts appear to have paid off both in terms of CCA filling its beds and gaining contracts to build new prisons (Berestein 2008). In 2007, CCA spent almost $2.5 million to lobby on legislations and regulations related to the private prison industry, and it spent $2 million in 2009.[8] At the beginning of 2000, CCA was awarded a contract to house 1,000 detainees at the CCA-owned San Diego Correctional Facility. CCA was to be paid $89.50 per day for each detainee it held. This was the beginning of a comeback for CCA. In July 2007, CCA announced that it was building a new 1,688 bed correctional facility in Adams County Mississippi, at a cost of $105 million. CCA built this facility without a management contract, because the company did not foresee difficulties in finding people to fill those prison beds. In fact, CCA had plans for 4,500 additional beds in 2007.[9] With the constantly expanding detention of immigrants, CCA could fully expect to fill those beds.

In 2009, CCA was awarded a Federal Bureau of Prisons contract for the facility. By that time, they had expanded the capacity to 2,232 beds. In addition, CCA was constructing a 3,060-bed facility in Eloy, Arizona, that would house immigrant detainees, and a 2,040-bed facility in Trousdale County, Tennessee. And, in 2008, CCA was awarded a contract from the Office of Federal Detention Trustees to build and manage a new correctional facility in Pahrump, Nevada, to house detainees as well as inmates. Business has been booming for CCA.[10]

CCA has been able to obtain favorable government contracts in part because of its ties to current and former elected officials. The former head of the Federal Bureau of Prisons, J. Michael Quinlan, is one of CCA's top executives. Both the CCA and the Geo Group have dominated the private prison sector because of their political influence. "Both benefit from extensive and intimate connections with state and local politics and the public corrections sector as well as from the usual interlocking directorships with other corporations in prison services, construction, the media, and finance" (Wood 2007: 231).

The private prison industry is just one example of how private companies benefit from the increased surveillance and punishment of immigrants. Telephone companies such as MCI and Evercom have significant contracts inside immigrant detention centers, where they charge exponentially more for phone calls than they do at phones not in prisons (Fernandes 2006: 198). Overall, DHS awards billions of dollars of contracts each year. Many of the names are familiar: Lockheed Martin, Northrop Grumman, Boeing, IBM, Unisys and, not surprisingly, Halliburton. In January 2006, the DHS awarded a $385 million contingency contract to Halliburton subsidiary, KBR, to build facilities to temporarily house immigrant detainees (Scott 2006). In many ways, the increased surveillance of the foreign born in the United States has turned out handsome profits for well-connected corporations. This is in large part because "DHS was conceived and created in a way that made it possible for private industry to become the driving force behind much of its operations. DHS was born with a massive budget, and those who were present at its creation undoubtedly saw the huge revenue potential for big business." (Fernandes 2006: 172–173).

Creating the "Other": Using Fear as Political Ploy

With the military build-up during the Cold War, the "others" were communists. With the prison expansion of the 1990s, the "others" were criminals (often racialized and gendered as black men). With the expansion of the immigration industrial complex, the "others" are "illegals" (racialized as Mexicans). In each case, the creation of an undesirable "other" creates popular support for government spending to safeguard the nation. Ideas of racial otherness play an important role in the demonization of criminals and undocumented migrants. This other-ization allows politicians to play on public fears and portray these groups as threatening public safety. As Michael Welch argues, the punitive legislation passed in the last decades of the twentieth century to control crime and immigration are "not only poorly formulated, but also unjust and discriminatory against the poor and people of color" (2002: 14). Welch further contends that these laws are passed in the context of a "moral panic, a turbulent and exaggerated response to a putative social problem" (2002: 8).

The PIC relies on the production of criminals through repressive laws and the policing of communities to fill the prisons it builds (Richie 2005). The creation of increasingly strict crime laws is partly due to campaign tactics used by politicians who aim to play on fear of crime to capture more votes. One of the most famous examples of a politician using the fear of crime as a campaign tactic is known as the "Willie Horton" case. In the 1988 run for presidential office, the George Bush campaign was able to play on white Americans' fear of crime and racial prejudices against blacks through the use of an ad that featured "Willie Horton." William Horton, a young black man, escaped from prison while on a weekend pass. He then "kidnapped and brutally assaulted a white couple in their home, raping the woman and stabbing the man" (Mendelberg 1997). An ad that featured this story and a mug shot of Mr. Horton was used by the Bush campaign to portray the opposing party as being lax on crime. This ad was part of Bush's successful campaign for keeping the presidential office in Republican hands. This is just one of many examples of politicians using the fear of crime for political gain. Notably, the Willie Horton case used both the fear of crime and the fear of black men to push forward a political agenda.

Just as fear of crime is racialized, so is fear of immigration. As Kevin Johnson (2004) points out, the majority of immigrants are people of color. Fewer than 20 percent of immigrants come from Europe, Canada, or Australia. Thus, any discourse about immigration today has the subtext of minority incorporation into society. The racialization of immigrants, and especially of undocumented migrants, became clear in the campaign to push forward Proposition 187 in California—a ballot initiative that would deny social services and educational opportunities to the undocumented.

When Proposition 187 was being debated, California was on the verge of becoming a majority-minority state, and demographic changes were at the heart of the fears of many supporters of the Proposition. In Robin Dale Jacobson's interviews with Proposition 187 supporters, one of her respondents told her that Proposition 187 was a response to the "Mexican impact on the state of California." Another interviewee was more forthright: "So, I just wanted something to be done about too many Mexican people all of a sudden" (Jacobson 2008: 39). These fears of the growth in the Mexican population were exacerbated by public perception of Mexicans as "illegals" and "criminals." Supporters of the proposition often took the fact that undocumented migrants had crossed the border illegally or overstayed their visas as an indication that they were prone to criminal activity. Governor Pete Wilson put flame to this fire by "widely publicizing the estimated costs of keeping illegal aliens in prison" (Jacobson 2008: 55). In addition to criminalizing undocumented immigrants, much of the discourse surrounding Proposition 187 racialized undocumented immigrants as Mexican. Thus, many of these supporters interpreted the "invasion" of undocumented workers as a racial takeover of California (Jacobson 2008: 117).

Political campaigns that promoted the passage of Proposition 187 drew from unmistakably racial imagery. Television ads supported by California Governor Pete Wilson "showed shadowy Mexicans crossing the border in large numbers" (Johnson 2004: 43). In another case, a political leader, Ron Prince, drew parallels to lynching by referring to a "posse" and a "rope" (Jacobson 2008; Johnson 2004). Johnson (2004) argues that the Proposition 187 campaign was a clear manifestation of the racial fears of white Californians. Although it would have been politically unsavory to launch an attack on domestic minorities, undocumented immigrants were seen as an appropriate target. The campaign for Proposition 187 had clear political benefits for Pete Wilson. Governor Wilson was on the verge of losing his reelection campaign in 1994 when he decided to put his support behind Proposition 187.

Governor Pete Wilson's anti-illegal stance, combined with the large voter turnout for Proposition 187, helped Wilson retain his position as the governor of California (Diamond 1996). Although there was no clear connection between the presence of a large undocumented population and the hard economic times California was experiencing, gubernatorial and state legislature candidates in California were able to use the presence of undocumented people to their advantage by advocating for harsh policies that were not guaranteed to improve the fiscal health of the state. Politicians used undocumented immigrants as scapegoats by blaming them for poor economic conditions. Their promises to get tough on illegal immigration helped them to win elections.

The scapegoating of undocumented immigrants is a political ploy used not only by politicians at national and state levels, but at local ones as well. For example, Sheriff Joe Arpaio, county sheriff for Maricopa County, has used anti-illegal rhetoric to gain votes, along with creatively using state laws to imprison and eventually deport thousands of undocumented immigrants in Maricopa County. Arpaio requires that victims and witnesses of crimes prove their immigration status to testify; this leads many not to report crimes at all. He encourages racial profiling and frequently asks Latino citizens to prove their right to be here. These harsh tactics have repeatedly assured his incumbency.

In 2008, Governor Janet Napolitano took $1.6 million from Arpaio's budget to redirect it to find fugitives, which was supposed to be his job (Robbins 2008). Undeterred, Arpaio continued with his dehumanizing campaigns. In February 2009, he shackled 200 undocumented migrants, dressed them in prison stripes, and forced them to walk under armed guard from the prison where they were being held to a new tent city. This was a media ploy designed to attract attention. It worked. A parade of TV cameras filmed the show and showed it around the world.[11] Shortly afterward, four leading members of the U.S. House Judiciary Committee asked Attorney General Janet Napolitano to investigate Arpaio for possible civil rights violations.[12]

The tactics used by these politicians have been successful insofar as they play on voters' fears of a rising tide of immigrants. Thus, even though getting tough on immigration primarily has the consequence of making life difficult for immigrants and does not reduce levels of immigration, politicians repeatedly advocate for such tactics, in efforts to win elections and reelections. This parallels the case of drug laws: it is widely accepted that "education and drug treatment are the most effective means of reducing the demand for illegal drugs" (Díaz-Cotto 2005: 148), yet politicians continue to advocate for repressive legislation and longer prison terms for drug users and sellers.

In Whose Interest?

The failure of immigration policy has created profits for government contractors, given fodder to politicians, and made undocumented migrants the targets of mass media talk show hosts, while creating a climate of dependency on migrants for certain sectors, such as food processing. The combination of fear, political maneuvers, and corporate profits has created a confluence of interests in the militarization of immigration enforcement, despite the negative consequences and limited efficacy of these actions. Although border militarization and interior immigration law enforcement are unlikely to alleviate any of the challenges associated with the presence of a large undocumented population in the United States, they have created new social problems.

There are many reasons to be opposed to having a large undocumented population in the United States. They present a security risk insofar as there are too many people who are unaccounted for, who are fundamentally disenfranchised, and who have no investment in a nation that chooses to ignore their contributions to society. The practical solution is not to try to remove all of them or to scare them away, but to encourage them to come out of the shadows by offering them an incentive to do so.

Increased militarization of the border will lead to handsome profits for certain corporations as well as increased funding for the DHS. It will not, however, lead to a reduction in the flow of migrants. Unfortunately, it is likely to increase the death toll at the border. The solution, however, is not to make more use of tactics destined to fail, but to encourage people to request permission to enter the United States by making the process less cumbersome and rendering the quotas more in line with actual labor needs in the United States. The growth of the immigration industrial complex, however, has ensured that practical solutions are unlikely to be enacted. As long as powerful companies, politicians, and media conglomerates stand to gain from the growth of the immigration industrial complex, it will be nearly impossible to enact viable reforms.

One of the aims of this book is to change the discourse on undocumented migration—to compel people to see that immigrants are not commodities or potential terrorists, but human beings with fundamental rights. The evidence, as discussed, shows that it will be difficult to change this discourse, partly because of the powerful interests behind the dehumanization of migrants. To begin to change the discourse, I want to conclude my discussion by laying out how immigration policies violate principles enshrined in human rights doctrine and set out a vision of how immigration policy would look in a world where human rights were valued and respected.

CONCLUSION

IMMIGRATION POLICY AND HUMAN RIGHTS

Immigration policy is based on the premise that states have the right to determine who can and cannot be a citizen and decide which noncitizens have the right to enter and remain within a state's borders. These premises are upheld in human rights tradition, which recognizes the right of states to national sovereignty, and the right of people to belong to a state.[1] The human rights tradition, then, does not require states to have open borders. It does, however, compel states to respect the fundamental dignity of all persons within and outside their borders, regardless of citizenship status. In this respect, the United States falls short. The current immigration policy regime in the United States does not respect the human rights of migrants.

Immigration policies and enforcement practices in the United States are in violation of international human rights treaties. Deportations without due process; detention without access to lawyers; separation of families; and racial profiling are some of the ways that immigration policies and practices violate immigrants' and citizens' human rights. These rights are violated through laws that mandate detention and deportation, strategies that include immigration raids and racial profiling, and the militarization of the border. It is crucial to record these violations and to develop policies and practices that respect the human rights of migrants. Throughout this book, I have mentioned several human rights treaties. In the conclusion, I revisit these treaties to develop policy suggestions that respect the human rights tradition.

Immigration Policy and Human Rights Violations

The human rights violations embedded in U.S. immigration policy and practice can be boiled down to five key rights violations:

1. The right to form a family
2. The right to due process
3. The right to freedom from discrimination
4. The right to freedom from arbitrary detention
5. The right to not experience cruel or unusual punishment

These rights are enshrined both in human rights treaties that the United States has signed and ratified as well as those to which the United States is not party.

The U.S. government has ratified the International Covenant on Civil and Political Rights (ICCPR), the Convention on the Elimination of All Forms of Racial Discrimination (CERD), and the Convention Against Torture and Other Cruel Inhuman or Degrading Treatment or Punishment (CAT). It has signed, but not ratified, the American Convention on Human Rights (ACHR). Finally, as a member of the Organization of American States, the United States is party to the American Declaration on the Rights and Duties of Man (The American Declaration). All of these documents contain provisions applicable to the treatment of immigrants.

The Right to Form a Family

The right to form a family is a fundamental aspect of human rights doctrine. The ICCPR states in Article 17 that no one shall be "subjected to arbitrary or unlawful interference with his privacy, family, home or correspondence," and in Article 23 that "the family is the natural and fundamental group unit of society and is entitled to protection by society and the state" and that all men and women have the right "to marry and to found a family." The right to found a family includes the right "to live together." Article 6 of the American Declaration states: "Every person has the right to establish a family, the basic element of society, and to receive protection therefor." The forced separation of citizens from their families through deportations is an example of how the right to form a family is violated. Deported parents often leave children behind. Spouses face the choice of giving up their homeland or losing their marriage. Deportation forces U.S. citizens to choose between their right to family unity and their right to remain in this country.

Any state has the right to deny entry for reasons of national security, yet many people have been denied entry to or removed from the United States on the basis of fairly minor infractions. As we saw in Chapter 4, "The Impossible Choice: Family Versus Citizenship in U.S. Immigration Policies," Sergio, who is married to Melissa, a U.S. citizen, has been ordered deported because he violated the terms of his visa. Melissa and Sergio's case is not isolated. Human Rights Watch researchers estimated, based on census data, that approximately 1.6 million spouses and children living in the United States have been separated from their parents or spouses due to deportations since 1996 (Capps et al. 2007).

The Right to Due Process

Article 13 of the ICCPR states, "An alien lawfully in the territory of a State party to the present covenant may be expelled therefrom only in pursuance of a decision reached in accordance with law and shall, except when compelling reasons of national security otherwise require, be allowed to submit the reasons against his expulsion and to have his case reviewed by, and be represented for the purpose before, the competent authority or a person or persons especially designated by the competent authority." In addition, the ACHR states, "Every person has the right to a hearing, with due guarantees and within a reasonable time, by a competent, independent and impartial tribunal, previously established by law." The absence of judicial review in deportation hearings of legal permanent residents accused of aggravated felonies violates these treaties, both of which have been signed by the U.S. government.

In a groundbreaking case, the Inter-American Commission on Human Rights (IACHR) concluded in July 2010 that the United States stands in violation of Articles V, VI, VII, XVIII, and XXVI of the American Declaration. The decision specified that

> it is well-recognized under international law that a Member State must provide non-citizen residents an opportunity to present a defense against deportation based on humanitarian and other considerations ... Each Member State's administrative or judicial bodies, charged with reviewing deportation orders, must be permitted to give meaningful consideration to a non-citizen resident's defense, balance it against the State's sovereign right to enforce reasonable, objective immigration policy, and provide effective relief from deportation if merited. The United States did not follow these international norms in the present case.[2]

The IACHR found that the United States' decision to deport Hugo Armendariz and Wayne Smith, both long-term legal permanent residents, of the United States was in violation of international standards insofar as Armendariz and Smith did not have the opportunity to present evidence of their rehabilitation, their family ties, or other equities in their favor. As legal permanent residents convicted of aggravated felonies, Armendariz and Smith were not granted judicial review of their deportation orders. In addition to violating their right to establish a family, their deportation violated the rights of their children to special protections. The best interests of their citizen children were not taken into account. The IACHR recommended that the United States "implement laws to ensure that non-citizen residents' right to family life, as protected under Articles V, VI, and VII of the American Declaration, are duly protected and given due process on a case-by-case basis in U.S. immigration removal proceedings." The United States asserted its right to sovereignty and has not resolved to change immigration laws on the basis of this decision.[3]

The Right to Freedom from Discrimination

The right to freedom from discrimination is a civil right resting on the principle that people should not be treated differently based on their race or ethnicity. In Chapter 3, "Racism and the Consequences of U.S. Immigration Policy," we saw how immigration law enforcement disproportionately affects Latin American and Caribbean nationals. Because of stereotypes about what undocumented migrants look like, Latinos in the United States are most often the victims of punitive immigration policies. Racial profiling was at the heart of the spring 2010 debates over Arizona Senate Bill (SB) 1070. When Arizona Governor Jan Brewer signed SB 1070 on April 23, 2010, the law required local law enforcement agents to check the immigration status of anyone they suspected to be an undocumented migrant. Opponents argued that the law mandated racial profiling. The enactment of House Bill (HB) 2162 changed the language but left racial profiling intact. In July 2010, Judge Susan Bolton issued a preliminary injunction that stopped this requirement because of concerns over racial profiling. Although not mandated by law, for now at least, racial profiling persists in immigration law enforcement. The following case is one documented example of racial profiling and elucidates how this practice occurs.

In July 2008, a group of farm workers stopped at a gas station to fuel their tank in rural Illinois. The gas station attendant called the Coles County sheriff's office to report what he suspected to be undocumented immigrants. The sheriff's office in turn called U.S. Immigration and Customs Enforcement (ICE) to report the vehicle. Agents from the Springfield ICE office apprehended the people and interviewed twenty-four of them. Eight of them turned out not to be undocumented immigrants; two were legal permanent residents from

Mexico, and six were U.S.-citizen children. The legal permanent residents, the children, and their parents were released, although the undocumented parents were told to return to their trial the following Monday. The eleven people who were neither legal residents nor parents were taken into ICE custody and placed in deportation proceedings.

This is a clear case of racial profiling by the gas station attendant, who presumed that all the people were undocumented migrants. The legal permanent residents and citizens in the group were perceived to be undocumented, based on how they looked and the fact that they were speaking Spanish. It is not possible to distinguish a legal permanent resident from an undocumented migrant based on appearance. Yet, people who look as though they may be noncitizens face discrimination when they are thought to be undocumented, as this example shows. Racial profiling violates people's rights to freedom from discrimination, which is enshrined both in international human rights documents and the U.S. legal tradition.

CERD stipulates, in Article 2, section 2, "No State shall encourage, advocate or lend its support, through police action or otherwise, to any discrimination based on race, colour or ethnic origin by any group, institution or individual." The actions of both the county sheriff and the Springfield ICE office violated this statute insofar as they used police action to respond to the presence of suspected undocumented migrants. These suspicions were racially discriminatory insofar as the assumption that they were undocumented was made on the basis of these individuals' physical appearance.

The Right to Freedom from Arbitrary Detention

By granting asylum to noncitizens with a well-founded fear of persecution, the United States is in line with international human rights doctrine. However, the United States stands in violation of human rights doctrine with its policy of mandatory detention of asylum seekers. When asylum seekers arrive into the United States, their detention is mandatory under provisions of the 1996 laws. An asylum seeker can subsequently be released on parole. However, this decision is not made by an independent judge, but by local ICE officials. The decision as to whether an asylum seeker will be granted parole is made by the same body that detains them. ICE plays the role of both judge and jailer. In 2007, only 4.5 percent of parole requests were granted (Human Rights First 2009).

Article 9 of the ICCPR states, "Everyone has the right to liberty and security of person. No one shall be subjected to arbitrary arrest or detention. No one shall be deprived of his liberty except on such grounds and in accordance with such procedure as are established by law." It further states, "Anyone who is deprived of his liberty by arrest or detention shall be entitled to take proceedings before a court, in order that that court may decide without delay on the lawfulness of his detention and order his release if the detention is not lawful." The mandatory detention of asylum seekers and the lack of an independent parole review are in violation of these statutes.

The Right to Not Experience Cruel or Unusual Punishment

The U.S. Constitution as well as several international treaties provide that no one shall be subjected to torture or cruel or unusual punishment. These treaties include Article 7 of the ICCPR and the CAT. Article 7 of the ICCPR states, "No one shall be subjected to torture or to cruel, inhuman or degrading treatment or punishment." The punishment inflicted on Francisco Castañeda by ICE officials described in Chapter 2, "The Department of Homeland Security and the Immigration Enforcement Regime of the Twenty-First Century," was in violation of these treaties. U.S. District Judge Dean Pregerson argued that the officials' alleged withholding of the necessary tests and treatments for Castañeda's extreme pain was "beyond cruel and unusual" punishment, and that this was a "textbook case" of what cruelty looks like.[4] Denials such as these of medical treatment to detainees abound, indicating that migrant detainees often face cruel and unusual punishment.

The conflation of undocumented migration with national security and the enforcement regime response has created a situation in which human rights violations are widespread in the United States. To stop this human rights disaster, it is necessary to change the way immigration policies are viewed in the United States and to put the human rights of migrants and their families at the core of immigration policy. In this spirit, there is one more human rights convention worth reviewing, although the United States is not party to this convention.

The International Convention on the Protection of the Rights of All Migrant Workers and Members of Their Families

The United Nations has put forth a convention on migrant rights, titled the International Convention on the Protection of the Rights of All Migrant Workers and Members of Their Families (ICPRMW). This convention currently has fifty-seven signatories, most of whom are migrant-sending nations. The United States, like most migrant-receiving nations, is not one of the signatories. This convention goes a bit further than the aforementioned conventions in terms of the rights and protections of migrant workers.

The ICPRMW specifies that migrants should not be treated as criminals when their legal status is in question. For example, this convention stipulates, "It shall not be the general rule that while awaiting trial [migrants] shall be detained in custody, but release may be subject to guarantees to appear for trial." United States laws that mandate the detention of most migrants while awaiting trial are in contravention of this treaty. This treaty further stipulates, "Any migrant worker or member of his or her family who is detained in a State of transit or in a State of employment for violation of provisions relating to migration, shall be held, in so far as practicable, separately from convicted persons or persons detained pending trial." The common practice of placing immigrant detainees in county jails together with convicted criminals is in contravention to this Article.

The ICPRMW makes it clear that the right to be with one's family should extend to migrant workers. Article 44 of this convention stipulates

> 1. States Parties, recognizing that the family is the natural and fundamental group unit of society and is entitled to protection by society and the State, shall take appropriate measures to ensure the protection of the unity of the families of migrant workers. 2. States Parties shall take measures that they deem appropriate and that fall within their competence to facilitate the reunification of migrant workers with their spouses or persons who have with the migrant worker a relationship that, according to applicable law, produces effects equivalent to marriage, as well as with their minor dependent unmarried children.

United States laws, policies, and practices violate this Article in a variety of ways, including mandatory deportations, long waiting lists for family reunification, and guest worker programs that fail to account for family and community ties. The United States government would do well to ratify this treaty and make it part of our legal tradition.

Immigration Policy with a Human Rights Vision

A crucial first step in immigration policy reform involves ensuring that immigration policies in the United States do not violate provisions of international human rights treaties. However, as I will argue below, current human rights treaties fall short insofar as they guarantee only the right to leave one's country, and not the right to enter another. I argue for the following three-step approach to immigration policy reform in the United States.

1. Implement policies that do not violate international human rights conventions.
2. Pave the way for legalization for all migrants currently in the United States.
3. Align migrant entry policies with the reality of globalization.

Step 1: Implement Policies That Do Not Violate International Human Rights Conventions

To meet the norms established by international human rights conventions, immigration policy must respect the rights outlined previously. First, all people have *the right to be with their families.* This means that immigration policy must allow for anyone who comes to the United States to bring their spouses and children with them. Further, it requires that family ties be considered in deportation cases and that previously deported migrants have the opportunity to appeal their cases on the basis of family ties.

Second, it requires *the right to due process* in all immigration cases. This means that people who are living in the United States and are facing deportation have the right to a fair trial by an independent judge, that they have the right to present equities in their favor, and that they have the right to a public defender.

Third, all people have *the right to freedom from discrimination.* This right would be realized in part with the ending of 287(g) programs that require police officers to racially profile people and report suspected undocumented migrants to immigration authorities. The realization of this right also requires Customs and Border Patrol (CBP) agents not to operate inside the United States, but to restrict their activities to the border.

Fourth, *the right to not be arbitrarily detained* requires ending the mandatory detention of noncitizens. Prior to being detained, noncitizens deserve a hearing that assesses their risk to society.

Finally, *the right to not face cruel or unusual punishment* would be achieved through a reform of the immigration detention system. This would be facilitated by the massive reduction in detainees we would see once mandatory detention was eliminated. The implementation of policies that are in line with international human rights conventions is a crucial first step and would lead to a more humane immigration system. However, the fulfillment of the human rights of migrants and their families requires us to go beyond existing human rights conventions.

Step 2: Pave the Way for Legalization for All Migrants Currently in the United States

Human rights doctrine respects the fundamental dignity of all human beings. A society that has a large population of undocumented migrants who lack a variety of basic rights is not a society that recognizes the dignity and equality of all. According to the most recent estimates, there are about eleven million undocumented migrants in the United States. Undocumented migrants live in a state of fear and uncertainty and are vulnerable to abuse and exploitation. To become a more equal society, the United States must do something with regard to this problem.

There are three general policy responses to the challenge presented by the presence of eleven million undocumented migrants in the United States:

1. Deportation for all
2. Attrition through enforcement
3. Legalization for all

The first policy option of deporting all undocumented migrants carries an astronomical human and economic cost. The Center for American Progress estimates the cost of removing undocumented migrants to be more than $200 billion (Hinojosa-Ojeda 2010). This figure, which does not take into account the economic impact on U.S. businesses and the U.S. treasury associated with the loss of productive labor and taxes, amounts to more than three times the annual budget of the Department of Homeland Security (DHS) of $60 billion and eight times the annual budget of the Department of Justice (DOJ) of $24 billion. More shocking than the economic cost is the social cost. Mass deportation would require raiding schools, homes, and worksites; would tear apart families; and would be yet another stain on the history of the United States.

The second policy option of attrition through enforcement describes the current policy of deporting 400,000 immigrants a year and facilitating cooperation between law enforcement officials and immigration enforcement agents. The goal of this strategy is to make life difficult enough for undocumented migrants that they will opt to return to their countries of origin. Proponents argue that once undocumented migrants are unable to obtain employment, driver's licenses, or housing, they will return to their birth countries. This approach is currently not working. One of the problems with it is that there is not an effective system to ensure that undocumented migrants do not obtain the necessary paperwork to work. Instead of preventing undocumented migrants from working, more stringent systems lead to more criminal organizations becoming involved in the production of fake documents that migrants can use to work. The tactic of using police officers to enforce immigration law has two central problems:

1. It breaks down the trust between communities and police, making this a strategy unpopular among police officers.[5]
2. It leads to civil rights violations insofar as police officers cannot distinguish between legal permanent residents and undocumented migrants.

Attrition through enforcement does not work in large part because there are too many people in the United States that do not want it to work. These people include employers who depend on undocumented migrants for their labor power, the family members of undocumented migrants, and advocates for immigrants that recognize the valuable contributions of immigrants to our society. Instead of leading to massive self-deportation, attrition through enforcement exacerbates human rights violations in the United States.

Legalization for all is the approach advocated by immigrant rights groups throughout the United States. It is the most cost-effective approach. The Congressional Budget Office (CBO) estimated that the legalization program proposed in 2006 would have cost $54 billion, yet it would have generated $66 billion in revenue (Congressional Budget Office 2006). More importantly, a path to legalization for all undocumented migrants would greatly reduce the human rights violations generated through the current policy of attrition through enforcement.

The legislative proposals we have seen thus far in Congress have not actually offered legalization for all. Instead, they provide a path to legalization for those who qualify. These proposals, although better than attrition through enforcement, fall short insofar as they do not fully dismantle the harms created by the 1996 laws. It is not unreasonable for legalization programs to come with some qualifications. For example, a drug mule who is serving time in a U.S. prison should not be granted automatic legalization upon her release. However, she and other undocumented migrants should be given the opportunity to present the reasons against their deportation. Any legalization reform must be accompanied by a reform of the judicial system with the aim of granting due process to migrants.

Legalization for all would improve wages and working conditions for everyone, because unscrupulous employers would not be able to take advantage of the undocumented status of migrants. Legalization for all would make the United States safer by allowing all undocumented migrants to come out of the shadows and obtain proper documentation to work, to drive vehicles, and to participate in U.S. society. Legalization for all would allow U.S. citizens to remain with their families and not to feel threatened by the possibility of deportation. Legalization for all would take us a long way toward fulfilling the human rights of migrants in the United States.

However, legalization for all is not enough. Legalizing all undocumented migrants in the United States without reforming the entry policies and addressing the issues of due process highlighted in this book would be shortsighted. Even if all undocumented migrants in the United States were able to legalize today, ten years from now, we would find ourselves in the same situation with a new population of undocumented migrants. This is the unspoken truth that rarely makes its way into debates over legalization. For this reason, immigration reform must include a dramatic revision of entry policies.

Step 3: Align Migrant Entry Policies with the Reality of Globalization

In the human rights tradition, the right to leave one's country is recognized. However, the right to enter another country does not form part of existing human rights conventions and treaties. This leads many critics to argue that the right of mobility is a serious omission in human rights treaties. The right to emigrate is effectively useless if there is no country to which one can migrate (Pécoud and Paul de Guchteneire 2006). Joseph Nevins (2003) adds to this discussion the fact that, in a globalizing world rampant with economic inequality, the human rights to free choice of employment and to an adequate standard of living enshrined in the Universal Declaration of Human Rights (UDHR) are difficult to achieve without the ability to leave one's country of origin.

Throughout this book, I have invoked international human rights doctrines and explained how U.S. immigration policies violate these doctrines. Yet, I would contend that human rights doctrines do not go far enough insofar as these doctrines do not grant the right to mobility. Human rights tradition recognizes the right of states to determine who can and cannot enter their territories. However, there are no guidelines for determining how states should regulate entry into their countries. If human beings had the right to mobility, states would have to provide compelling reasons to deny anyone the right to enter their territories.

In most countries, it is much easier to transport goods across borders than it is for people to cross borders themselves. Under current U.S. law, it is exceedingly difficult for most people in the world to enter the United States. The vast majority of temporary-visa requests to enter the United States are denied, and it is virtually impossible for most people to obtain permanent visas that allow them to reside in the United States (Mau 2010). In contrast, it is much less difficult for goods to enter the country. A Chinese businessman, for example, may be able to send daily shipments of plastic toys for sale at Walmart yet could be unable himself to enter the United States. The current policies for entry into the United States for goods and people are diametrically opposed. Most goods can enter the United States unless there is a compelling reason for them *not* to enter. Most people, however, must have a compelling reason for them to enter, or they have no hope of ever coming to the United States. The fact that a toy was made in China makes it only marginally more difficult to sell in the United States than if it were made in Arkansas. In contrast, the accident of one's birth in China could make it impossible for a person to ever enter the United States.

If we take seriously the proposition that all human beings possess fundamental human dignity and are worthy of basic rights, it is hard to find an argument against allowing more people to migrate legally to the United States. As I mentioned, immigration restrictions will inevitably lead to an undocumented population that is marginalized and vulnerable. Moreover, there are many people whose human rights would only be fulfilled were they allowed to migrate to the United States. If the aforementioned Chinese businessman wanted to travel to the United States because his young children were U.S. citizens and lived in San Francisco, he would have to wait until they were twenty-one years of age and then would have to wait years after that for his visa to be approved. His right to be with his minor children is not recognized in U.S. immigration law. If he had no family ties in the United States, his chances of moving to the United States to attain an adequate standard of living would be practically null.

There is one convincing counter-argument to allowing higher numbers of immigrants to come to the United States: the claim that increased migration inhibits the ability of poor U.S. citizens to maintain an adequate standard of living. This argument, however, does not take into account the fact that it is not the mere presence of immigrants that pulls down wages. Instead, wages are low when unscrupulous employers take advantage of the vulnerable status of migrants. The appropriate response is not to shut the door on immigrants, but to first legalize immigrants and then to reform and more heavily enforce labor laws such that employers will not be able to pay less than living wages or to have workers in unsafe labor conditions.

As I have maintained, there is a clear case for reforming immigrant entry policies in the United States. Yet, the question of how open these policies should be is an imperative one. I would suggest one possibility would be to shift the burden of proof, such that states are required to provide reasons a person should not enter as opposed to the current situation whereby it is up to an individual to prove that he deserves to enter another country. This would be one way of incorporating the right to mobility into human rights doctrine. Can we imagine human rights doctrines saying, "States shall, except when compelling reasons of national security otherwise require, allow noncitizens to enter their territories"? What does the right to mobility mean? What would it actually look like? Crucially, does the right to mobility require open borders?

These questions remain unanswered for human rights scholars (Pécoud and Paul de Guchteneire 2006; Bauböck 2009). There certainly are many immigration scholars who argue for open borders, including, for example, Nandita Sharma, Kevin Johnson, Jonathan Moses, Jane Guskin and David Wilson. As Guskin and Wilson (2007) point out, open borders would save us billions of dollars in immigration law enforcement, increase tax revenues because all workers would pay payroll taxes, raise wages and improve work conditions because we would no longer have a disenfranchised workforce, and eliminate criminal activity associated with undocumented migration, such as identity theft and human trafficking.

It is now time for human rights scholars to take on these questions and to begin a conversation within the United Nations that explores the extent to which a right to mobility could be incorporated into human rights doctrine. In such a conversation, human rights scholars would do well to pay attention to what social scientists have to say about migration, especially that

1. People often migrate because of specific ties between their country of origin and their destination country.
2. Emigration affects sending communities because of the transnational ties it creates and the social and economic remittances migrants send.
3. Temporary migrants often become permanent in response to immigration controls.

4. The impacts of immigrants in receiving communities are often profound, and, frequently, positive.

A discussion of the right to mobility is an ethical and moral debate, but it also must be based on social scientific evidence of the inevitability and consequences of emigration and immigration to create effective policy.

Notes

Introduction

1. NewBedfordRelief. 2007. "New Bedford." YouTube video. http://www .youtube.com/comment_servlet?all_comments&v=a-8ke8gd60g&fromurl=/ watch%3Fv%3Da-8ke8gd60g. Accessed July 15, 2009.

2. In the United States District Court for the District of Arizona United States of America, Plaintiff, vs. State of Arizona; and Janice K. Brewer, Governor of the State of Arizona, in her Official Capacity, Defendants. No. CV 10-1413-PHX-SRB ORDER. http://graphics8.nytimes.com/packages/pdf/national/20100729_ARIZONA_DOC. pdf. Accessed October 20, 2010.

3. "Breaking the Piggy Bank: How Illegal Immigration Is Sending Schools into the Red." http://www.fairus.org/site/PageServer?pagename=research_researchf6ad. Accessed April 5, 2010.

4. ICE. December 1, 2003. "Changes to the NSEERS Program." http:// www.ice.gov/pi/news/factsheets/NSEERSFAQ120103.htm. Accessed February 15, 2010.

5. The Associated Press. 2007. "High Profile Raids Leave Immigrants Across U.S. Living in Fear." *International Herald Tribune.* Feb. 20, 2007. http://www.iht. com/articles/ap/2007/02/21/america/NA-GEN-U.S.-Immigration-Raids-Fear.php. Accessed March 20, 2007.

6. "Worksite Enforcement Overview." ICE. November 25, 2008. Online at http:// www.ice.gov/doclib/pi/news/factsheets/worksite.pdf. Accessed January 16, 2009.

7. DHS FY 08 Budget Priorities. http://www.dhs.gov/xabout/budget/ gc_1170797368531.shtm. Accessed January 16, 2009.

8. "Goal 1: Protect Our Nation from Dangerous People." http://www.dhs.gov/ xnews/testimony/gc_1170955059184.shtm.

9. The name Don Franco, as well as the names of all the other undocumented migrants, their family members, and deportees in this book, are pseudonyms, with the exception of those names derived from human rights reports and newspaper articles.

Chapter 1

1. Despite popular rhetoric that undocumented migrants are criminals, most undocumented migrants are not in violation of criminal statutes, and, if encountered by federal immigration enforcement agents, they are processed through civil immigration courts, not criminal courts. If found to be undocumented, migrants are not punished; they are deported. Deportation is a civil sanction, not a punishment.

2. http://www.dhs.gov/files/statistics/data/DSLPR03c.shtm and http://hdr .undp.org/en/reports/global/hdr2010/

3. "Country Data: Brazil." *The Economist.* http://www.economist.com/countries/ Brazil/profile.cfm?folder=Profile%2DEconomic%20Data. Accessed July 15, 2009.

4. "Segundo as Grandes Regiões, Unidades da Federação e Municípios—2002–2005; Tabela 1—Produto Interno Bruto a Preços Correntes e Produto Interno Bruto per Capita." Instituto Brasileiro de Geografia e Estatística. http://www.ibge.gov.br/home/estatistica/ economia/pibmunicipios/2005/tab01.pdf. Accessed July 15, 2009.

5. Ibid; Elena Zúñiga Herrera, 2004. "Tendencias y Características de la Migración Mexicana a los Estados Unidos." http://www.conapo.gob.mx/publicaciones/ migra2006_01/01.pdf. Accessed May 2007. Zúñiga Herrera provides another measure: there are 2,443 municipalities in Mexico, and in 2000, 96 percent of these municipalities sent migrants to the United States.

6. Statistical Report of Consejo Nacional de Población. "Población Nacida en México Residente en Estados Unidos por Entidad Federativa de Nacimiento, 1990, 2000 y 2003." http://www.conapo.gob.mx/mig_int/series/070103.xls. Accessed May 2007.

7. "Cato Handbook for Congress: 12. USA PATRIOT Act and Domestic Detention Policy." Robert Levy 2005. http://www.cato.org/pubs/handbook/hb108/ hb108-12.pdf. Accessed July 17, 2009.

8. Ibid.

9. "Who Is Boycotting Arizona?" http://www.azcentral.com/business/articles/ 2010/05/13/20100513immigration-boycotts-list.html. Accessed October 2, 2010.

10. American Immigration Lawyers Association. Case No.: CIV-10-1061-SRB 07/14/10. Brief of Amicus Curiae. http://www.aila .org/content/default .aspx?bc=9418|11708|32246. Accessed October 20, 2010.

11. In the United States District Court for the District of Arizona United States of America, Plaintiff, vs. State of Arizona; and Janice K. Brewer, Governor of the State of Arizona, in her Official Capacity, Defendants. No. CV 10-1413-PHX-SRB ORDER. http://graphics8.nytimes.com/packages/pdf/national/20100729_ARIZONA_DOC .pdf. Accessed October 20, 2010.

12. In fact, Rumbaut and Ewing (2009) note that noncitizens are much less likely to commit crimes than their native-born counterparts.

Chapter 2

1. "U.S. Urged to Apologize for 1930s Deportations." April 5, 2006. *USA TODAY*. Wendy Koch. http://www.usatoday.com/news/nation/2006-04-04-1930s-deportees-cover_x.htm. Accessed January 21, 2009.

2. Office of Immigration Statistics, Department of Homeland Security, Table 38. "Aliens Removed by Criminal Status and Region and Country of Nationality: Fiscal Years 2000 to 2009."

3. Evans, Becky. 2008. "In a Remote Guatemalan Village, Links to New Bedford Abound." *South Coast Today*. March 5. http://www.southcoasttoday.com/apps/pbcs.dll/article?AID=/20080306/NEWS/803060348/-1/special21. Accessed July 15, 2009.

4. Fieldnotes, April 24, 2008. Our Lady of Tepeyac Social Club. Chicago, Illinois.

5. "Worksite Enforcement Overview." April 30, 2009. Immigration and Customs Enforcement. http://www.ice.gov/pi/news/factsheets/worksite.htm. Accessed July15, 2009.

6. "Homeland Security: Budget in Brief. Fiscal Year 2005." Department of Homeland Security. http://www.dhs.gov/xlibrary/assets/FY_2005_BIB_4.pdf. Accessed July 15, 2009.

7. "Immigration and Naturalization Service Budget 1975–2003." Department of Justice. http://www.usdoj.gov/archive/jmd/1975_2002/2002/html/page104-108.htm. Accessed July 15, 2009.

8. "Immigration Enforcement Spending Since IRCA." 2005. Migration Policy Institute. http://www.migrationpolicy.org/ITFIAF/FactSheet_Spending.pdf. Accessed July 15, 2009.

9. "A Day to Remember." Shadowblogger YouTube Video. 2006. http://www.youtube.com/watch?v=QvRhhAQorPw. Accessed July 15, 2009.

10. Ibid.

11. "Swift Justice" 2007. LittleVoiceProd. http://www.youtube.com/watch?v=YXztFiLql48. Accessed July 15, 2009.

12. "Ice Raids—One Year Later: Interview with Helen Somersall of Catholic Charities Northern." December 12, 2007. Chris Casey. *The Tribune*. http://www.greeleytrib.com/article/20071212/NEWS/112120110. Accessed July 15, 2009.

13. "Federal Trade Commission 2006 ID Theft Report." 2007. Synovate. http://www.ftc.gov/os/2007/11/SynovateFinalReportIDTheft2006.pdf. Accessed July 15, 2009.

14. "Testimony of Women Detained by ICE." NewBedfordRelief. 2007. YouTube video. http://www.youtube.com/watch?v=qADLyZctfok&feature=related. Accessed July 15, 2009.

15. "Immigration Matters: The Anatomy of an Immigration Raid." New America Media, News Analysis, Mary Holper, Posted: May 21, 2007. http://news

.newamericamedia.org/news/view_article.html?article_id=f9a8d584602ed96b1602b 54ce054a550. Accessed July 15, 2009.

16. "New Bedford." NewBedfordRelief. 2007. YouTube video. http://www .youtube.com/watch?v=a-8ke8gd60g. Accessed July 15, 2009.

17. "Immigration Raid Rips Families: Illegal Workers in Massachusetts Separated from Children." Robin Shulman, Washington Post Staff Writer. March 18, 2007; Page A06. http://www.washingtonpost.com/wp-dyn/content/article/2007/03/17/ AR2007031701113.html. Accessed July 15, 2009.

18. "New Bedford Detainee Testimony." NewBedfordRelief. 2007. YouTube video. http://www.youtube.com/watch?v=2qG6FZbr9rM&feature=related. Accessed July 15, 2009.

19. "New Bedford." NewBedfordRelief. 2007. YouTube video. http://www .youtube.com/watch?v=a-8ke8gd60g. Accessed July 15, 2009.

20. "Timeline of the New Bedford Raid." 2007. *The Boston Globe.* http://www .boston.com/news/local/articles/2007/03/15/timeline_of_the_new_bedford_raid/. Accessed July 15, 2009.

21. "New Bedford Detainee Testimony." NewBefordRelief. 2007. YouTube video. http://www.youtube.com/watch?v=2qG6FZbr9rM&feature=related. Accessed July 15, 2009.

22. "Testimony of Woman Detained by ICE" NewBedfordRelief 2007. YouTube video. http://www.youtube.com/watch?v=qADLyZctfok Accessed 15 July 2009.

23. "Fight to Free Bianco Workers Dominates Mayan Ceremony." Becky Evans. Standard-Times staff writer. October 01, 2007. http://www.southcoasttoday.com/apps/ pbcs.dll/article? AID=/20071001/NEWS/710010333. Accessed July 15, 2009.

24. "A Year After Raid, Immigration Cases Drag On for Many." Maria Sacchetti. *Boston Globe.* March 6, 2008. http://www.boston.com/news/local/ articles/2008/03/06/a_year_after_raid_immigration_cases_drag_on_for_many/. Accessed July 15, 2009.

25. "Illegal Immigrant Father Reunited with Family." Becky Evans. *Standard-Times,* June 06, 2007. http://www.southcoasttoday.com/apps/pbcs.dll/ article?AID=/20070606/NEWS/706060363. Accessed July 15, 2009.

26. "A Year After Raid, Immigration Cases Drag On for Many." Maria Sacchetti. *Boston Globe.* March 6, 2008. http://www.boston.com/news/local/ articles/2008/03/06/a_year_after_raid_immigration_cases_drag_on_for_many/. Accessed July 16, 2009.

27. "ICE Raids Chicago Neighborhood—Again." World War IV Report. September 20, 2008. http://www.ww4report.com/node/6052. Accessed July 16, 2009.

28. Fieldnotes. April 24, 2008. Our Lady of Tepeyac Social Club. Chicago, Illinois.

29. "Operator of a Chicago 'Little Village' Photo Shop—Nuevo Foto Muñoz— Charged with Participating in Fraudulent Identification Document Conspiracy." U.S.

ICE May 30, 2007. http://www.ice.gov/pi/news/newsreleases/articles/070530chicago
.htm. Accessed March 3, 2010.

30.   "ID Bust: A Woman's Terror Fears Have Taken Down One of the Largest Fake
Document Rings in the U.S." Joe Contreras. *Newsweek*. February 29, 2008. http://
www.newsweek.com/id/117121. Accessed July 16, 2009.

31.   "Guatemalan Natives Talk About Postville Immigration Raid." GazetteOnline
May 14, 2008. http://www.youtube.com/watch?v=blIUTdU9IF8. Accessed July 16,
2009.

32.   Although Camayd-Freixas is an interpreter and not a lawyer or a social scientist,
his recounting is unique and important insofar as he had privileged access to the proceedings. Others, such as anthropologist Mark Grey and public health professor Michele
Devlin, recount that they were not able to gain access to the Waterloo Cattle Congress,
and thus also have to rely on Camayd-Freixas's account of the proceedings.

33.   Flores-Figueroa v. United States. Certiorari to the United States Court of Appeals for the Eighth Circuit No. 08–108. Argued February 25, 2009—Decided May 4,
2009. http://www.supremecourtus.gov/opinions/08pdf/08-108.pdf. Accessed March
11, 2010.

34.   "About the U.S. Detention and Deportation System." http://www
.detentionwatchnetwork.org/aboutdetention. Accessed March 23, 2009.

35.   "Alien Detention Standards: Telephone Access Problems Were Pervasive at
Detention Facilities; Other Deficiencies Did Not Show a Pattern of Noncompliance."
GAO. June 6, 2007. http://www.gao.gov/htext/d07875.html Accessed 16 July 2009
and "Immigrant Detention: Can ICE Meet Its Legal Imperative and Case Management
Responsibilities?" Donald Kerwin and Serena Yi-Ying Lin. September 2009. Migration
Policy Institute. http://www.migrationpolicy.org/pubs/detentionreportSept1009.pdf.
Accessed March 2010.

36.   October 4, 2007. Francisco Castaneda's testimony before Congress. http://
www.aclu.org/images/asset_upload_file841_32062.pdf and United States District Court
Central District of California Francisco Castaneda, Plaintiff, Case No. CV 07-07241
DDP (JCx) Amended Order Denying Motion to Dismiss. http://www.cacd.uscourts
.gov/CACD/RecentPubOp.nsf/bb61c530eab0911c882567cf005ac6f9/6d9b8d3d31
42d7be8825740b0053dbdc/$FILE/CV07-07241DDP.pdf. Accessed July 15, 2009.

37.   Ibid.

38.   "Detained and Deprived of Rights: Children in the Custody of the U.S. Immigration and Naturalization Service." Human Rights Watch. 1998. http://www.hrw
.org/reports98/ins2/. Accessed July 16, 2009.

39.   Ibid.

40.   Ibid.

41.   Ibid.

42.   "Locking Up Family Values: The Detention of Immigrant Families." 2007.
Women's Commission for Refugee Women and Children and Lutheran Immigration

and Refugee Service. http://www.womenscommission.org/pdf/famdeten.pdf. Accessed July 16, 2009.

43. "ICE Detention Reform: Principles and Next Steps: Secretary Napolitano Announces New Immigration Detention Reform Initiatives." DHS. October 9, 2009. http://www.docstoc.com/docs/12873022/ICE-detention-reform. Accessed March 11, 2010.

44. "Urge Release of Palestinian Salim Y." CLINIC. July 12, 2004. http://www.lifeorliberty.org/action_alerts/urge_release_of_palestinian_sa.html. Accessed July 17, 2009.

45. "Systemic Problems Persist in U.S. Ice Custody Reviews for "Indefinite" Detainees." 2005. Kathleen Glynn and Sarah Bronstein. CLINIC. http://idc.rfbf.com.au/wp-content/uploads/2009/06/clinicindefinitereportfinal.pdf. Accessed July 17, 2009; "Palestinian Children Living in Detention: Family in U.S. Illegally Can't Stay, Can't Go Home." January 31, 2007. Paul Meyer and Frank Trejo. *The Dallas Morning News.* http://www.dallasnews.com/sharedcontent/dws/news/localnews/stories/020107 dnmetpalfamily.3b835587.html. Accessed August 25, 2009.

46. Zadvydas v. Davis. http://supct.law.cornell.edu/supct/html/99-7791.ZO.html.

47. *Borjes-Brindis v. Gunja and Ashcroft.* U.S. Tenth Circuit Court of Appeals. May 26, 2004. http://ca10.washburnlaw.edu/cases/2004/05/03-1447.htm.

48. "§ 1226a. Mandatory detention of suspected terrorists; habeas corpus; judicial review." http://www.law.cornell.edu/uscode/8/usc_sec_08_00001226---a000-.html. Accessed May 11, 2011.

49. "Systemic Problems Persist in U.S. Ice Custody Reviews for "Indefinite" Detainees." 2005. Kathleen Glynn and Sarah Bronstein. CLINIC. http://idc.rfbf.com.au/wp-content/uploads/2009/06/clinicindefinitereportfinal.pdf. Accessed July 17, 2009.

50. "ICE's Compliance with Detention Limits for Aliens with a Final Order of Removal from the United States." Office of Inspector General. OIG-07-28. 2007. http://www.dhs.gov/xoig/assets/mgmtrpts/OIG_07-28_Feb07.pdf. Accessed July 17, 2009.

Chapter 3

1. DHS/OIS Table 37d: 2007.

2. DHS/OIS Table 38: Aliens Removed by Criminal Status and Region and Country of Nationality: Fiscal Years 2000 to 2009.

3. As mentioned above, although the War on Terror has had negative consequences for people from the Middle East and parts of Asia, the numbers of deportees from that region is relatively small. In FY 2009, 315 Pakistanis were deported, and 48 people from Yemen. DHS Table 38, FY 2009.

4. Because of the lack of diplomatic relations between the United States and Cuba, Cubans are rarely deported from the United States. The situation is similar for Vietnam.

5. "Profiling's Enabler: High Court Ruling Underpins Arizona Immigration Law." Gabriel J. Chin and Kevin R. Johnson. *Washington Post*. Tuesday, July 13, 2010. A15. http://www.washingtonpost.com/wp-dyn/content/article/2010/07/12/AR2010071204049.html. Accessed October 18, 2010.

6. "Understanding SB1070 from the Lens of Institutionalized Racism and Civil Rights." Bill Ong Hing. 2010. The Race Equity Project. http://www.equity.lsnc.net/understanding-sb1070-from-the-lens-of-institutionalized-racism-and-civil-rights/. Accessed April 3, 2011.

7. New York Times/CBS Poll from April 28 to May 2, 2010. http://documents.nytimes.com/new-york-timescbs-news-poll-immigration-overhaul?ref=us. Accessed April 3, 2011.

8. "Hispanics of Honduran Origin in the United States, 2007." Pew Hispanic Center. October 15, 2009. http://pewhispanic.org/files/factsheets/55.pdf. Accessed March 12, 2010.

9. "Delegation of Immigration Authority Section 287(g) Immigration and Nationality Act." ICE. August 18, 2008. http://www.ice.gov/partners/287g/Section287_g.htm. Accessed March 12, 2010.

10. Rytina, Nancy, and John Simanski. 2009. "Apprehensions by the U.S. Border Patrol: 2005–2008." June 2009. http://www.dhs.gov/xlibrary/assets/statistics/publications/ois_apprehensions_fs_2005-2008.pdf. Accessed March 24, 2010. And Table 35. Deportable Aliens Located by Program and Border Patrol Sector and Investigations Special Agent in Charge (Sac) Jurisdiction: Fiscal Years 1999 to 2008. 2008 OIS Statistics Yearbook. http://www.dhs.gov/xlibrary/assets/statistics/yearbook/2008/table35.xls. Accessed March 24, 2010.

11. OIS/DHS Table 2008.

12. ICE Annual Report FY 2008. http://www.ice.gov/doclib/pi/reports/ice_annual_report/pdf/ice08ar_final.pdf. Accessed October 18, 2010.

13. "House Report 110-181—Department of Homeland Security Appropriations Bill, 2008." http://ecip.loc.gov/cgi-bin/cpquery/?&sid=cp1101pqt3&refer=&r_n=hr181.110&db_id=110&item=&sel=TOC_126353&. Accessed October 20, 2010.

14. Gardner, Trevor, and Aarti Kohli. 2009. "The C.A.P. Effect: Racial Profiling in the ICE Criminal Alien Program." http://www.law.berkeley.edu/files/policybrief_irving_FINAL.pdf.

15. Ibid.

16. "Forced Apart: By the Numbers." April 2009 Human Rights Watch. http://www.hrw.org/en/reports/2009/04/15/forced-apart-numbers. Accessed March 23, 2010.

17. "What Has Been Learned from Self-Reports About Criminal Careers and

the Causes of Offending?" 2001 David P. Farrington, Ph.D. Institute of Criminology, University of Cambridge. http://www.homeoffice.gov.uk/rds/pdfs/farrington.pdf. Accessed July 17, 2009.

18. "Drug Use Trends" 2002. Executive Office of the President Office of National Drug Control Policy. http://www.whitehousedrugpolicy.gov/publications/factsht/druguse/drugusetrends.pdf. Accessed July 17, 2009.

19. "United States: Punishment and Prejudice: Racial Disparities in the War on Drugs." Human Rights Watch. May 2000 Vol. 12, No. 2. http://www.hrw.org/legacy/reports/2000/usa/. Accessed July 17, 2009.

20. "Racial Disparities in Imprisonment." 1998. Pamela Oliver. http://www.ssc.wisc.edu/~oliver/RACIAL/Reports/meparticledraft3.htm. Accessed July 20, 2009.

21. Thanks to Helen Marrow for providing me with this data.

22. I have included Cuba and Vietnam in these figures because of their high numbers among the foreign-born. However, due to the lack of diplomatic ties with these two countries, people are rarely deported to either.

23. "Drug Use Trends." 2002. Executive Office of the President Office of National Drug Control Policy. http://www.whitehousedrugpolicy.gov/publications/factsht/druguse/drugusetrends.pdf. Accessed July 17, 2009.

24. Department of Homeland Security Office of Inspector General. January 2009. "Removals Involving Illegal Alien Parents of United States Citizen Children" http://www.dhs.gov/xoig/assets/mgmtrpts/OIG_09-15_Jan09.pdf. Accessed March 24, 2010.

25. "Strangers in a Strange Land." *New York Times* video. Produced by Brent Renaud and Craig Renaud. March 20, 2011. http://video.nytimes.com/video/2011/03/20/world/americas/100000000733274/deportees.html. Accessed April 7, 2011.

Chapter 4

1. "State Felon Voting Laws" 2008. ProCon.org. http://felonvoting.procon.org/viewresource.asp?resourceID=286. Accessed July 17, 2009.

2. "Immigration: Adjustment to Permanent Resident Status Under Section 245(i)" CRS Report for Congress
Andorra Bruno. 2002. http://fpc.state.gov/documents/organization/10087.pdf. Accessed 17 July 2009.

3. Ibid.

4. Harzig, Christiane. 2003. "Immigration Policies: A Gendered Historical Comparison." In Mirjana Morokvasic-Müller, Umut Erel, Kyoko Shinozaki, eds., *Gender on the Move*. Vol. 1 in the ifu-series: Crossing Borders and Shifting Boundaries. Opladen: Leske und Budrich: 35–58. http://www.siyanda.org/docs/harzig_immigration.pdf.

5. Institute for Latino Studies: "Mexican Women in Chicago: A Report to the Secretaría de Desarrollo Social de México." Departamento de Estudios Internacionales—ITAM

& Institute for Latino Studies, University of Notre Dame. January 2005, pp.35. http://latinostudies.nd.edu/pubs/pubs/Sedesol.pdf. Accessed October 20, 2010.

Chapter 5

1. "Illegal Immigration: Border-Crossing Deaths Have Doubled Since 1995; Border Patrol's Efforts to Prevent Deaths Have Not Been Fully Evaluated. Government Accountability Office." 2006. http://www.gao.gov/new.items/d06770.pdf. Accessed August 25, 2009.

2. "Price of Admission: Along the Border, Sexual Assault Has Become Routine." Tim Vanderpool. *Tucson Weekly.* http://www.tucsonweekly.com/tucson/price-of-admission/Content?oid=1091501.

3. The reversal of the 100-to-1 sentencing disparity between crack and powder cocaine is one example of a policy that did change, in response to research and pressure. This change, however, took more than twenty years, despite abundant evidence that the logic behind the policy was flawed.

4. Bureau of Justice Prison Statistics. June 2008. http://www.ojp.usdoj.gov/bjs/prisons.htm. Accessed October 20, 2009.

5. This is partly related to the fact that it is impossible to incarcerate all nonviolent offenders. Most people who commit nonviolent crimes such as illegal drug use, petty theft, and forgery are never caught. Increasing the numbers of people who are caught and prosecuted thus has little effect on the rates of crime.

6. Introduction of S. 1038. Dianne Feinstein. Congressional Record. http://thomas.loc.gov/cgi-bin/query/F?rl11:l:./temp/~rl11DtvtZW:e24262. Accessed May 11, 2011.

7. "Blood, Sweat and Fear." http://www.hrw.org/reports/2005/usa0105/1.htm#_Toc88546710, page 1. Accessed September 1, 2010.

8. "CCA Released Q4 Lobbying Numbers." Private Prison Watch. http://private-prisonwatch.net/2010/03/26/cca-releases-q4-lobbying-numbers.aspx. Accessed April 6, 2010.

9. "Corrections Corporation of America Commences Construction of a New Prison and an Expansion of an Existing Prison." July 2, 2007. Press release. CCA Website. http://investor.shareholder.com/cxw/releasedetail.cfm?ReleaseID=252246. Accessed July 22, 2009.

10. CCA Quarterly Report to the SEC. August 4, 2008. http://apps.shareholder.com/sec/viewerContent.aspx?companyid=CXW&docid=6086086. Accessed July 22, 2009.

11. "Shackling Immigrants in Arpaio's America." *New York Times.* http://www.iht.com/articles/2009/02/06/opinion/edarpaio.1-424179.php. Accessed July 17, 2009.

12. "Chairman of the U.S. House Judiciary Committee Calls for Investigation of Arpaio." February 14, 2009. *Hispanic News.* http://hispanic.cc/chairman_of_the_u.s._house_judiciary_committee_calls_for_investigation_of_arpaio.htm. Accessed March 23, 2009.

Conclusion

1. Universal Declaration of Human Rights. Article 13. (2): "Everyone has the right to leave any country, including his own, and to return to his country."

2. The Inter-American Commission on Human Rights. Report No. 81/10. Publication. Case 12.562. Wayne Smith, Hugo Armendariz, et al. v. United States. Online at http://cejil.org/sites/default/files/Final%20Report_CIDH_Wayne_Smith.pdf.

3. Ibid.

4. United States District Court Central District of California Francisco Castaneda, Plaintiff, Case No. CV 07-07241 DDP (JCx). Amended Order Denying Motion to Dismiss. http://www.cacd.uscourts.gov/CACD/RecentPubOp.nsf/bb61c530eab0911c88 2567cf005ac6f9/6d9b8d3d3142d7be8825740b0053dbdc/$FILE/CV07-07241DDP .pdf.

5. http://www.nytimes.com/2010/04/09/opinion/09fri3.html.

BIBLIOGRAPHY

Acker, Alison. *Honduras: The Making of a Banana Republic.* Boston: South End Press, 1989.

ACLU. 2007. "Family Profiles in the ACLU's Challenge to the Hutto Detention Center." 3.6.07. http://www.aclu.org/immigrants-rights/family-profiles-aclus-challenge-hutto-detention-center. Accessed October 18, 2010.

Akers Chacón, Justin. "The War on Immigrants." Pp. 173–260 in *No One Is Illegal Fighting Racism and State Violence on the US-Mexico Border.* Edited by Justin Akers Chacón and Mike Davis. Chicago: Haymarket Books, 2006.

Aldana, Raquel. "Of Katz and 'Aliens': Privacy Expectations and the Immigration Raids." *UC Davis Law Review* 41 (2008): 1081–1136.

Alvarez, R. Michael, and Tara L. Butterfield. "The Resurgence of Nativism in California? The Case of Proposition 187 and Illegal Immigration." *Social Science Quarterly* 91, no.1 (2000): 167–179.

Andreas, Peter. *Border Games: Policing the U.S.-Mexico Divide.* Ithaca: Cornell University Press, 2000.

Anguiano Téllez, Maria Eugenia. "Detour Through the Sonora-Arizona Desert: New Routes of Mexican Emigration to the United States." *The Journal of Latino–Latin American Studies* 2, no. 4 (2007): 4–19.

Avila, José Luis, Carlos Fuentes, and Rodolfo Tuirán. "Tiempos de Estancia de los Trabajadores Temporales en los Estados Unidos: Situación Actual y Perspectivas." In La Situación Demográfica de México, 2000. Consejo Nacional de Población. Mexico. http://www.conapo.gob.mx/publicaciones/2000/pdf/13Migracion.pdf. Accessed May 2007.

Azmy, Baher, Bassina Farbenblum, Scott Michelman, R. Scott Thompson, Scott L. Walker, and Heather C. Bishop 2008. First Amended Complaint in Argueta et al. vs Meyers et al. http://law.shu.edu/ProgramsCenters/PublicIntGovServ/CSJ/upload/amended_complaint.pdf. Accessed October 18, 2010.

Bacon, David. *Children of Nafta.* Berkeley: University of California Press, 2004.

Bacon, David. "Justice Deported." *The American Prospect.* December 14, 2006. http://www.prospect.org/web/page.ww?section=root&name=ViewWeb&articleId=12297. Accessed October 10, 2008.

Bacon, David. "The Real Political Purpose of the ICE Raids." *New America Media*. March 30, 2007. http://news.newamericamedia.org/news/view_article .html?article_id= e5a3be40ba1f338650f2c0f793d11c3d. Accessed October 10, 2008.

Bacon, David. *Illegal People: How Globalization Creates Migration and Criminalizes Immigrants*. Boston: Beacon Press, 2008.

Balderrama, Francisco, and Raymond Rodríguez. *Decade of Betrayal: Mexican Repatriation in the 1930s (Second Edition)*. Albuquerque, NM: University of New Mexico Press, 2006.

Banco Central de Honduras. 2001. "La Actividad Maquiladora en Honduras 1998–2000." Tegucigalpa, Honduras. http://www.bch.hn/download/maquila/maquila-2000 .pdf. Accessed October 28, 2010.

Bankoff, Greg. "Regions of Risk: Western Discourses on Terrorism and the Significance of Islam." *Studies in Conflict & Terrorism* 26 (2003): 413–428.

Baubök, Rainer. "Global Justice, Freedom of Movement and Democratic Citizenship." *European Journal of Sociology/Archives Européennes de Sociologie* 50 (2009): 1–31.

Bean, Fran, B. Lindsay Lowell, and Lowell J. Taylor. "Undocumented Mexican Immigrants and the Earnings of Other Workers in the United States." *Demography* 25, no.1 (1988): 35–52.

Bean, Frank D, Edward E. Telles, and B. Lindsay Lowell. "Undocumented Migration to the United States: Perceptions and Evidence." *Population and Development Review* 13, no. 4 (1987): 671–690.

Beckett, Katherine, and Bruce Western. "Governing Social Marginality: Welfare, Incarceration and the Transformation of State Policy." *Punishment and Society* 3, no. 1 (2001): 43–59.

Berestein, Leslie. "Detention Dollars: Tougher Immigration Laws Turn the Ailing Private Prison Sector into a Revenue Maker." *San Diego Tribune*, May 4, 2008.

Bernstein, Nina. "Few Details on Immigrants Who Died in Custody." *New York Times*. May 5, 2008. http://www.nytimes.com/2008/05/05/nyregion/05detain.html. Accessed October 28, 2010.

Bhabha, Jacqueline. "The 'Mere Fortuity' of Birth? Are Children Citizens?" *Differences* 15 (2004): 91–117.

Biao, Xiang. "Emigration from China: A Sending Country Perspective." *International Migration* 41, no. 3 (2003): 21–48.

Birman, Dina, and Edison Trickett. "Cultural Transitions in First-Generation Immigrants: Acculturation of Soviet Jewish Refugee Adolescents and Parents." *Journal of Cross-Cultural Psychology* 32, no. 4 (2001): 456–477.

Blau, Judith, and Alberto Moncada. *Human Rights: Beyond the Liberal Vision*. Lanham, Maryland: Rowman and Littlefield, 2005.

Blau, Judith, and Albert Moncada. *Justice in the United States: Human Rights and the U.S. Constitution*. Lanham, Maryland: Rowman & Littlefield, 2006.

Bonilla-Silva, Eduardo. "From Bi-Racial to Tri-Racial: Towards a New System of Racial Stratification in the USA." *Ethnic and Racial Studies* 27, no. 6 (2004): 931–950.

Borjas, George. "Increasing the Supply of Labor through Immigration: Measuring the Impact on Native-Born Workers." *Center for Immigration Studies* 2004. http://www.cis.org/articles/2004/back504.pdf. Accessed October 28, 2010.

Boyd, Monica. "Oriental Immigration: The Experience of the Chinese, Japanese, and Filipino Populations in the United States." *International Migration Review* 5, no.1 (1971): 48–61.

Brands, H.W. "Decisions on American Armed Intervention: Lebanon, Dominican Republic, and Grenada." *Political Science Quarterly* 102, no. 4 (1987): 607–624.

Brewer, Rose M and Nancy Heitzeg. "The Racialization of Crime and Punishment: Criminal Justice, Color-Blind Racism, and the Political Economy of the Prison Industrial Complex." *American Behavioral Scientist* 51, no. 5 (2008): 625–644.

Buchanan, Pat. *State of Emergency.* New York: St Martin's Press, 2006.

Bybee, Roger, and Carolyn Winter. "Immigration Flood Unleashed by NAFTA's Disastrous Impact on Mexican Economy." *Common Dreams,* April 25, 2006. http://www.commondreams.org/views06/0425-30.htm. Accessed October 10, 2008.

Calavita, Kitty. "Contradictions of Immigration Lawmaking: The Immigration Reform and Control Act of 1986." *Law and Policy* 11, no. 1 (1989): 17–48.

Camarota, Steven. "The High Cost of Cheap Labor: Illegal Immigration and the Federal Budget." *Center for Immigration Studies,* 2004. http://www.cis.org/articles/2004/fiscal.pdf. Accessed October 28, 2010.

Camayd-Freixas, Erik. 2008. "Statement of Dr. Erik Camayd-Freixas, Federally Certified Interpreter at the US District Court for the Northern District of Iowa Regarding a Hearing on 'The Arrest, Prosecution, and Conviction of 297 Undocumented Workers in Postville, Iowa from May 12 to 22, 2008' before the Subcommittee on Immigration, Citizenship, Refugees, Border Security, and International Law." July 24, 2008.

Capps, Randy, Rosa Maria Castañeda, Ajay Chaudry, and Robert Santos. "Paying the Price: The Impact of Immigration Raids on America's Children." Report for the Urban Institute for the National Council of La Raza. 2007. http://www.urban.org/UploadedPDF/411566_immigration_raids.pdf. Accessed December 2, 2008.

Champlin, Dell, and Eric Hake. "Immigration as Industrial Strategy in American Meatpacking." *Review of Political Economy.* 18: 1: (2006): 49–70.

Chaudry, Ajay, Randy Capps, Juan Manuel Pedroza, Rosa Maria Castañeda, Robert Santos, and Molly M. Scott. "Facing Our Future: Children in the Aftermath of Immigration Enforcement." Report for the Urban Institute. April 7, 2010. http://carnegie.org/fileadmin/Media/Publications/facing_our_future.pdf. Accessed October 28, 2010.

Chavez, Linda. "The Realities of Immigration." *Commentary* July–August, 2006. http://www.commentarymagazine.com/viewarticle.cfm/the-realities-of-immigration-10094. Accessed October 10, 2008.

Chellaraj, Gnanaraj, Keith E.Maskus, and Aaditya Mattoo. "Skilled Immigrants, Higher

Education, and U.S. Innovation." In: *International Migration, Remittances, and the Brain Drain,* edited by: Caglar Ozden and Maurice Schiff. 245–260. New York: Palgrave MacMillan 2006. http://team.univ-paris1.fr/teamperso/DEA/Cursus/M1/internation%20migration%20remittances%20brain%20drain%20world%20bank.pdf#page=261. Accessed November 19, 2007.

Chermak, Steven M. "Body Count News: How Crime Is Presented in the News Media." *Justice Quarterly* 11, no. 4 (1994): 561–582.

Cheshier, Eric. "Corrections Corp of America (CXW) Is Out of Lock-Down." *Financial News.* 2008. http://thestockmasters.com/article-CXW-05072008.html. Accessed July 11, 2008.

Chiswick, Barry, and Michael Wenz. 2005. "The Linguistic and Economic Adjustment of Soviet Jewish Immigrants in the United States, 1980 to 2000" IZA DP No. 1726. Available online at ftp://repec.iza.org/RePEc/Discussionpaper/dp1238.pdf.

Chiswick, Barry. "Illegal Immigration and Immigration Control." *Journal of Economic Perspectives* 2, no. 3 (1988): 101–115.

Chiswick, Barry. "Soviet Jews in the United States: An Analysis of Their Linguistic and Economic Adjustment." *International Migration Review* 27, no. 2 (1993): 260–285.

Chiu, Bess, Lynly Egyes, Peter L. Markowitz, and Jaya Vasandani. 2009. Constitution on ICE: A Report on Immigration Home Raid Operations Cardozo Immigration Justice Clinic. http://www.cardozo.yu.edu/uploadedFiles/Cardozo/Profiles/immigrationlaw-741/IJC_ICE-Home-Raid-Report%20Updated.pdf. Accessed November 11, 2010.

Cobb, Stephen. "Defense Spending and Defense Voting in the House: An Empirical Study of an Aspect of the Military-Industrial Complex Thesis." *The American Journal of Sociology* 82, no. 1 (1976): 163–182.

Collier, Michael, and Eduardo Gamarra. "The Colombian Diaspora in South Florida." Presentation, Latin American Studies Association International Congress. Dallas, Texas. March 27–29, 2003.

Collins, Patricia Hill. *Black Sexual Politics.* New York: Routledge, 2004.

Colvin, Amanda. "Birthright Citizenship in the United States: Realities of De Facto Deportation and International Comparisons Toward Proposing a Solution." *Saint Louis University Law Journal* 53 (2008): 219–246.

Congressional Budget Office. "Cost Estimate: S. 2611: Comprehensive Immigration Reform Act of 2006." May 16, 2006. Available online at http://www.cbo.gov/ftpdocs/72xx/doc7208/s2611.pdf. Accessed April 3, 2011.

Congressional Research Services. "U.S. Immigration Policy on Asylum Seekers." Updated May 5, 2005. Ruth Ellen Wasem. http://www.fas.org/sgp/crs/misc/RL32621.pdf. Accessed April 2, 2011.

Cook, Melissa. "Banished for Minor Crimes: The Aggravated Felony Provision of the Immigration and Nationality Act as a Human Rights Violation." *Boston College Third World*

Law Journal 23, no. 2 (2003): 213–274. http://www.bc.edu/dam/files/schools/law/lawreviews/journals/bctwj/23_2/03_TXT.htm. Accessed November 12, 2010.

Cornelius, Wayne, and Marc. R. Rosenblum. "Immigration and Politics." *Annual Review of Political Science* 8 (2005): 99–119.

Cornelius, Wayne. "Controlling 'Unwanted' Immigration: Lessons from the United States, 1993–2004." *Journal of Ethnic and Migration Studies* 31, no. 4 (2005). http://www.cri.uci.edu/pdf/JEMS—final.pdf. Accessed November 12, 2010.

Cornelius, Wayne. "Impacts of Border Enforcement on Unauthorized Mexican Migration to the United States." *Border Battles*. Published on September 26, 2006. http://borderbattles.ssrc.org/Cornelius/. Accessed April 3, 2011.

Coutin, Susan Bibler. "'Differences' within Accounts of U.S. Immigration Law." *PoLAR: Political and Legal Anthropology Review* 19, no. 1 (1996): 11–20.

Coutin, Susan Bibler. "Questionable Transactions as Grounds for Legalization: Immigration, Illegality and the Law." *Crime, Law and Social Change* 37 (2002): 19–36.

Cuamea Velázquez, Felipe. "Approaches to the Study of International Migration: A Review." *Estudios Fronterizos* 1, no. 1 (2000): 137–168.

Danticat, Edwidge. *Brother, I'm Dying*. New York: Alfred A. Knopf, 2007.

Davis, Angela. "Masked Racism: Reflections on the Prison Industrial Complex." *Colorlines* 2, 1998. http://www.colorlines.com/article.php?ID=309&p=1. Accessed October 10, 2008.

Davis, Mike. "Hell Factories in the Field: A Prison-Industrial Complex." *Radical Urban Theory*, 1995. http://www.radicalurbantheory.com/mdavis/hellfactories.html. Accessed July 11, 2008.

de Genova, Nicholas. *Working the Boundaries: Race, Space, and "Illegality" in Mexican Chicago*. Durham, North Carolina: Duke University Press, 2005.

Diamond, Sara. "Right-Wing Politics and the Anti-Immigration Cause" *Social Justice*. 23, no. 3 (1996): 154–169.

Díaz-Cotto, Juanita. "Latinas and the War on Drugs in the United States, Latin America, and Europe." In *Global Lockdown: Race Gender and the Prison-Industrial Complex*. Edited by Julia Sudbury, Pp. 137–153, New York: Routledge, 2005.

Do Valle, Alice, Vanessa Huang, and Mari Spira. "The Prison Industrial Complex: A Deliberation." *International Feminist Journal of Politics* 8, no. 1 (2006): 130–144.

Donato, Katharine, Jorge Durand, and Douglas S. Massey. "Stemming the Tide?: Assessing the Deterrent Effects of the Immigration Reform and Control Act." *Demography* 29, no. 2 (1992): 139–157.

Dougherty, Mary, Denise Wilson, and Amy Wu. 2006. "Immigration Enforcement Actions: 2005." *Department of Homeland Security, Office of Immigration Statistics*. http://www.dhs.gov/xlibrary/assets/statistics/yearbook/2005/Enforcement_AR_05.pdf. Accessed November 12, 2010.

Dow, Mark. *American Gulag*. Berkeley: University of California Press, 2004.

Dunn, Timothy. "Border Militarization via Drug and Immigration Enforcement: Human Rights Implications." *Social Justice* 28, no. 2 (2001): 7–30.

Dyer, Joel. "Meatpacking Industry Has a Long History of Reliance on Immigrant Labor." *The Fort Collins Weekly,* 2006. http://www.greeleytribune.com/article/20061226/ NEWS/112230087. Accessed April 6, 2010.

Eckstein, Susan, and Lorena Barberia. "Grounding Immigrant Generations in History: Cuban Americans and Their Transnational Ties." *International Migration Review* (2002) 36, no. 3: 799–837.

Eisenhower, Dwight. "Eisenhower's Farewell Address to the Nation." January 17, 1961. http://www.informationclearinghouse.info/article5407.htm. Accessed October 10, 2008.

Emiliano del Toro, Guillermo. "Foreign Direct Investment in Mexico and the 1994 Crisis: A Legal Perspective." *Houston Journal of International Law* 20 (1997). Online at http://findarticles.com/p/articles/mi_hb3094/is_n1_20/ai_n28695475/. Accessed November 12, 2010.

Escobar, Cristina. "Dual Citizenship and Political Participation: Migrants in the Interplay of United States and Colombian Politics." *Latino Studies* 2, no.1 (2004): 45–69.

Evans, Becky. "In a Remote Guatemalan Village, Links to New Bedford Abound." *South Coast Today,* Bedford, Massachusetts. March 5, 2008. http://www.southcoasttoday .com/apps/pbcs.dll/article?AID=/20080306/NEWS/803060348/-1/special21. Accessed July 11, 2008.

Feagin, Joe. *Racist America.* New York: Routledge, 2000.

Fernandes, Deepa. *Targeted: Homeland Security and the Business of Immigration.* New York: Seven Stories Press, 2006.

Fix, Michael, and Wendy Zimmermann. "All Under One Roof: Mixed-Status Families in an Era of Reform." *International Migration Review* 35, no. 2 (2001): 397–419.

FONAMIH. 2005. "Honduras 2005: Ejes de un Proceso Migratorio Nacional." http://aci -erp.hn/doct/Fonamih/Ejes_Proceso_Migratorio.pdf. Accessed November 12, 2010.

Fragomen, Austin T., and Steven Bell. "Entry of Aliens to the United States: The Basic Structure" in *Immigration Fundamentals: A Guide to Law and Practice.* New York: Practicing Law Institute. 2007.

Fragomen, Austin. T. "The Illegal Immigration Reform and Immigrant Responsibility Act of 1996: An Overview." *International Migration Review* 31, no. 2 (1997): 438–460.

Frelick, Bill. "US Detention of Asylum Seekers and Human Rights." *Migration Policy Institute.* March, 2005. http://www.migrationinformation.org/Feature/display. cfm?ID=296. Accessed April 6, 2010.

Fukuyama, Francis. "Identity Crisis: Why We Shouldn't Worry About Mexican Immigration." *Slate Friday.* June 4, 2004.

Fusco, Wilson. 2005. "A Formação de Comunidades-Filhas No Fluxo de Brasileiros Para os Estados Unidos." *São Paulo Perspectives* 19, no. 3 (2005): 55–63. http://www

.scielo.br/scielo.php?script=sci_arttext&pid=S0102-88392005000300005&lng=pt. Accessed February 6, 2008.

Gabriel, Jackie. "Organizing the Jungle: Industrial Restructuring and Immigrant Unionization in the American Meatpacking Industry." *Working USA* 9: 3: (2006) 337–359.

García, María Cristina. *Seeking Refuge: Central American Migration to Mexico, the United States and Canada.* Berkeley: University of California Press, 2006.

Garrison, Vivian, and Carol Weiss. "Dominican Family Networks and United States Immigration Policy: A Case Study." *International Migration Review* 13, no. 2 (1979): 264–283.

Gfroerer, Joseph C., and Lucilla L. Tan. "Substance Use Among Foreign-Born Youths in the United States: Does the Length of Residence Matter?" *American Journal of Public Health* 93, no. 11 (2003): 1892–1895.

Gilmore, Ruth. *Golden Gulag: Prisons, Surplus, Crisis and Opposition in Globalizing California.* Berkeley: University of California Press, 2007.

Golash-Boza, Tanya, and Douglas Parker. "Human Rights in a Globalizing World: Who Pays the Human Cost of Migration?" *The Journal of Latino-Latin American Studies* 2, no. 4 (2007): 34–46.

Gonzales, Juan. "Asian Indian Immigration Patterns: The Origins of the Sikh Community in California." *International Migration Review* 20, no.1 (1986): 40–54.

Goodman, Amy. 2010. "Earthquake Frees Haitian Prisoners from Port-au-Prince Jail, 80% Never Charged with a Crime." Democracy Now, January 21. http://www .democracynow.org/2010/1/21/earthquake_frees_haitian_prisoners_from_port. Accessed May 26, 2011.

Gordon, Charles, Stanley Mailman, and Stephen Yale-Loehr. 2008. *Immigration Law and Procedure*: Section 71.01. Matthew Bender Company: New York.

Gouveia, Lourdes, and Donald Stull. "Latino Immigrants, Meatpacking, and Rural Communities: A Case Study of Lexington, Nebraska." JSRI Research Report #26, 1997. The Julian Samora Research Institute, Michigan State University, East Lansing, Michigan.

Goza, Franklin. "Brazilian Immigration to North America." *International Migration Review* 28, no. 1 (1994): 136–152.

Gregory, Steven. *The Devil Behind the Mirror: Globalization and Politics in the Dominican Republic.* Berkeley: University of California Press, 2007.

Grey, Mark, Michele Devlin, and Aaron Goldsmith. *Postville U.S.A.: Surviving Diversity in Small Town America.* Boston: Gemmamedia, 2009.

Guarnizo, Luis Eduardo, and Luz Marina Díaz. "Transnational Migration: A View from Colombia." *Ethnic and Racial Studies* 22, no. 2 (1999): 397–421.

Guerette, Rob. "Immigration Policy, Border Security, and Migrant Deaths: An Impact Evaluation Under the Border Safety Initiative." *Criminology & Public Policy* 6, no. 2 (2007): 245–266.

Gupta, Vanita, and Lisa Graybill. "Justice Denied: Immigrant Families Detained at Hutto" in *Human Rights Begins at Home* ed. ACLU 23–28. 2008. http://www.udhr60.org/justice_denied.pdf. Accessed April 6, 2010.

Guskin, Jane, and David Wilson. *The Politics of Immigration: Questions and Answers.* New York: St. Martin's Press, 2007.

Haines, David, Dorothy Rutherford, and Patrick Thomas. "Family and Community among Vietnamese Refugees." *International Migration Review* 15, no. 1/2 (1981): 310–319.

Hamilton, Nora, and Norma Stoltz Chinchilla. "Central American Migration: A Framework for Analysis." *Latin American Research Review* 26, no. 1 (1991): 75–110.

Hanson, Gordon. 2007. "The Economic Logic of Illegal Immigration," in: The Bernard and Irene Schwartz Series on American Competitiveness Council Special Report No. 26. Council on Foreign Relations. http://www.cfr.org/content/publications/attachments/ImmigrationCSR26.pdf. Accessed November 12, 2010.

Hattery, Angela, and Earl Smith. "The Prison Industrial Complex." *Sociation Today* 4, no. 2 (2006). http://www.ncsociology.org/sociationtoday/v42/prison.htm. Accessed October 10, 2008.

Hernández, Ramona. "On the Age Against the Poor: Dominican Migration to the United States." *Journal of Immigrant & Refugee Services* 2, no. 1/2 (2004): 87–107.

Higham, Scott, and Robert O'Harrow. "Contracting Rush for Security Led to Waste, Abuse." *The Washington Post,* May 22, 2005: A01.

Hines, Barbara. "An Overview of US Immigration Law and Policy Since 9/11." *Texas Hispanic Journal of Law & Policy* 12 (2006): 9–28.

Hing, Bill Ong. "Misusing Immigration Policies in the Name of Homeland Security." *The New Centennial Review* 6, no. 1 (2006): 195–224.

Hinojosa-Ojeda, Raúl. "Raising the Floor for American Workers: The Economic Benefits of Comprehensive Immigration Reform" Center for American Progress, 2010. http://www.americanprogress.org/issues/2010/01/pdf/immigrationeconreport.pdf.Accessed April 4, 2011.

Holper, Mary. "Immigration Matters: The Anatomy of an Immigration Raid." *New American Media,* May 21, 2007. http://news.newamericamedia.org/news/view_article.html?article_id=f9a8d584602ed96b1602b54ce054a550. Accessed July 11, 2008.

Hsu, Spencer. "Immigration Raid Jars a Small Town: Critics Say Employers Should Be Targeted." *Washington Post Sunday.* May 18, 2008. http://www.washingtonpost.com/wp-dyn/content/article/2008/05/17/AR2008051702474.html. Accessed April 6, 2010.

Human Rights First. 2009. U.S. Detention of Asylum Seekers: Seeking Protection, Finding Prison. http://www.humanrightsfirst.org/wp-content/uploads/pdf/090429-RP-hrf-asylum-detention-report.pdf. Accessed April 3, 2011.

Human Rights Watch. 2007. Forced Apart. http://www.hrw.org/reports/2007/us0707/. Accessed April 6, 2010.

Human Rights Watch. 2009. Forced Apart (By the Numbers): Non-Citizens Deported Mostly for Non-Violent Offenses. Online at www.hrw.org/node/82173. Accessed April 6, 2010.

Huntington, Samuel. "Reconsidering Immigration." *Center for Immigration Studies*. November 2000. http://www.cis.org/articles/2000/back1100.html. Accessed October 9, 2008.

Huntington, Samuel. *Who Are We? The Challenges to American National Identity*. New York: Simon and Schuster, 2004.

Immigration and Customs Enforcement 2008a. "Fact Sheet: Frequently Asked Questions About Worksite Enforcement." 2008. http://www.ice.gov/pi/news/factsheets/worksite.htm. Accessed July 11, 2008.

Immigration and Customs Enforcement 2008b. "ICE Fiscal Year 2007 Annual Report." http://www.ice.gov/doclib/about/ice07ar_final.pdf. Accessed July 11, 2008.

Immigration and Customs Enforcement 2008c. "ICE Fiscal Year 2008 Annual Report." http://www.ice.gov/doclib/pi/reports/ice_annual_report/pdf/ice08ar_final.pdf. Accessed April 6, 2010.

Inda, Johnathan. *Targeting Immigrants: Government, Technology and Ethics*. Oxford: Blackwell Publishing, 2006.

International Federation for Human Rights. "Mexico: The North American Free Trade Agreement (NAFTA): Effects on Human Rights." No. 448, Volume 2. April 2006. http://www.fidh.org/IMG/pdf/Mexique448-ang2006.pdf. Accessed October 10, 2008.

Jackson, John. *The Globalizers: Development Workers in Action*. Baltimore: Johns Hopkins University Press, 2006.

Jacobson, Robin Dale. *The New Nativism: Proposition 187 and the Debate Over Immigration*. Minneapolis: University of Minnesota Press, 2008.

Jenson, Jane. 2001. "Building Citizenship: Governance and Service Provision in Canada." In *Building Citizenship: Governance and Service Provision in Canada*. CPRN Discussion Paper No. F/17. pp. 1–22. http://www.eric.ed.gov/ERICWebPortal/contentdelivery/servlet/ERICServlet?accno=ED476344. Accessed November 12, 2010.

Johnson, Kevin. *The 'Huddled Masses' Myth: Immigration and Civil Rights*. Philadelphia: Temple University Press, 2004.

Johnson, Kevin. *Opening the Floodgates: Why America Needs to Rethink Its Borders and Immigration Laws*. New York: New York University Press, 2009.

Johnson, Kevin. "The Forgotten "Repatriation" of Persons of Mexican Ancestry and Lessons for the 'War on Terror.'" *Pace Law Review* Paper 39 (2005). http://digitalcommons.pace.edu/lawrev/39.

Jones, Richard C. "Causes of Salvadoran Migration to the United States." *The Geographical Review* 79 (1989): 183–194.

Joppke, Christian. "Why Liberal States Accept Unwanted Immigration." *World Politics* 50, no. 2 (1998): 266–293.

Kanstroom, Daniel. "Deportation, Social Control, and Punishment: Some Thoughts About Why Hard Laws Make Bad Cases." *Harvard Law Review* 113 (2000): 1890–1935.

Keely, Charles. "Effects of the Immigration Act of 1965 on Selected Population Characteristics of Immigrants to the United States." *Demography* 8, no. 2 (1971): 157–169.

Kelly, Gail P. "Coping with America: Refugees from Vietnam, Cambodia, and Laos in the 1970s and 1980s." *Annals of the American Academy of Political and Social Science* 487 (1986): 138–149.

Kerwin, Donald, and Serena Yi-Ying Lin. "Immigrant Detention: Can ICE Meet Its Legal Imperatives and Case Management Responsibilities?" Migration Policy Institute. 2009. http://www.migrationpolicy.org/pubs/detentionreportSept1009.pdf. Accessed November 12, 2010.

Khadria, Binod. "India: Skilled Migration to Developed Countries, Labour Migration to the Gulf." *Migración y Desarrollo* 2, no. 7 (2006): 4–37.

King, Ryan, Marc Mauer, and Malcolm C. Young. "Incarceration and Crime: A Complex Relationship." *The Sentencing Project.* 2005. http://www.sentencingproject.org/Admin/Documents/publications/inc_iandc_complex.pdf. Accessed October 8, 2008.

Koerner, Brendan I. "The Security Traders." *Mother Jones.* September/October 2002.

Koulish, Robert. "Privatizing the Leviathan Immigration State." *Monthly Review Zine.* July 20, 2007. http://mrzine.monthlyreview.org/koulish200707.html. Accessed October 10, 2008.

Krikorian, Mark. *The New Case Against Immigration: Both Legal and Illegal.* New York: Sentinel, 2008.

Liang, Zai, and Hideki Morooka. "Recent Trends of Emigration from China: 1982–2000." *International Migration* 42, no. 3 (2004): 145–164.

Liu, John M., Paul M. Ong, and Carolyn Rosenstein. "Dual Chain Migration: Post-1965 Filipino Immigration to the United States." *International Migration Review* xxv, no. 3 (1991): 487–513.

López, Ann Aurelia. *The Farmworkers' Journey.* Berkeley: University of California Press, 2007.

Lopez, Mark Hugo, and Susan Minushkin. 2008 National Survey of Latinos: Hispanics See Their Situation in US Deteriorating; Oppose Key Immigration Enforcement Measures. Washington, DC: Pew Hispanic Center, September 2008.

Lynch, Michael. "Beating a Dead Horse: Is There Any Basic Empirical Evidence for the Deterrent Effect of Imprisonment?" *Crime, Law and Social Change* 31 (1999): 347–362.

Madhavan, M.C. "Indian Emigrants: Numbers, Characteristics, and Economic Impact." *Population and Development Review* 11, no. 3 (1985): 457–481.

ManTech. "Board of Directors." 2008. http://www.mantech.com/about/board.asp. Accessed July 11, 2008.

Marcella, Gabriel. "The United States and Colombia: The Journey from Ambiguity to Strategic Clarity." Strategic Studies Institute Report, US Army War College. 2003. http://www.strategicstudiesinstitute.army.mil/pdffiles/pub10.pdf. November 12, 2010.

Marshall, T. H. *Citizenship and Social Class.* Cambridge: Cambridge University Press, 1950.

Massey, Douglas, Jorge Durand, and Nolan J. Malone. *Beyond Smoke and Mirrors: Mexican Immigration in an Era of Economic Integration.* New York: Russell Sage Foundation, 2002.

Massey, Douglas. "Economic Development and International Migration in Comparative Perspective." *Population and Development Review* 14, no. 3 (1988): 383–413.

Massey, Douglas. "International Migration at the Dawn of the Twenty-First Century: The Role of the State." *Population and Development Review* 25, no. 2 (1999): 303–322.

Master, Maureen. "Due Process for All: Redressing Inequities in the Criminal Provisions of the 1996 Immigration Laws." United States Conference for Catholic Bishops. 2003. http://www.usccb.org/mrs/dueprocessforall.shtml. Accessed October 23, 2008.

Mattera, Philip, Mafruza Khan, and Stephen Nathan. "Corrections Corporation of America: A Critical Look at Its First Twenty Years." *Grassroots Leadership Report.* 2003. http://www.soros.org/initiatives/justice/articles_publications/publications/cca_20_years_20031201/CCA_Report.pdf. Accessed November 12, 2010.

Mau, Steffen. "Mobility Citizenship, Inequality, and the Liberal State: The Case of Visa Policies." *International Political Sociology* 4, no. 4 (2010): 339–361.

Mauer, Marc. "The Causes and Consequences of Prison Growth in the United States." *Punishment and Society* 3, 1 (2001): 9–20.

Mendelberg, Tali. "Executing Hortons: Racial Crime in the 1988 Presidential Campaign." *Public Opinion Quarterly* 61 (1997): 134–157.

Mendelson, Margot, Shayna Strom, and Michael Wishnie. 2009. "Collateral Damage: An Examination of ICE's Fugitive Operations Program." Migration Policy Institute. http://www.migrationpolicy.org/pubs/NFOP_Feb09.pdf. Accessed April 6, 2010.

Menjívar, Cecilia. "Liminal Legality: Salvadoran and Guatemalan Immigrants' Lives in the United States." *American Journal of Sociology* 111, no. 4 (2006): 999–1037.

Menjívar, Cecilia. "Men's Migration and Women's Lives: Views from Rural Armenia and Guatemala." *Social Science Quarterly* 88, no. 5 (2007): 1243–1262.

Migration Policy Institute Migration Information Source. "Family Unity: The New Geography of Family Life," by Kate Jastram, May 1, 2003. http://www.migrationinformation.org/Feature/display.cfm?ID=118. November 12, 2010.

Mills, Mark. "On My Mind: The Security-Industrial Complex." *Forbes.* November 29, 2004.

Min, Byung S. "Trade and Foreign Direct Investment Patterns in the Republic of Korea in the Aftermath of the 1997 Asian Financial Crisis." *Asia-Pacific Trade and Investment Review* 2, no. 1 (2006): 3–24.

Min, Pyong Gap. "Korean Immigrants in Los Angeles." *Institute for Social Science Research.* Working Papers, Los Angeles, California 1990.

Morawetz, Nancy. "Understanding the Impact of the 1996 Deportation Laws and the Limited Scope of Proposed Reforms." *Harvard Law Review* 113, 8 (2000): 1936–1962.

Morrison, Thomas. "The Relationship of U.S. Aid, Trade and Investment to Migration Pressures in Major Sending Countries." *International Migration Review* 16, no. 1 (1982): 4–26.

Moses, Johnathan. *International Migration: Globalization's Last Frontier.* London: Zed Books, 2006.

Moskos, Charles C. "The Concept of the Military-Industrial Complex: Radical Critique or Liberal Bogey?" *Social Problems* 21, no. 4 (1972): 498–512.

National Network for Immigrant and Refugee Rights. "Rights of Immigrants in and Migrants to the United States." Submitted by the National Network for Immigrant and Refugee Rights to the United Nations. 2008. http://www2.ohchr.org/english/bodies/cerd/docs/ngos/usa/USHRN3.doc. Accessed July 11, 2008.

Nevins, Joseph. "Thinking Out of Bounds: A Critical Analysis of Academic and Human Rights Writings on Migrant Deaths in the U.S.-Mexico Border Region." *Migraciones Internacionales* 2: 2 (2003): 171–190.

Ngai, Mae M. "The Strange Career of the Illegal Alien: Immigration Restriction and Deportation Policy in the United States, 1921–1965." *Law and History Review* 21, no. 1 (2003): 69–107.

Ngai, Mae. *Impossible Subjects: Illegal Aliens and the Making of Modern America.* Princeton: Princeton University Press, 2004.

Nguyen, Ngoc Anh, and Thang Nguyen. 2007. "Foreign Direct Investment in Vietnam: An Overview and Analysis of the Determinants of Spatial Distribution Across Provinces." MPRA Paper No. 1921. http://mpra.ub.uni-muenchen.de/1921. Accessed November 12, 2010.

Office of Inspector General, Department of Homeland Security. "Detention and Removal of Illegal Aliens. US Immigration and Customs Enforcement. April 14, 2006. http://trac.syr.edu/immigration/library/P737.pdf. Accessed November 12, 2010.

Office of Inspector General, Department of Homeland Security. "Removals Involving Illegal Alien Parents of United States Citizen Children." 2009. http://www.dhs.gov/xoig/assets/mgmtrpts/OIG_09-15_Jan09.pdf. Accessed November 12, 2010.

Office of Inspector General, Department of Homeland Security. "Treatment of Immigration Detainees at Immigration and Customs Enforcement Facilities." December 2006. http://www.dhs.gov/xoig/assets/mgmtrpts/OIG_07-01_Dec06.pdf. Accessed November 12, 2010.

Office of the Press Secretary 2007. "Interview of the President by Steve Scully, C-Span."

http://www.c-span.org/executive/gwbushinterview.asp. Accessed November 12, 2010.

O'Harrow, Robert, and Scott Higham. "US Border Security at a Crossroads: Technology Problems Limit Effectiveness of a US-VISIT Program to Screen Foreigners." *The Washington Post.* May 23, 2005: A01.

Oliver, Melvin, and Thomas Shapiro. *Black Wealth / White Wealth* 2006. Oxford University Press: New York.

Pakulski, J. "Cultural Citizenship." *Citizenship Studies* 1, no. 1 (1997): 73–86.

Passel, Jeffrey. "The Size and Characteristics of the Unauthorized Migrant Population in the US Estimates Based on the March 2005 Current Population Survey." Pew Hispanic Center. 2006. http://pewhispanic.org/files/execsum/61.pdf. Accessed October 10, 2008.

Patel, Sunita, and Tom Jawetz. 2007. "Conditions of Confinement in Immigration Detention Facilities." Briefing Materials. http://www.aclu.org/pdfs/prison/unsr_briefing_materials.pdf. Accessed October 10, 2008.

Patterson, Wayne. *The Korean Frontier in America: Immigration to Hawaii, 1896–1910.* Honolulu: University of Hawaii Press, 1988.

Pécoud, Antoine, and Paul de Guchteneire. "International Migration, Border Controls, and Human Rights: Assessing the Relevance of a Right to Mobility." *Journal of Borderlands Studies* 21: 1 (2006): 69–86.

Perez, Louis. *Cuba and the United States: Ties of Singular Intimacy, Third Edition.* Athens and London: University of Georgia Press, 2003.

Peterson, Cassie L. "An Iowa Immigration Raid Leads to Unprecedented Criminal Consequences: Why ICE Should Rethink the Postville Model." *Iowa Law Review* 95, no. 1 (2009): 323–346.

Pettit, Becky, and Bruce Western. "Mass Imprisonment and the Life Course: Race and Class Inequality in U.S. Incarceration." *American Sociological Review* 69 (2004): 151–169.

Pew Hispanic Center. "The Size and Characteristics of the Unauthorized Migrant Population in the U.S. Estimates Based on the March 2005 Current Population Survey." Pew Hispanic Center. 2006a. http://pewhispanic.org/files/reports/61.pdf. Accessed April 1, 2011.

Pew Hispanic Center. "Cubans in the United States." 2006b. http://pewhispanic.org/files/factsheets/23.pdf. Accessed October 8, 2008.

Pew Hispanic Center. "2007 National Survey of Latinos: As Illegal Immigration Issue Heats Up, Hispanics Feel a Chill." Washington, DC, December 2007. http://pewhispanic.org/reports/report.php?ReportID=84. Accessed April 1, 2011.

Priest, Dana, and Amy Goldstein. "System of Neglect: As Tighter Immigration Policies Strain Federal Agencies, The Detainees in Their Care Often Pay a Heavy Cost." *Washington Post.* Page A1; May 11, 2008. http://www.washingtonpost.com/wp-srv/nation/specials/immigration/cwc_d1p1.html. Accessed April 2, 2011.

Quan, Adan. "Through the Looking Glass: US Aid to El Salvador and the Politics of National Identity." *American Ethnologist* 32, no. 2 (2003): 276–293.

Reimers, David M. "Post-World War II Immigration to the United States: America's Latest Newcomers." *The ANNALS of the American Academy of Political and Social Science* 454, no. 1 (1981): 1–12.

Repak, Terry A. "Labor Recruitment and the Lure of the Capital: Central American Migrants in Washington, DC." *Gender and Society* 8, no. 4 (1994): 507–524.

Richardson, Diane. "Sexuality and Citizenship." *Sociology* 32, no. 1 (1998): 83–100.

Richie, Beth. "Queering Anti-Prison Work: African American Lesbians in the Juvenile Justice System." In *Global Lockdown: Race Gender and the Prison-Industrial Complex.* Edited by Julia Sudbury. New York: Routledge, 2005.

Ricketts, Erol. "US Investment and Immigration from the Caribbean." *Social Problems* 34, no. 4 (1987): 374–387.

Robbins, Ted. "America's Toughest Sheriff Takes on Immigration." Narrated by Ted Robbins. Morning Edition. National Public Radio. March 10, 2008. http://www.npr.org/templates/story/story.php?storyId=88002493. Accessed April 3, 2011.

Roediger, David. *Working Toward Whiteness: How America's Immigrants Became White.* New York: Basic Books, 2005.

Romer, Daniel, Kathleen Hall Jamieson, and Sean Aday. "Television News and the Cultivation of Fear of Crime." *Journal of Communication* 53, no. 1 (2003): 88–104.

Romero, Victor. *Everyday Law for Immigrants.* Boulder, CO: Paradigm Publishers, 2009.

Rosaldo, Renato. "Cultural Citizenship and Educational Democracy." *Cultural Anthropology* 9, no. 3 (1994): 402–411.

Rosas, Gilberto. "The Managed Violences of the Borderlands: Treacherous Geographies, Policeability, and the Politics of Race." *Latino Studies* 4, no. 4 (2006): 401–418.

Rumbaut, Rubén G., Roberto G. Gonzales, Golnaz Komaie, and Charlie V. Morgan. "Debunking the Myth of Immigrant Criminality: Imprisonment Among First- and Second-Generation Young Men." *Migration Information Source,* 2006. http://www.migrationinformation.org/USFocus/display.cfm?ID=403. Accessed October 8, 2008.

Rumbaut, Rubén. "Origins and Destinies: Immigration to the United States since World War II." *Sociological Forum* 9, no. 4 (1994): 583–621.

Rytina, Nancy. 2009. "Estimates of the Legal Permanent Resident Population in 2008." Office of Immigration Statistics, Department of Homeland Security. http://www.dhs.gov/xlibrary/assets/statistics/publications/ois_lpr_pe_2008.pdf. Accessed April 7, 2010.

Sacchetti, Maria. "A Year After Raid, Immigration Cases Drag On for Many." *Boston Globe.* March 6, 2008. http://www.boston.com/news/local/articles/2008/03/06/a_year_after_raid_immigration_cases_drag_on_for_many/. Accessed July 11, 2008.

Sachs, Jeffrey, Nirupam Bajpai, and Ananthi Ramiah. "Understanding Regional Economic

Growth in India."*Asian Economic Papers*. 2002. http://www.lexisnexis.com/us/lnacademic/auth/checkbrowser.do?ipcounter=1&cookieState=0&rand=0.814247 4194099402&bhcp=1. Accessed October 8, 2008.

Saenz, Rogelio, Janie Filoteo, and Aurelia Lorena Murga. "Are Mexicans in the United States a Threat to the American Way of Life?" *Du Bois Review: Social Science Research on Race*, 4, no. 2 (2007): 375–393.

Sanderson, Matthew R., and Jeffrey D. Kentor. "Foreign Direct Investment and International Migration: A Cross-National Analysis of Less-Developed Countries, 1985–2000." *International Sociology* 23 (2008): 514–539.

Sassen, Saskia. "America's 'Immigration Problem.'" World Policy 6, Fall (1989): 811–832.

Schlosser, Eric. "The Prison-Industrial Complex." *The Atlantic Monthly*. December 1998.

Scott, Peter Dale. "Homeland Security Contracts for Vast New Detention Camps." *Global Research*. February 6, 2006. http://www.globalresearch.ca/index .php?context=viewArticle&code=%20SC20060206&articleId=1897. Accessed July 11, 2008.

Scudeler, Valeria Cristina. 1998. "O Mercado de Trabalho dos EUA e Alguns Indicadores sobre a Primeira Inserção Socio-Ocupacional do Fluxo Migratório de Governador Valadares—MG." Anais do XI Encontro Nacional de Estudos Populacionais da ABEP. http://www.abep.nepo.unicamp.br/docs/anais/PDF/1998/a142.pdf.

Seattle University School of Law. 2008. "Voices from Detention: A Report on Human Rights Violations at the Northwest Detention Center." http://www.law.seattleu.edu/ documents/news/archive/2008/DRFinal.pdf. Accessed April 7, 2010.

Sharma, Nandita. *Home Economics: Nationalism and the Making of 'Migrant Workers' in Canada*. Toronto: University of Toronto Press, 2006.

Shulman, Robin. "Immigration Raid Rips Families: Illegal Workers in Massachusetts Separated from Children." *Washington Post*. March 18, 2007. http://www .washingtonpost.com/wp-dyn/content/article/2007/03/17/AR2007031701113 .html. Accessed July 11, 2008.

Simon, Johnathan. *Governing through Crime: How the War on Crime Transformed American Democracy and Created a Culture of Fear*. New York: Oxford University Press, 2007.

Sinclair, Upton. 1985 [1906]. *The Jungle*. Penguin Press: New York.

Siqueira, Sueli. 2007a. "O Sonho Frustrado e o Sonho Realizado: As Duas Faces da Migração para os EUA." Nuevo Mundo No. 7. Posted June 7. Accessed February 7, 2008. http://nuevomundo.revues.org/document5973.html.

Siqueira, Sueli. 2007b. "Emigracao Internacional e o Retorno a Terra Natal: Realizacoes e Frustracoes." XV Encontro Nacional Sobre Emigracao. Universidad Vale do Rio Doce, Minas Gerais, Brazil. http://www.abep.nepo.unicamp.br/docs/anais/ outros/5EncNacSobreMigracao/comunic_sec_2_emi_int_ret.pdf. Accessed February 7, 2008.

Skeldon, Ronald. "Migration from China." *Journal of International Affairs*. Winter

(1996). http://www.ciaonet.org/olj/jia/jia_win9622.html. Accessed February 7, 2008.

Sladkova, Jana. "Expectations and Motivations of Hondurans Migrating to the United States." *Journal of Community & Applied Social Psychology* 14 (2007): 187–202.

Smith, Judith. "Celebrating Immigration History at Ellis Island." *American Quarterly* 44, no. 1 (1992): 82–100.

Source Watch. 2008. "Rick Renzi." http://www.sourcewatch.org/index.php?title=Rick_ Renzi. Accessed July 11, 2008.

Stewart, Elizabeth. "International Human Rights Law and the Haitian Asylum Applicant Detention Cases." *Virginia Journal of International Law* 26 (1986): 173–218. http:// heinonline.org/HOL/Page?handle=hein.journals/vajint26&id=1&collection= journals&index=. Accessed October 8, 2008.

Storesletten, Kjetil. "Sustaining Fiscal Policy through Immigration." *Journal of Political Economy* 108, no. 2 (2000): 300–323.

Sweig, Julia. "What Kind of War for Colombia?" *Foreign Affairs* 81, no. 5 (2002): 122.

Talbot, Margaret. "The Lost Children: What Do Tougher Detention Policies Mean for Illegal Immigrant Families?" *The New Yorker*. March 3, 2008.

Teitelbaum, Michael. "Immigration, Refugees, and Foreign Policy." *International Organization* 38, no. 3 (1984): 429–450.

Texas Appleseed. 2010. "Justice for Immigration's Hidden Population: Protecting the Rights of Persons with Mental Disabilities in the Immigration Court and Detention System." March 2010.

Tonry, Michael. "Why Are US Incarceration Rates So High?" *Crime and Delinquency* 45, no. 4 (1999): 419–437.

Transnational Records Access Clearinghouse 2007. TRAC Immigration Website: http:// trac.syr.edu/immigration/.

Tumlin, Karen, Joaquin Linton, and Ranjana Natarajan. 2009. "A Broken System: Confidential Reports Reveal Failures in U.S. Immigrant Detention Centers." National Immigration Law Center. ACLU of Southern California. Holland & Knight.

United Nations Human Rights Council. 2008. "Promotion and Protection of All Human Rights, Civil, Political, Economic, Social and Cultural Rights, Including the Right to Development: Report of the Special Rapporteur on the Human Rights of Migrants. Jorge Bustamante. Addendum Mission to the United States of America. March 5, 2008.

Universal Declaration of Human Rights. 1948. United Nations. http://www.un.org/ Overview/rights.html. Accessed November 12, 2010.

U.S. Department of Agriculture. Economic Research Service. Food and Rural Economics Division. *U.S. Foreign Direct Investment in the Western Hemisphere Processed Food Industry,* by Christine Bolling, Steve Neff, and Charles Handy. *Agricultural Economic Report* 760, 1998. http://www.ers.usda.gov/publications/aer760/aer760.pdf. Accessed February 6, 2008.

U.S. Department of Justice. Bureau of Justice Statistics. *Prisoners in 2005* by Paige Harrison and Allen Beck. 2006. http://morehousemaleinitiative.com/wp-content/uploads/2008/11/doj-prison-stats2.pdf. Accessed November 12, 2010.

U.S. Department of Homeland Security. Office of Immigration Statistics. Policy Directorate. "Estimates of the Unauthorized Immigrant Population Residing in the United States: January 2010" by Michael Hoefer, Nancy Rytina, and Bryan C. Baker. 2011. http://www.dhs.gov/xlibrary/assets/statistics/publications/ois_ill_pe_2010.pdf. Accessed April 1, 2011.

U.S. Department of Homeland Security. Office of Immigration Statistics. Policy Directorate. "Estimates of the Unauthorized Immigrant Population Residing in the United States: January 2009" by Michael Hoefer, Nancy Rytina, and Bryan C. Baker. 2010a. http://www.dhs.gov/xlibrary/assets/statistics/publications/ois_ill_pe_2009.pdf. Accessed April 1, 2011.

U.S. Department of Homeland Security. Office of Immigration Statistics. Policy Directorate. "Immigration Enforcement Actions: 2009." 2010b. http://www.dhs.gov/xlibrary/assets/statistics/publications/enforcement_ar_2009.pdf. Accessed May 11, 2011.

U.S. Department of Homeland Security. Office of Immigration Statistics. Policy Directorate. "Estimates of the Unauthorized Immigrant Population Residing in the United States: January 2008" by Michael Hoefer, Nancy Rytina, and Bryan C. Baker. 2009a. http://www.dhs.gov/xlibrary/assets/statistics/publications/ois_ill_pe_2008.pdf. Accessed April 6, 2010.

U.S. Department of Homeland Security. Office of Immigration Statistics. Policy Directorate. "Estimates of the Legal Permanent Resident Population in 2008" by Nancy Rytina. 2009b. http://www.dhs.gov/xlibrary/assets/statistics/publications/ois_lpr_pe_2008.pdf Accessed April 1, 2011.

U.S. Department of Homeland Security. Office of Immigration Statistics. Policy Directorate. "Estimates of the Unauthorized Immigrant Population Residing in the United States: January 2007" by Michael Hoefer, Nancy Rytina, and Bryan C. Baker. 2008. http://www.dhs.gov/xlibrary/assets/statistics/publications/ois_ill_pe_2007.pdf. Accessed October 10, 2008.

U.S. Department of Homeland Security. Office of Immigration Statistics. Policy Directorate. "Estimates of the Unauthorized Immigrant Population Residing in the United States: January 2006" by Michael Hoefer, Nancy Rytina, and Christopher Campbell. 2007. http://www.dhs.gov/xlibrary/assets/statistics/publications/ill_pe_2006.pdf. Accessed October 10, 2008.

U.S. Department of Homeland Security. Office of Immigration Statistics. Policy Directorate." Estimates of the Legal Permanent Resident Population in 2006" by Nancy Rytina, 2006. http://www.dhs.gov/xlibrary/assets/statistics/publications/LPR_PE_2006.pdf. Accessed December 2, 2008.

U.S. House of Representatives. House Judiciary Committee. "Impacts of Border

Enforcement on Unauthorized Mexican Migration to the United States: Testimony Prepared for the House Judiciary Committee Field Hearing on Immigration." Wayne Cornelius. San Diego, California, August 2, 2006. http://judiciary.house.gov/media/pdfs/cornelius080206.pdf. Accessed July 11, 2008.

U.S. House of Representatives. Committee on the Judiciary. Subcommittee on Immigration, Border Security, and Claims. "Testimony of Rosemary Jenks on "Identification Document Fraud" prepared for the US House of Representatives Committee on the Judiciary Subcommittee on Immigration, Border Security, and Claims. Rosemary Jenks, Washington, D.C., May 13, 1997. http://www.cis.org/articles/1997/jenks51397.htm. Accessed October 10, 2008.

U.S. House of Representatives. 2008a. Committee on the Judiciary. Subcommittee on Immigration, Citizenship, Refugees, Border Security, and International Law. "Statement of David Wolfe Leopold on Behalf of the American Immigration Lawyers Association Before the Subcommittee on Immigration, Citizenship, Refugees, Border Security, and International Law, Committee on the Judiciary, United States House of Representatives 'Hearing on the Arrest, Prosecution, and Conviction of Undocumented Workers in Postville, Iowa from May 12 to May 22, 2008.'" David Wolfe Leopold, Washington, D.C., July 24, 2008.

U.S. House of Representatives. 2008b. Committee on the Judiciary. Subcommittee on Immigration, Citizenship, Refugees, Border Security, and International Law. "Statement of Gary E. Mead, Deputy Director, Office of Detention and Removal Operations, ICE, DHS. 'Problems with ICE interrogation, Detention and Removal Procedures' February 13 before House Subcommittee on Immigration, Citizenship, Refugees, Border Security and International Law." Gary Mead, Washington, D.C. February 13, 2008.

U.S. House of Representatives. 2008c. Committee on the Judiciary. Subcommittee on Immigration, Citizenship, Refugees, Border Security, and International Law. "Statement of Deborah Rhodes, Senior Associate Deputy Attorney General, United States Department of Justice Before the United States House of Representatives Committee on the Judiciary, Subcommittee on Immigration, Citizenship, Refugees, Border Security, and International Law. Hearing Entitled 'Immigration Raids: Postville and Beyond.'" Deborah Rhodes, Washington, D.C., July 24, 2008.

U.S. Immigration and Customs Enforcement. 2007. "ICE Fiscal Year 2007 Annual Report." http://www.ice.gov/doclib/news/library/reports/annual-report/2007annual-report.pdf. Accessed April 3, 2011.

Van Etten, Ida M. "Russian Jews as Desirable Immigrants." *Forum* 15 (1993): 172–182.

Waldman, Paul, Elbert Ventura, Robert Savillo, Susan Lin, and Greg Lewis. "Fear and Loathing in Prime Time: Immigration Myths and Cable News." *Media Matters Action Network*. 2008. http://mediamattersaction.org/reports/fearandloathing/online_version. Accessed October 8, 2008.

Wallerstein, Immanuel. "Citizens All? Citizens Some!: The Making of the Citizen." *Society for the Comparative Study of Society and History* 0010-4175, no. 03 (2003): 650–679.

Wang, John. "Illegal Chinese Immigration into the United States: A Preliminary Factor Analysis." *International Journal of Offender Therapy and Comparative Criminology* 45, no. 3 (2001): 345–355.

Warner, Judith Ann. "The Social Construction of the Criminal Alien in Immigration Law, Enforcement Practice and Statistical Enumeration: Consequences for Immigrant Stereotyping." *Journal of Social and Ecological Boundaries* 1, no. 2 (2005): 56–80.

Welch, Michael and Liza Schuster. "Detention of Asylum Seekers in the US, UK, France, Germany, and Italy: A Critical View of the Globalizing Culture of Control." *Criminal Justice* 5 (2005): 331–355.

Welch, Michael. *Detained: Immigration Laws and the Expanding I.N.S. Jail Complex* Philadelphia: Temple University Press, 2002.

Welch, Michael. "Ironies of Social Control and the Criminalization of Immigrants." *Crime Law and Social Change* 39 (2003): 319–337.

Western, Bruce. *Punishment and Inequality in America.* New York: Russell Sage Foundation, 2006.

Western, Bruce. 2007. "Testimony Before the Joint Economic Committee of the U.S. Congress." October 4. http://www.wjh.harvard.edu/soc/faculty/western/pdfs/western_jec_testimony.pdf. Accessed October 13, 2008.

White, Michael, Ann E. Biddlecom, and Shenyang Guo. "Immigration, Naturalization, and Residential Assimilation among Asian Americans in 1980." *Social Forces* 72, no. 1 (1993): 93–117.

White House. "Economic Report of the President." 2005. http://www.gpoaccess.gov/eop/2005/2005_erp.pdf. Accessed October 8, 2008.

Wiarda, Howard. "Review: The United States and the Dominican Republic: Intervention, Dependency and Tyrannicide." *Journal of Interamerican Studies and World Affairs* 22, no. 2 (1980): 247–260.

Wood, Phillip J. "Globalization and Prison Privatization: Why Are Most of the World's For-Profit Adult Prisons to Be Found in the American South?" *International Political Sociology* 1 (2007): 222–239.

Zúñiga Herrera, Elena. 2006a. "Tendencias y Características de la Migración Mexicana a los Estados Unidos." Consejo Nacional de Población. http://www.conapo.gob.mx/publicaciones/migra2006_01/01.pdf. Accessed May 2007.

Zúñiga Herrera, Elena. 2006b. "Origen y Destino de la Migración Reciente de Mexicanos a los Estados Unidos." Consejo Nacional de Población. http://www.conapo.gob.mx/publicaciones/migra2006_01/02.pdf. Accessed May 2007.

Index

ABOUT THE AUTHOR

Tanya Golash-Boza is the author of *Yo Soy Negro: Blackness in Peru* (2011), in addition to more than a dozen peer-reviewed articles and book chapters in journals such as *Social Forces, Social Problems,* and *Ethnic and Racial Studies.* She's also written dozens of essays in online and print magazines, including *The Nation, Counterpunch, Dissident Voice,* and *Racism Review.* Her innovative scholarship recently earned the Distinguished Early Career Award of the Racial and Ethnic Minorities Studies Section of the American Sociological Association.

Her most recent work is on the consequences of mass deportation. With funding from a Fulbright-Hays Faculty Research Abroad Award, she completed more than 150 interviews with deportees in Brazil, Guatemala, Jamaica, and the Dominican Republic. She currently is writing a new book based on those interviews, tentatively titled *Deported: The Casualties of Mass Deportation from the United States.*

Tanya Golash-Boza graduated with a BA in philosophy from the University of Maryland, a certificate of anthropology from L'Ecole d'Anthropologie in Paris, and an MA and PhD in sociology from the University of North Carolina at Chapel Hill. She lives in Lawrence, Kansas, with her husband and three school-age children. She speaks fluent English, Spanish, Portuguese, and French.

As an assistant professor of sociology and American studies at the University of Kansas, Tanya Golash-Boza teaches courses on race, immigration, and globalization.